Contents

THE
POINT
OF
LAW

THE
Employment
Relations Act
explained
RICHARD HEMMINGS

London: The Stationery Office

© The Stationery Office 2000

Applications for reproduction should be made in writing to The Stationery Office Limited, St Crispins, Duke Street, Norwich NR3 1PD.

The information contained in this publication is believed to be correct at the time of manufacture. Whilst care has been taken to ensure that the information is accurate, the publisher can accept no responsibility for any errors or ommissions or for changes to the details given. Every effort has been made to trace copyright holders and to obtain permission for the use of copyright material. The publishers will gladly receive any information enabling them to rectify any errors or omissions in subsequent editions.

Richard Hemmings has asserted his moral rights under the Copyright, Designs and Patents Act 1988, to be identified as the author of this work.

Crown copyright material reproduced with permission of Her Majesty's Stationery Office

A CIP catalogue record for this book is available from the British Library

A Library of Congress CIP catalogue record has been applied for

First published 2000

ISBN 0 11 702395 7

Printed in the United Kingdom for The Stationery Office by Albert Gait Ltd.

TJ000054 C10 02/00 9385 11948

The Employment Relations Act 1999 explained

The Employment Relations Act 1999 explained, was written by Richard Hemmings LLM Solicitor.

His law firm - The Law Offices of Richard Hemmings - specialises in employment law. During his first ten years in the profession he practised as a criminal defence advocate in East Anglia. By 1985 the level of employment law work enabled him to specialise exclusively in that field. He was fascinated by an area of law which was growing and changing rapidly as a result of year-on-year legislation by the Government and the significant impact of European law and the Decisions of the European Courts of Justice. During the same time the HR function in many organisations had gained long overdue respect as a worthy discipline in its own right, allowing employment lawyers and personnel professionals to develop strong collaborative relationships.

Richard is also an Employment Tribunal Chairman sitting part-time in London, a Consultant with solicitors Taylor Vinters of Cambridge and author of the Employment Acts explained, in the Point of Law series covering the Employment Rights (Dispute Resolution) Act 1998, the National Minimum Wage Act 1998 and the Public Interest Disclosure Act 1998.

The Law Offices of Richard Hemmings LLM

Sandy Lane
Barham
Ipswich
IP6 OPB

Tel: 01473 833844
Fax: 01473 833230

Website: http://www.hemmings.co.uk

Disclaimer

This publication is intended to provide a brief commentary on the Employment Relations Act 1999, and should not be relied upon by any party without taking further legal advice.

Introduction

The aim of this book is to explain how the provisions of the Employment Relations Act 1999 will affect those who are covered by its provisions. In an increasingly knowledge-based world, the propositions that knowledge is power and that you are what you know, are relentlessly validated.

The reader will be given a full understanding of the practical implications of the Act by means of comprehensive annotations to their provisions drawn from published and unpublished sources, Ministerial commitments and explanations and personal analysis, in order to place these important additions to the body of employment law in context.

Employment Law can be loosely defined as the collection of rules, enforceable in the Employment Tribunal, County Court or High Court, which govern what happens in the workplace. Legal rules do not exist in a vacuum. They have a purpose - primarily to strike a fair balance between the interests of an individual working within an organisation and the interests of the organisation employing that person's skills and commitment. What amounts to a fair balancing of often competing interests at any particular point of time is judged by the Government of the day - politicians acting as social engineers to identify what they consider to be wrong and to fix it. The social engineering is promoted through changing the existing law e.g. reducing the qualifying period for protection against unfair dismissal from two years to one year, or by introducing new law such as the statutory right to paid annual leave introduced by the Working Time Regulations 1998.

The law is a precision tool in the hands of those lawyers who are expert in their field - craftsmen in their chosen specialisms. However the primary audience for the law is not lawyers but those affected by it - individuals and organisations. The law needs to be accessible to those affected by it and those advising them, particularly HR professionals, Trade Unions, CAB's and Law Centres. Accordingly, the explanatory notes alongside each section are written in plain English. Although this necessarily involves a loss of the precision of the statutory text, the user-friendly purpose of this volume in the Point of Law series would otherwise by lost. The expert lawyer will undoubtedly move swiftly from the explanatory note into the detail of the statutory text. At the other end of the spectrum, there will be those for whom the explanatory notes alone meet their purpose and only occasional reference to the statutory text will be needed. For many readers, starting with the explanatory note and moving into the statutory text as necessary will provide the knowledge and understanding they seek.

Explanatory Notes prepared by the Department of Trade and Industry have also been issued. This source of non-statutory guidance may represent a valuable additional source of explanation and insight from those involved in translating the Government's policy objectives into draft legislation and steering the legislation through the Parliamentary process. The DTI Explanatory Notes do not form part of the Act, nor have they been endorsed by Parliament. Nevertheless, lawyers and personnel practitioners will find them helpful, particularly their indicative, but non-binding, value when addressing Employment Tribunals or the higher Courts on the proper construction of the statutory language of the Act itself. The Explanatory Notes and further guidance are available on www.dti.gov.uk

The Structure of this Guide

The next section of this chapter - An Overview of the Act - summarises the major provisions of the Act. It is intended to provide an introduction to the key provisions as a constructive starting point for those unfamiliar with the legislation and as a refresher to the main components of the Act for those who already have a working knowledge of the legislation.

There then follows the Act itself with explanatory annotations, and the statutory Regulations on Maternity and Parental Leave.

Wherever reference is made to a commencement date a related Commencement Order will have been made and referred to. At the time of publication there have been three Commencement Orders, The Employment Relations Act 1999 (Commencement No. 1 and Transitional Provisions) Order 1999 SI1999No.2509 (C.63), The Employment Relations Act 1999 (Commencement No. 2 and Transitional and Savings Provisions) Order 1999 SI1999No.2830 (C.72), and The Employment Relations Act 1999 (Commencement No. 3 and Transitional Provision) Order 1999 SI 1999 No.3374 (C.90) – available on www.legislation.hmso.gov.uk

An Overview of the Act

A number of pre-election manifesto commitments on changes to Employment and Trade Union Law were incorporated in the Government's White Paper *Fairness at Work* published in May 1998 (Cm 3968) and later evolved in the light of consultation. The Act received Royal Assent on 27 July 1999. The majority of the Act consists of amendments to the two primary codifying Acts dealing with collective and individual employment law, respectively the Trade Union & Labour Relations (Consolidation) Act 1992 (the 1992 Act) and the Employment Rights Act 1996 (the 1996 Act). The Act also empowers the Secretary of State to make Regulations regarding a range of statutory rights e.g Parental Leave, implementing the Parental Leave Directive in the United Kingdom in compliance with its obligation to meet the European standards in this area of family-friendly policies designed to assist parents combining careers with family life. The consultative process regarding the draft Regulations on Maternity and Parental Leave began in September 1999 with the Secretary of State announcing on 4 November 1999 the Government's post-consultative decisions on the detail of the Regulations. Those Regulations, set out further in this publication, came into effect on 15 December 1999.

The reader's first impression of the Employment Relations Act 1999 may be daunting. The 47 sections covering 21 pages are dwarfed by the 9 Schedules occupying five times as many pages, the Act itself totalling 125 pages. The size of the Schedules simply reflects the primary status of the Act as an amending one, the Schedules setting out in particular the amendments, and additional clauses, to the 1992 and 1996 Acts in particular. Schedule One of the 1999 Act (dealing with statutory Trade Union recognition has itself 172 paragraphs. However the author's advice is to resist any temptation to paralysis. The Act readily divides into smaller digestible portions. Provided the reader can locate that most elusive of commodities – quiet uninterrupted reading time – the main principles, the underlying purpose, and the steps which personnel practitioners will need to take to evolve compliant policies and systems will be readily absorbed and evaluated. Nevertheless there are aspects of the Act where the language is opaque and the effect unclear. This will ultimately be resolved only by case law rulings. This has led to justifiable criticism by informed commentators e.g. the description of the 1999 Act as "a monster of discretions and uncertainties"

In summary, much of the Act has to be cut-and-pasted into the 1992 and 1996 Acts. The balance is largely enabling legislation, providing the statutory power to introduce changes through detailed Regulations. Copies of the amended versions of the 1992 and 1996 Acts, incorporating the 1999 Act are essential and simplifying tools for those whose role requires an expert exploration of the details. Overall implementation of all aspects of the Act will ultimately extend well into Year 2000. At the time of publication, not all the enabling provisions have been triggered by Commencement Orders and only the Maternity and Parental Leave Regulations have come into force.

The principal provisions are:

- Procedures for the statutory, as opposed to voluntary, recognition of Trade Unions for collective bargaining and the statutory scheme applying to recognition and derecognition of Trade Unions. This includes:

  - The process of seeking recognition
  - Automatic recognition and balloted recognition
  - Consequences of recognition
  - Identifying the bargaining unit
  - Subsequent changes affecting the bargaining unit
  - Derecognition e.g. where Union is not independent
  - The right not to suffer detriment for actions relating to recognition/ derecognition process

- Individual employment rights related to Trade Unions:

  - Protection against discrimination by omission on the grounds of Trade Union membership or non-membership or Trade Union activities
  - Protection against blacklisting on the grounds of Trade Union membership or activities
  - Balloting/Call-out on Industrial Action

- Removal of requirement for Trade Unions to identify to employer those workers to be balloted or called out on industrial action

- Family-related employment rights:
  - Simplification and extension of existing maternity rights
  - Three months parental leave
  - Time off for urgent reasons relating to dependants

- Right to be accompanied – employee right to accompanied by their chosen fellow employee or Trade Union representative in disciplinary and grievance procedures

- Other individual rights:
  - Protection from dismissal for taking part in lawfully organised official industrial action
  - Prohibition of waivers for unfair dismissal in fixed term contracts
  - Regulation-making powers for the Secretary of State to ensure compliance with the Part-time Work Directive
  - Exempting residential members of religious and other such communities from the National Minimum Wage Act 1998
  - Enabling powers for Secretary of State to extend some or all existing statutory employment rights to specified categories of workers not presently protected

- Compensatory and other awards:
  - The maximum compensatory award for unfair dismissal increases from £12,000 to £50,000
  - Special and additional awards for non-compliance with an Employment Tribunal Order are consolidated
  - Removal of the upper limit of compensation for whistle-blowing under the Public Interest Act 1998
  - Removal of the upper limit of compensation for unfair dismissal where the reason relates to Health and Safety

- Miscellaneous
  - Redefinition of role of the Central Arbitration Committee (CAC)
  - Abolition of the Commissioner for the Rights of Trade Union Members and the Commissioner for Protection against Unlawful Industrial Action
  - ACAS general duty redefined as "to promote the improvement of industrial relations"
  - ACAS, CAC and the Certification Officers' Annual Reports to be published on financial (not calendar) year basis.
  - Statutory authority for the Secretary of State to provide funds to develop partnerships at work
  - A range of amendments to empower the Secretary of State to alter the regulatory framework affecting Employment Agencies
  - The removal of certain limits restricting certain employment rights affecting those who ordinarily work in Great Britain

- Empowering the Secretary of State to make Regulations to provide TUPE-type protection in particular cases
- Authorisation of Inland Revenue Officers to pass information internally regarding the National Minimum Wage Act 1998 to colleagues in other Government Agencies
- A technical amendment to the School Standards and Framework Act 1998 consequent on the reduction on 1 June 1999 in the qualifying period for protection against unfair dismissal from two years to one year
- Reducing the Ministerial scope to exclude Crown servants from certain statutory employment rights
- Increased powers of the Certification Officer in disputes between Unions and their members

Employment Relations Act 1999
1999 Chapter 26

An Act to amend the law relating to employment, to trade unions and to employment agencies and businesses.

[27th July 1999]

Be it enacted by the Queen's most Excellent Majesty, by and with the advice and consent of the Lords Spiritual and Temporal, and Commons, in this present Parliament assembled, and by the authority of the same, as follows:-

Trade unions

1.– (1) The Trade Union and Labour Relations (Consolidation) Act 1992 shall be amended as follows.

(2) After Chapter V of Part I (rights of trade union members) there shall be inserted-

"CHAPTER VA

COLLECTIVE BARGAINING: RECOGNITION

Recognition of trade unions.

70A. Schedule A1 shall have effect."

(3) Immediately before Schedule 1 there shall be inserted the Schedule set out in Schedule 1 to this Act.

s.1
A new Chapter – CHAPTER VA COLLECTIVE BARGAINING : RECOGNITION is inserted into the 1992 Act between Chapter V and Chapter VI. Chapter VA contains three sections; s.70A, s.70B and s.70C. Sections 70B and 70C deal with training and are inserted by s.5 of the 1999 Act. Schedule 1 to the 1999 Act which inserts Schedule A1 to the 1992 Act - i.e the detailed scheme running to 172 paragraphs, providing for statutory recognition of an independent Trade Union for collective bargaining purposes. For commentary on this see below at Schedule 1.

Commencement – At the time of publication, s.1 and Schedule 1 have not come into force and no commencement date has been appointed.

2. Schedule 2 shall have effect.

> **s.2** – *Sections 146-150 inclusive of the 1992 Act provide a remedy for* action *short of dismissal taken by an employer on grounds related to Union membership or activity. See <u>Associated Newspapers v. Wilson and Associated British Ports v. Palmer [1995] ICR406</u>. The effect of s.2 is to extend the current law to include not only protection against positive action but also protection against* omissions *on such Union grounds (e.g. withholding a pay increase). The amendments are set out in s.2 and Schedule 2.*
>
> Commencement – *this section came into force on 25 October 1999 under Commencement Order No.2.*

3.– (1) The Secretary of State may make regulations prohibiting the compilation of lists which-

    (a) contain details of members of trade unions or persons who have taken part in the activities of trade unions, and

    (b) are compiled with a view to being used by employers or employment agencies for the purposes of discrimination in relation to recruitment or in relation to the treatment of workers.

> **s.3**
> **s3(1)** – *With effect from 25 October 1999 (by virtue of Commencement Order No. 2) the Secretary of State has been empowered to make Regulations prohibiting the compilation of blacklists of Trade Union members or activists prepared with a view to being used by employers or employment agencies to discriminate in the recruitment or treatment of workers. The secondary legislation requires affirmative resolution – see s.42.*

(2) The Secretary of State may make regulations prohibiting-

    (a) the use of lists to which subsection (1) applies;

    (b) the sale or supply of lists to which subsection (1) applies.

> **s3(2)** – *The Regulations prohibiting compilation of lists may also prohibit the use, sale or supply of such lists.*

(3) Regulations under this section may, in particular-

(a) confer jurisdiction (including exclusive jurisdiction) on employment tribunals and on the Employment Appeal Tribunal;

(b) include provision for or about the grant and enforcement of specified remedies by courts and tribunals;

(c) include provision for the making of awards of compensation calculated in accordance with the regulations;

(d) include provision permitting proceedings to be brought by trade unions on behalf of members in specified circumstances;

(e) include provision about cases where an employee is dismissed by his employer and the reason or principal reason for the dismissal, or why the employee was selected for dismissal, relates to a list to which subsection (1) applies;

(f) create criminal offences;

(g) in specified cases or circumstances, extend liability for a criminal offence created under paragraph (f) to a person who aids the commission of the offence or to a person who is an agent, principal, employee, employer or officer of a person who commits the offence;

(h) provide for specified obligations or offences not to apply in specified circumstances;

(i) include supplemental, incidental, consequential and transitional provision, including provision amending an enactment;

(j) make different provision for different cases or circumstances.

s3(3) – *The Secretary of State is empowered to provide in the Regulations for a range of matters including giving jurisdiction to Employment Tribunals and the EAT, power to grant and enforce specified remedies, award compensation to blacklisted individuals, and provide remedies for employees dismissed or selected for dismissal because they have been blacklisted; allowing Trade Unions to institute proceedings on behalf of blacklisted members; and creating criminal offences committed not only by the principal offender but also by e.g. an accomplice or agent of the offender, or their employee or employer.*

(4) Regulations under this section creating an offence may not provide for it to be punishable-

(a) by imprisonment,

(b) by a fine in excess of level 5 on the standard scale in the case of an offence triable only summarily, or

(c) by a fine in excess of the statutory maximum in the case of summary conviction for an offence triable either way.

s3(4) – *The penalties for criminal offences created by Regulations made by the Secretary of State are limited. The offences cannot be punishable by imprisonment; offences which are specified in the Regulations to be triable only in the Magistrates' Court will carry a maximum in accordance with level 5 on the standard scale (currently £5,000). Any offence specified to be triable either in the Magistrates' Court or in the Crown Court will be subject to the prevailing statutory maximum for a summary conviction for a case triable either way. The penalties are comparable to the criminal sanctions in the Data Protection Act 1998 (see the Data Protection Act explained by James Mullock and Piers Leigh-Pollitt in the Point of Law explained series).*

(5) In this section-

"list" includes any index or other set of items whether recorded electronically or by any other means, and

"worker" has the meaning given by section 13.

s3(5) – *Is interpretative. "List" is widely defined to include any index or other set of items however recorded. Accordingly it will apply to lists stored electronically on computer systems, personal computers, laptops, notepads, organisers, on databases in advanced mobile phones, or on confidential pass-worded websites. "By any other means", covers not only conventional storage systems but also information storage technologies yet to emerge.*

"Worker" is allocated the extended definition set out in s.13 of this Act and therefore includes agency workers, home workers, persons in Crown employment and Parliamentary staff as well as those within the definition of "worker" in s.230(3) of the 1996 Act.

(6) Subject to subsection (5), expressions used in this section and in the Trade Union and Labour Relations (Consolidation) Act 1992 have the same meaning in this section as in that Act.

s3(6) – *Apart from "list" and "worker" the expressions used in s.3 have the same meanings as in the 1992 Act.*

The Government intends to issue draft Regulations and consult on them before reaching a decision on the final text of the Regulations.

At the time of publication the consultative document and draft Regulations have not been issued by the DTI.

Commencement – *Commencement Order No. 2 empowered the Secretary of State, with effect from 25 October 1999 to make Regulations under this section. At the time of publication no Regulations have been made.*

4. Schedule 3 shall have effect.

s.4 – *Section 4 gives effect to Schedule 3 which seeks to clarify and simplify the complex rules relating to industrial action, ballots and notices set out in s.226-235 of the 1992 Act. The Government have incorporated a number of proposals from those who responded during the consultation process regarding* Fairness at Work. *See the notes to Schedule 3.*

Commencement – *At the time of publication, no Commencement Order has been made specifying the date on which this section comes into force.*

5. In Chapter VA of Part I of the Trade Union and Labour Relations (Consolidation) Act 1992 (collective bargaining: recognition) as inserted by section 1 above, there shall be inserted after section 70A-

s.5 – *Adds two new sections to Chapter VA - s.70(B) and s.70(C), both dealing with training:*

"**Training.**

70B.– (1) This section applies where-

    (a) a trade union is recognised, in accordance with Schedule A1, as entitled to conduct collective bargaining on behalf of a bargaining unit (within the meaning of Part I of that Schedule), and

    (b) a method for the conduct of collective bargaining is specified by the Central Arbitration Committee under paragraph 31(3) of that Schedule (and is not the subject of an agreement under paragraph 31(5)(a) or (b)).

(2) The employer must from time to time invite the trade union to send representatives to a meeting for the purpose of-

(a) consulting about the employer's policy on training for workers within the bargaining unit,

(b) consulting about his plans for training for those workers during the period of six months starting with the day of the meeting, and

(c) reporting about training provided for those workers since the previous meeting.

(3) The date set for a meeting under subsection (2) must not be later than-

(a) in the case of a first meeting, the end of the period of six months starting with the day on which this section first applies in relation to a bargaining unit, and

(b) in the case of each subsequent meeting, the end of the period of six months starting with the day of the previous meeting.

(4) The employer shall, before the period of two weeks ending with the date of a meeting, provide to the trade union any information-

(a) without which the union's representatives would be to a material extent impeded in participating in the meeting, and

(b) which it would be in accordance with good industrial relations practice to disclose for the purposes of the meeting.

(5) Section 182(1) shall apply in relation to the provision of information under subsection (4) as it applies in relation to the disclosure of information under section 181.

(6) The employer shall take account of any written representations about matters raised at a meeting which he receives from the trade union within the period of four weeks starting with the date of the meeting.

(7) Where more than one trade union is recognised as entitled to conduct collective bargaining on behalf of a bargaining unit, a reference in this section to "the trade union" is a reference to each trade union.

(8) Where at a meeting under this section (Meeting 1) an employer indicates his intention to convene a subsequent meeting (Meeting 2) before the expiry of the period of six months beginning with the date of Meeting 1, for the reference to a period of six months in subsection (2)(b) there shall be substituted a reference to the expected period between Meeting 1 and Meeting 2.

(9) The Secretary of State may by order made by statutory instrument amend any of subsections (2) to (6).

(10) No order shall be made under subsection (9) unless a draft has been laid before, and approved by resolution of, each House of Parliament.

s70(B) – *Provided certain conditions are met an employer must invite Union representatives to a meeting to consult on the employer's training policy, the training planned during the period up to the date of the next such meeting (or if a date has not been set, the training plans for the next six months), and report on the training undertaken since the last meeting. The two conditions are that firstly there is statutory recognition of the Union under the Schedule A1 procedure in the 1992 Act and secondly there is no agreement between the employer and Union under paragraph 31(5) of Schedule A1 that such statutory recognition should not be legally binding. The above obligations regarding training only apply to workers within the bargaining unit. The first meeting must take place within six months of the CAC imposing the method of collective bargaining and the interval between subsequent meetings must be no longer than six months. At least two weeks before such meetings, the employer must provide any information without which the Union would be impeded in participating in the meeting and which is in line with good industrial relations practice to provide, subject to certain exceptions e.g. where the provision of information would disclose the identity of individuals without their consent. The employer must take into account any written representations on the training issues discussed at the meeting which the Union submits, in writing to the employer, during the period of four weeks after the meeting.*

70C.– (1) A trade union may present a complaint to an employment tribunal that an employer has failed to comply with his obligations under section 70B in relation to a bargaining unit.

(2) An employment tribunal shall not consider a complaint under this section unless it is presented-

(a) before the end of the period of three months beginning with the date of the alleged failure, or

(b) within such further period as the tribunal considers reasonable in a case where it is satisfied that it was not reasonably practicable for the complaint to be presented before the end of that period of three months.

(3) Where an employment tribunal finds a complaint under this section well-founded it-

(a) shall make a declaration to that effect, and

(b) may make an award of compensation to be paid by the employer to each person who was, at the time when the failure occurred, a member of the bargaining unit.

(4) The amount of the award shall not, in relation to each person, exceed two weeks' pay.

(5) For the purpose of subsection (4) a week's pay-

(a) shall be calculated in accordance with Chapter II of Part XIV of the Employment Rights Act 1996 (taking the date of the employer's failure as the calculation date), and

(b) shall be subject to the limit in section 227(1) of that Act.

(6) Proceedings for enforcement of an award of compensation under this section-

(a) may, in relation to each person to whom compensation is payable, be commenced by that person, and

(b) may not be commenced by a trade union."

s70(C) – *Provides complaints machinery to an Employment Tribunal for the Union to present a claim alleging a breach of the employer's obligations under s.70(B) e.g. inadequate provision of information in advance of meetings, failure to hold meetings or excessive intervals between meetings. Action appears possible for each failure to hold a meeting. In accordance with conventional time limits a complaint to an Employment Tribunal must be presented within three months of the alleged failure. If the complaint is upheld, the Tribunal may award compensation to each member of the bargaining unit up to a maximum of two weeks pay, a potentially significant sum even in a relatively small bargaining unit of e.g. in a unit consisting of 260 workers the award could be equivalent to one worker's pay for ten years.*

Commencement – *At the time of publication, no Commencement Order has been made specifying the date on which this section comes into force.*

6. In sections 128(1)(b) and 129(1) of the Employment Rights Act 1996 (interim relief) after "103" there shall be inserted "or in paragraph 161(2) of Schedule A1 to the Trade Union and Labour Relations (Consolidation) Act 1992".

s.6 – *This section must be read in conjunction with paragraph 161 of Schedule 1 to this Act. Paragraph 161 provides for a dismissal to be automatically unfair in specified circumstances where the dismissal is connected with Union recognition or derecognition. The effect of s.6 is to allow an employee who presents a complaint of unfair dismissal under paragraph 161 to claim interim relief under the long-established provisions set out in s.128-131 of the 1996 Act. Provided an employee presents a complaint within seven days of dismissal, alleging that the employer's reason for dismissal is connected with Union recognition or derecognition, and the Tribunal considers it is likely that the dismissal will be found to be unfair, the Tribunal may order the employer to either re-employ the worker immediately on terms at least as favourable as before the dismissal or run the risk of a substantial award of extra compensation to an employee who is successful on a full merits hearing. In an industrial dispute, the threat of collective Tribunal applications under the interim relief provisions in the 1996 Act, particularly multi-applicant proceedings combined under Rule 18 of the Employment Tribunals Rules of Procedure, can be a significant and sometimes determinative factor in the ultimate outcome of the dispute.*

Commencement – *At the time of publication, no Commencement Order has been made specifying the date on which this section comes into force.*

Leave for family and domestic reasons

7. The provisions set out in Part I of Schedule 4 shall be substituted for Part VIII of the Employment Rights Act 1996.

s.7 – *This section gives effect to Part I of Schedule 4 of this Act. The familiar maternity provisions in Part VIII of the 1996 Act are repealed in their entirety and substituted by Part I of Schedule 4 which provides for basic rights and regulation-making powers relating to maternity and parental leave. The substituted Part VIII of the 1996 Act extends the existing maternity leave rights and establishes a new right to parental leave for men and women. Employees are protected from detriment or dismissal for exercising these rights and complaints will be dealt with primarily in Employment Tribunals. The aim is to simplify the maternity leave scheme by providing a basic statutory framework, with the detailed provisions contained within a single set of Regulations. The new provisions evolved from informal consultation with particular interest groups e.g. Maternity Alliance, incorporated in* Fairness at Work *and then the subject of public consultation. Draft Regulations were issued with the consultative document in September 1999 and further refinements announced by the DTI earlier in November 1999. See the notes to Part I of Schedule 4 and the notes to the Maternity and Parental Leave etc Regulations 1999.*

Commencement - Commencement Order No. 2 empowered the Secretary of State, with effect from 15 December 1999 to make Regulations under this section. The Maternity and Parental Leave etc Regulations 1999 SI.1999 No. 3312 which came into force on 15 December 1999 but most of the maternity provisions only apply if the expected week of childbirth is on or after 30 April 2000.

8. The provisions set out in Part II of Schedule 4 shall be inserted after section 57 of that Act.

s.8 – *This section and Part II of Schedule 4 implements the part of the Parental Leave Directive not implemented by s.7. s.57A and s.57B are added after s.57 of the 1996 Act, giving employees the right to take a reasonable amount of unpaid time off work to deal with specific matters affecting a dependent. s.57A sets out the circumstances in which the employee's right to time off is triggered e.g. to help a dependent who falls ill, gives birth or is injured, or when a dependent dies, or when care arrangements for a dependent unexpectedly break down. It also covers circumstances where there is an unexpected incident involving a dependent child during school hours or on a school trip or in other circumstances when the school has responsibility for the child. The definition of a dependent, the obligation to inform the employer and the process for presenting a complaint to an Employment Tribunal are set out in detail in the new sections 57A and 57B. For commentary on this see below at Schedule 4 Part II.*

Commencement - Commencement Order No. 2 empowered the Secretary of State, with effect from 15 December 1999 to make Regulations under this section. The Maternity and Parental Leave Regulations have been in force since 15 December 1999.

9. Part III of Schedule 4 (which makes amendments consequential on sections 7 and 8) shall have effect.

s.9 – *This section gives effect to Part III of Schedule 4 which confers a right not to suffer detriment for reasons connected with maternity, parental leave or time off and makes dismissal for any such reason automatically unfair. Otherwise Part III of Schedule 4 deals with the technical changes to the existing legislation consequential on the introduction of additional rights in respect of maternity leave, parental leave and time off to deal with matters concerning dependants. The protective measures contained in Part III of Schedule 4 reflect requirements of the Parental Leave Directive and proposals set out in* Fairness at Work.

Commencement - *Commencement Order No. 2 empowered the Secretary of State, with effect from 15 December 1999 to make Regulations under this section. The Maternity and Parental Leave Regulations have been in force since 15 December 1999. For commentary on this see below at Schedule 4 Part III.*

Disciplinary and grievance hearings

10.– (1) This section applies where a worker-

    (a) is required or invited by his employer to attend a disciplinary or grievance hearing, and

    (b) reasonably requests to be accompanied at the hearing.

s.10 *– Creates a statutory right for a worker to be accompanied by a fellow worker or Trade Union official of the worker's choice ("a companion") during grievance and disciplinary procedures. Although s.3 of the 1996 Act obliges employers with 20 or more employees to incorporate within the statutory written employment particulars required by Part I of that Act, a statement specifying any applicable disciplinary rules, the person to whom the employee can apply if dissatisfied with any disciplinary decision, and the person to whom an employee can apply to redress any employment related grievance and the procedure involved, there is no statutory obligation to incorporate the standards in the ACAS Code of Practice on Disciplinary Practice and Procedures in Employment. The Code states that disciplinary procedures should give individuals the right to be accompanied by a Trade Union representative or by a fellow employee of their choice at disciplinary interviews. The Code represents good practice and Employment Tribunals must take into account the Code where it appears relevant. However, like the Highway Code and references to it during prosecutions for driving offences, the Code itself has no direct legal force. S.10 creates a specific statutory right to be accompanied and s.11 to s.15 contain the detailed provisions. The right to be accompanied arises where a worker is required or invited by the employer to attend a disciplinary or grievance hearing and the worker* reasonably *requests to be accompanied at the hearing. It should be noted that unlike Part I of the 1996 Act this section covers all "workers" (as defined in s.13: see below), not just employees.*

(2) Where this section applies the employer must permit the worker to be accompanied at the hearing by a single companion who-

    (a) is chosen by the worker and is within subsection (3),

(b) is to be permitted to address the hearing (but not to answer questions on behalf of the worker), and

(c) is to be permitted to confer with the worker during the hearing.

> **s10(2)** – *The employer must permit the worker to be accompanied by a companion of the worker's own choice. The companion may be (1) a Trade Union official employed by the Trade Union, (2) a Trade Union official not employed by the Trade Union but certified by the Union to have been trained or experienced in acting as a worker's companion at disciplinary or grievance hearings, (3) another of the employer's workers. The companion must be permitted to address the hearing (but not, without the employer's consent, to answer questions on behalf of the worker) and the employer must permit the worker and the companion to confer during the hearing.*

(3) A person is within this subsection if he is-

(a) employed by a trade union of which he is an official within the meaning of sections 1 and 119 of the Trade Union and Labour Relations (Consolidation) Act 1992,

(b) an official of a trade union (within that meaning) whom the union has reasonably certified in writing as having experience of, or as having received training in, acting as a worker's companion at disciplinary or grievance hearings, or

(c) another of the employer's workers.

(4) If-

(a) a worker has a right under this section to be accompanied at a hearing,

(b) his chosen companion will not be available at the time proposed for the hearing by the employer, and

(c) the worker proposes an alternative time which satisfies subsection (5),

the employer must postpone the hearing to the time proposed by the worker.

> **s10(4)** – *If the worker's chosen companion will not be available at the proposed hearing and the worker proposes an alternative reasonable time within five working days of the hearing fixed by the employer, the hearing must be postponed to the proposed alternative time.*

(5) An alternative time must-

(a) be reasonable, and

(b) fall before the end of the period of five working days beginning with the first working day after the day proposed by the employer.

(6) An employer shall permit a worker to take time off during working hours for the purpose of accompanying another of the employer's workers in accordance with a request under subsection (1)(b).

(7) Sections 168(3) and (4), 169 and 171 to 173 of the Trade Union and Labour Relations (Consolidation) Act 1992 (time off for carrying out trade union duties) shall apply in relation to subsection (6) above as they apply in relation to section 168(1) of that Act.

> **s10(7)** – *The employer must allow the companion time off during working hours for the purpose of attending the hearing. The well-established rules regarding time off for carrying out Trade Union duties in the 1992 Act apply to a companion's function.*
>
> Commencement – *at the time of publication, no Commencement Order has been made specifying the date on which this section comes into force.*

11.– (1) A worker may present a complaint to an employment tribunal that his employer has failed, or threatened to fail, to comply with section 10(2) or (4).

(2) A tribunal shall not consider a complaint under this section in relation to a failure or threat unless the complaint is presented-

(a) before the end of the period of three months beginning with the date of the failure or threat, or
(b) within such further period as the tribunal considers reasonable in a case where it is satisfied that it was not reasonably practicable for the complaint to be presented before the end of that period of three months.

(3) Where a tribunal finds that a complaint under this section is well-founded it shall order the employer to pay compensation to the worker of an amount not exceeding two weeks' pay.

(4) Chapter II of Part XIV of the Employment Rights Act 1996 (calculation of a week's pay) shall apply for the purposes of subsection (3); and in applying that Chapter the calculation date shall be taken to be-

(a) in the case of a claim which is made in the course of a claim for unfair dismissal, the date on which the employer's notice of dismissal was given or, if there was no notice, the effective date of termination, and
(b) in any other case, the date on which the relevant hearing took place (or was to have taken place).

(5) The limit in section 227(1) of the Employment Rights Act 1996 (maximum amount of week's pay) shall apply for the purposes of subsection (3) above.

(6) No award shall be made under subsection (3) in respect of a claim which is made in the course of a claim for unfair dismissal if the tribunal makes a supplementary award under section 127A(2) of the Employment Rights Act 1996 (internal appeal procedures).

s.11 *– Provides for a complaint to be brought by a worker to an Employment Tribunal that his employer has failed, or threatened to fail, to comply with the statutory requirement to allow an employee to be accompanied or the statutory right to seek a reasonable postponement. A complaint to a Tribunal must be brought within three months of the date of the failure or threat unless it was not reasonably practicable for the complaint to be presented within that timescale. Where a Tribunal finds that the complaint is well-founded it must order the employer to pay compensation, such sum not to exceed two weeks pay. The provisions in the 1996 Act regarding the calculation of a week's pay are imported. The amount of a week's pay is capped in accordance with s.227(1) of 1996 Act – currently £230 per week. No compensation can be awarded by the Tribunal if it also awards a supplementary award under s.127(A)(2) of the 1996 Act, introduced on 1 January 1999 by s.13 Employment Rights (Dispute Resolution) Act 1998 which provides that where the employer has a dismissal appeals procedure but prevented the employee from using it, the Employment Tribunal must include a supplementary award of such amount as it considers just and equitable, but not exceeding two weeks actual pay.*

Commencement *– at the time of publication, no Commencement Order has been made specifying the date on which this section comes into force.*

12.– (1) A worker has the right not to be subjected to any detriment by any act, or any deliberate failure to act, by his employer done on the ground that he-

(a) exercised or sought to exercise the right under section 10(2) or (4), or
(b) accompanied or sought to accompany another worker (whether of the same employer or not) pursuant to a request under that section.

s.12
s12(1) - Provides a right not to be subjected to any detriment as an individual on the grounds of having sought to exercise the right to be accompanied by a Trade Union or worker companion.

(2) Section 48 of the Employment Rights Act 1996 shall apply in relation to contraventions of subsection (1) above as it applies in relation to contraventions of certain sections of that Act.

s12(2) – *Provides for the enforcement procedure before Employment Tribunals contained in s.48 of the 1996 Act to apply. Where the reason for the worker's dismissal is that the worker exercised or sought to exercise the right to be accompanied or the reason was that a worker accompanied or sought to accompany another worker (i.e. to be the companion) that dismissal will be automatically unfair. The protection provided to workers by this section is not governed by length of service or upper age limit. Accordingly a worker with less than one year's service or over the normal age of retirement can nevertheless make a claim of unfair dismissal. An application for interim relief under the 1996 Act is also available (see the Note to s.[ ])*

Commencement - *at the time of publication, no Commencement Order has been made specifying the date on which this section comes into force.*

s.13 – *Provides definitions of worker, agency worker, home worker, disciplinary hearing, grievance hearing, working day. Home workers and agency workers as defined are within the generic definition. A disciplinary hearing is a hearing which could result in:*

* *the administration of a formal warning to a worker by his employer*

* *the taking of some other action in respect of a worker by his employer, or*

* *the confirmation of a warning issued or some other action taken*

A grievance hearing is a hearing which concerns the performance of a duty by an employer in relation to a worker.

Commencement – *this section came into force on 25 October 1999 in respect of the definitions 1, 2, and 3 of s.13 (worker, agency worker and home worker)*

(3) A worker who is dismissed shall be regarded for the purposes of Part X of the Employment Rights Act 1996 as unfairly dismissed if the reason (or, if more than one, the principal reason) for the dismissal is that he-

    (a) exercised or sought to exercise the right under section 10(2) or (4), or
    (b) accompanied or sought to accompany another worker (whether of the same employer or not) pursuant to a request under that section.

(4) Sections 108 and 109 of that Act (qualifying period of employment and upper age limit) shall not apply in relation to subsection (3) above.

(5) Sections 128 to 132 of that Act (interim relief) shall apply in relation to dismissal for the reason specified in subsection (3)(a) or (b) above as they apply in relation to dismissal for a reason specified in section 128(1)(b) of that Act.

(6) In the application of Chapter II of Part X of that Act in relation to subsection (3) above, a reference to an employee shall be taken as a reference to a worker.

13.– (1) In sections 10 to 12 and this section "worker" means an individual who is-

   (a) a worker within the meaning of section 230(3) of the Employment Rights Act 1996,

   (b) an agency worker,

   (c) a home worker,

   (d) a person in Crown employment within the meaning of section 191 of that Act, other than a member of the naval, military, air or reserve forces of the Crown, or

   (e) employed as a relevant member of the House of Lords staff or the House of Commons staff within the meaning of section 194(6) or 195(5) of that Act.

(2) In subsection (1) "agency worker" means an individual who-

   (a) is supplied by a person ("the agent") to do work for another ("the principal") by arrangement between the agent and the principal,

   (b) is not a party to a worker's contract, within the meaning of section 230(3) of that Act, relating to that work, and

   (c) is not a party to a contract relating to that work under which he undertakes to do the work for another party to the contract whose status is, by virtue of the contract, that of a client or customer of any professional or business undertaking carried on by the individual;

and, for the purposes of sections 10 to 12, both the agent and the principal are employers of an agency worker.

(3) In subsection (1) "home worker" means an individual who-

   (a) contracts with a person, for the purposes of the person's business, for the execution of work to be done in a place not under the person's control or management, and

   (b) is not a party to a contract relating to that work under which the work is to be executed for another party to the contract whose status is, by virtue of the contract, that of a client or customer of any professional or business undertaking carried on by the individual;

and, for the purposes of sections 10 to 12, the person mentioned in paragraph (a) is the home worker's employer.

(4) For the purposes of section 10 a disciplinary hearing is a hearing which could result in-

   (a) the administration of a formal warning to a worker by his employer,

   (b) the taking of some other action in respect of a worker by his employer, or

   (c) the confirmation of a warning issued or some other action taken.

(5) For the purposes of section 10 a grievance hearing is a hearing which concerns the performance of a duty by an employer in relation to a worker.

(6) For the purposes of section 10(5)(b) in its application to a part of Great Britain a working day is a day other than-

(a) a Saturday or a Sunday,

(b) Christmas Day or Good Friday, or

(c) a day which is a bank holiday under the Banking and Financial Dealings Act 1971 in that part of Great Britain.

s.14 – *Certain restrictions on contracting out contained in s.203 of the 1996 Act, are imported into this Act to restrict contracting-out of the worker's rights under the provisions in s.10 to s.13. S.14 also provides for ACAS conciliation in Tribunal claims relating to the statutory rights under s.10 to s.13 and for compromise agreements to settle claims and potential claims under ss.10-13.*

Commencement - *at the time of publication, no Commencement Order has been made specifying the date on which this section comes into force*

14. Sections 10 to 13 of this Act shall be treated as provisions of Part V of the Employment Rights Act 1996 for the purposes of-

(a) section 203(1), (2)(e) and (f), (3) and (4) of that Act (restrictions on contracting out), and

(b) section 18(1)(d) of the Employment Tribunals Act 1996 (conciliation).

15. Sections 10 to 13 of this Act shall not apply in relation to a person employed for the purposes of-

(a) the Security Service,

(b) the Secret Intelligence Service, or

(c) the Government Communications Headquarters.

s.15 – *Excludes employee of the Security Service, Secret Intelligence Service and GCHQ from the statutory rights conferred under s.10 to s.13 of this Act*

Commencement - *at the time of publication, no Commencement Order has been made specifying the date on which this section comes into force.*

Other rights of individuals

16. Schedule 5 shall have effect.

s.16 – This section changes the law regarding the right to make a claim of unfair dismissal by workers dismissed for taking part in industrial action. S.16 gives effect to Schedule 5 which extends the limited protection of the 1992 Act against unfair dismissal of those engaged in industrial action, to protect those who lawfully take organised official industrial action. It achieves this by adding a new s.238A after s.238 of the 1992 Act. S.238A does not extend protection to those involved in unofficial industrial action and are dismissed. S.238A introduces the concept of "protected industrial action".

In summary the protection exists during the first eight weeks, and beyond eight weeks if the employee has ceased industrial action before the expiry of the eight week period or if the employee is still engaged in industrial action beyond the eight week period but the employer has failed to follow such procedural steps as would have been reasonable to resolve the dispute. The employee is only protected if induced to commit the industrial action by his Union and the circumstances are such that the Union itself is protected under s.219 of the 1992 Act (protection from liability in tort for inducement to break, or interfere with, contract). The eight weeks runs from when the employee first takes part in the industrial action; it covers any industrial action, not just strikes, and the consequences of the action being protected is that dismissal is automatically unfair.

When assessing whether the employers have taken reasonable procedural steps to resolve the dispute, the Tribunal should take into particular account whether the employer or the Union have followed agreed disputes-resolution procedures, whether the employer or the Union have offered or agreed to commence or reopen negotiations after the action began; and whether the employer or the Union have unreasonably refused to involve a third party (usually ACAS) to help resolve the dispute through conciliation or through non-binding recommendations on procedural matters only from a mediator. The Tribunal must not involve itself in judging the merits of the dispute. See the notes to Schedule 5.

Commencement – *at the time of publication, no Commencement Order has been made specifying the date on which this section comes into force.*

17.– (1) The Secretary of State may make regulations about cases where a worker-

(a) is subjected to detriment by his employer, or
(b) is dismissed,

on the grounds that he refuses to enter into a contract which includes terms which differ from the terms of a collective agreement which applies to him.

(2) The regulations may-

    (a) make provision which applies only in specified classes of case;

    (b) make different provision for different circumstances;

    (c) include supplementary, incidental and transitional provision.

(3) In this section-

"collective agreement" has the meaning given by section 178(1) of the Trade Union and Labour Relations (Consolidation) Act 1992; and

"employer" and "worker" have the same meaning as in section 296 of that Act.

(4) The payment of higher wages or higher rates of pay or overtime or the payment of any signing on or other bonuses or the provision of other benefits having a monetary value to other workers employed by the same employer shall not constitute a detriment to any worker not receiving the same or similar payments or benefits within the meaning of subsection (1)(a) of this section so long as-

    (a) there is no inhibition in the contract of employment of the worker receiving the same from being the member of any trade union, and

    (b) the said payments of higher wages or rates of pay or overtime or bonuses or the provision of other benefits are in accordance with the terms of a contract of employment and reasonably relate to services provided by the worker under that contract.

s.17 – This section empowers the Secretary of State to make Regulations to protect workers from dismissal, or detriment short of dismissal, arising from a refusal to enter into an individual contract which includes terms different to those in a collective agreement which would otherwise apply. The definition of "a collective agreement" in s.178 of the 1992 Act is imported into the 1999 Act for these purposes.

Commencement – at the time of publication no Commencement Order has been made empowering the Secretary of State to make Regulations under this section. The Government have indicated that they propose to issue draft Regulations and consult on them before the Regulation themselves are made.

18.– (1) In section 197 of the Employment Rights Act 1996 (fixed-term contracts) subsections (1) and (2) (agreement to exclude unfair dismissal provisions) shall be omitted; and subsections (2) to (5) below shall have effect in consequence.

> **s.18** – *The usual position regarding statutory employment rights is that employees are not able to waive those rights by entering into an agreement with the employer to sign the rights away. There are however exceptions, including the right for workers on fixed term contracts lasting one year or more to enter into a written agreement, before the contract expires, waiving their right to claim unfair dismissal arising from a failure to renew the contract. The detailed rules are contained in s.197 and require careful reading as there are exceptions to the exceptions e.g. refusing to work on Sundays. A shop worker who has signed a waiver, and whose fixed term contract is not renewed because of a refusal to work Sundays, can nevertheless make a claim of unfair dismissal.*
>
> **s18(1)** – *This sub-section repeals s.197(1) of the 1996 Act. S.197(1) permits workers on fixed term contracts lasting one year or more to waive their rights to claim unfair dismissal arising from a failure to renew the contract. S.197(2) prevents a worker from waiving such protection e.g. where the reason for non-renewal is a refusal to work on Sundays. With the repeal of s.197(1) of the 1996 Act by s.18(1) a worker on a fixed term contract cannot waive unfair dismissal rights. S.197(2) of the 1996 Act is repealed because it is no longer necessary.*

(2) In sections 44(4), 46(2), 47(2), 47A(2) and 47B(2) of that Act-

    (a) the words from the beginning to "the dismissal," shall be omitted, and

    (b) for "that Part" there shall be substituted "Part X".

> **s18(2)** – *This sub-section repeals, as no longer necessary once s.18(1) is in force, those specified provisions in the 1996 Act which protect employees from detriment where, had they been dismissed, such dismissal would be regarded as automatically unfair e.g. health and safety cases.*

(3) In section 45A(4) of that Act the words from ", unless" to the end shall be omitted.

> **s18(3)** – *This sub-section makes equivalent consequential amendments to similar provisions on detriment in respect of working time in the 1996 Act.*

(4) In section 23 of the National Minimum Wage Act 1998, for subsection (4) there shall be substituted-

    "(4) This section does not apply where the detriment in question amounts to dismissal within the meaning of-

    (a) Part X of the Employment Rights Act 1996 (unfair dismissal), or

    (b) Part XI of the Employment Rights (Northern Ireland) Order 1996 (corresponding provision for Northern Ireland),

except where in relation to Northern Ireland the person in question is dismissed in circumstances in which, by virtue of Article 240 of that Order (fixed term contracts), Part XI does not apply to the dismissal."

s18(4) – *This sub-section makes equivalent consequential amendments to similar provisions on detriment in respect of The National Minimum Wage Act 1998.*

(5) In paragraph 1 of Schedule 3 to the Tax Credits Act 1999, for sub-paragraph (3) there shall be substituted-

"(3) This paragraph does not apply where the detriment in question amounts to dismissal within the meaning of-

    (a) Part X of the Employment Rights Act 1996 (unfair dismissal), or

    (b) Part XI of the Employment Rights (Northern Ireland) Order 1996 (corresponding provision for Northern Ireland),

except where in relation to Northern Ireland the employee is dismissed in circumstances in which, by virtue of Article 240 of that Order (fixed term contracts), Part XI does not apply to the dismissal."

s18(5) – *This sub-section makes equivalent consequential amendments to similar provisions on detriment in respect of The Tax Credits Act 1999.*

(6) Section 197(1) of the Employment Rights Act 1996 does not prevent Part X of that Act from applying to a dismissal which is regarded as unfair by virtue of section 99 or 104 of that Act (pregnancy and childbirth, and assertion of statutory right).

s18(6) – *This sub-section provides that where a fixed term contract is not renewed on grounds of pregnancy or maternity, or because the employee has asserted a statutory employment right, an existing unfair dismissal waiver under s.197(1) of the 1996 Act will not deprive the employee of a remedy for unfair dismissal. It was enacted, to allow earlier rectification of an anomaly, by Commencement Order No. 1 which brought sub-section (6) into effect on 30 September 1999. It has now been repealed by provisions coming into force under Commencement Order No. 2.*

Commencement – *Commencement Order No. 2 brought sub-sections (1)-(5) into effect on 25 October 1999 with transitional provisions for pre-25.10.99 waivers in para 2 of Schedule 3.*

19.– (1) The Secretary of State shall make regulations for the purpose of securing that persons in part-time employment are treated, for such purposes and to such extent as the regulations may specify, no less favourably than persons in full-time employment.

s.19

s.19(1) – Requires the Secretary of State to make Regulations to ensure that part-time workers receive equal treatment with full-time workers in accordance with the EU Directive on part-time work (Council Directive 97/81/EC). The aim of the Council Directive and the Framework Agreement between the European Social Partners is to remove discrimination against part-timers and improve the quality of part-time work. The Secretary of State requires statutory authority in the terms of s.19(1) because Directives which implement Framework Agreements cannot, under the Treaty of Amsterdam, cover pay. The Government have indicated that they do not wish to legislate piecemeal and wish to address pay as well as terms and conditions of employment at the same time.

(2) The regulations may-

   (a) specify classes of person who are to be taken to be, or not to be, in part-time employment;
   (b) specify classes of person who are to be taken to be, or not to be, in full-time employment;
   (c) specify circumstances in which persons in part-time employment are to be taken to be, or not to be, treated less favourably than persons in full-time employment;
   (d) make provision which has effect in relation to persons in part-time employment generally or provision which has effect only in relation to specified classes of persons in part-time employment.

s.19(2) – The Regulations may define what constitutes a part-time worker and a full-time worker. Without definitions the scope of protection would be unclear.

(3) The regulations may-

(a) confer jurisdiction (including exclusive jurisdiction) on employment tribunals and on the Employment Appeal Tribunal;

(b) create criminal offences in relation to specified acts or omissions by an employer, by an organisation of employers, by an organisation of workers or by an organisation existing for the purposes of a profession or trade carried on by the organisation's members;

(c) in specified cases or circumstances, extend liability for a criminal offence created under paragraph (b) to a person who aids the commission of the offence or to a person who is an agent, principal, employee, employer or officer of a person who commits the offence;

(d) provide for specified obligations or offences not to apply in specified circumstances;

(e) make provision about notices or information to be given, evidence to be produced and other procedures to be followed;

(f) amend, apply with or without modifications, or make provision similar to any provision of the Employment Rights Act 1996 (including, in particular, Parts V, X and XIII) or the Trade Union and Labour Relations (Consolidation) Act 1992;

(g) provide for the provisions of specified agreements to have effect in place of provisions of the regulations to such extent and in such circumstances as may be specified;

(h) include supplemental, incidental, consequential and transitional provision, including provision amending an enactment;

(i) make different provision for different cases or circumstances.

s.19(3) – *The Secretary of State may specify that any disputes may be heard only by Employment Tribunals, that appeals will lie to the Employment Appeal Tribunal and that certain related conduct may constitute a criminal offence. The Regulations may set up a procedure for requiring information from the employer, probably along the model of the existing discrimination questionnaires.*

(4) Without prejudice to the generality of this section the regulations may make any provision which appears to the Secretary of State to be necessary or expedient-

(a) for the purpose of implementing Council Directive 97/81/EC on the framework agreement on part-time work in its application to terms and conditions of employment;

(b) for the purpose of dealing with any matter arising out of or related to the United Kingdom's obligations under that Directive;

(c) for the purpose of any matter dealt with by the framework agreement or for the purpose of applying the provisions of the framework agreement to any matter relating to part-time workers.

s.19(4) – *Provides expressly that the scope of the Regulations is related to the Council Directive and the Framework Agreement on part-time work.*

Commencement - *At the time of publication no Commencement Order has been made empowering the Secretary of State to make Regulations under this section. The Government have indicated in* Fairness at Work *that it would implement the Directive before April 2000. The consultative document, containing draft Regulations, has a response deadline of 7 January 2000.*

(5) Regulations under this section which create an offence-

    (a) shall provide for it to be triable summarily only, and

    (b) may not provide for it to be punishable by imprisonment or by a fine in excess of level 5 on the standard scale.

20.– (1) The Secretary of State may issue codes of practice containing guidance for the purpose of-

    (a) eliminating discrimination in the field of employment against part-time workers;

    (b) facilitating the development of opportunities for part-time work;

    (c) facilitating the flexible organisation of working time taking into account the needs of workers and employers;

    (d) any matter dealt with in the framework agreement on part-time work annexed to Council Directive 97/81/EC.

(2) The Secretary of State may revise a code and issue the whole or part of the revised code.

(3) A person's failure to observe a provision of a code does not make him liable to any proceedings.

(4) A code-

    (a) is admissible in evidence in proceedings before an employment tribunal, and

    (b) shall be taken into account by an employment tribunal in any case in which it appears to the tribunal to be relevant.

s.20 – *The Secretary of State may issue Codes of Practice relating to part-time work. Breach of such a Code would not alone amount to a breach of a statutory employment right but the Tribunal may take into account the provisions of such a Code if it considers it to be relevant.*

Commencement – *The Commencement Order No. 2 empowers the Secretary of State, with effect from 25 October 1999 to make Regulations under this section.*

21.– (1) Before issuing or revising a code of practice under section 20 the Secretary of State shall consult such persons as he considers appropriate.

(2) Before issuing a code the Secretary of State shall-

    (a) publish a draft code,

    (b) consider any representations made to him about the draft,

    (c) if he thinks it appropriate, modify the draft in the light of any representations made to him.

(3) If, having followed the procedure under subsection (2), the Secretary of State decides to issue a code, he shall lay a draft code before each House of Parliament.

(4) If the draft code is approved by resolution of each House of Parliament, the Secretary of State shall issue the code in the form of the draft.

(5) In this section and section 20(3) and (4)-

    (a) a reference to a code includes a reference to a revised code,

    (b) a reference to a draft code includes a reference to a draft revision, and

    (c) a reference to issuing a code includes a reference to issuing part of a revised code.

> **s.21** – *The section sets out the process by which a Code can be issued or revised. There must be prior consultation on any draft Code or revision, responses to the consultative process must be taken into account before laying the Code or the revision before both Houses of Parliament and there must be an affirmative resolution of both Houses before the Code or revision can be issued.*
>
> Commencement - *This section came into force on 25 October 1999 under Commencement Order No.2. However, no draft Code has been issued for consultation at the date of publication.*

22. The following shall be inserted after section 44 of the National Minimum Wage Act 1998 (exclusions: voluntary workers)-

    "**44A.**– (1) A residential member of a community to which this section applies does not qualify for the national minimum wage in respect of employment by the community.

    (2) Subject to subsection (3), this section applies to a community if-

        (a) it is a charity or is established by a charity,

        (b) a purpose of the community is to practise or advance a belief of a religious or similar nature, and

        (c) all or some of its members live together for that purpose.

    (3) This section does not apply to a community which-

(a) is an independent school, or

(b) provides a course of further or higher education.

(4) The residential members of a community are those who live together as mentioned in subsection (2)(c).

(5) In this section-

(a) "charity" has the same meaning as in section 44, and

(b) "independent school" has the same meaning as in section 463 of the Education Act 1996 (in England and Wales), section 135 of the Education (Scotland) Act 1980 (in Scotland) and Article 2 of the Education and Libraries (Northern Ireland) Order 1986 (in Northern Ireland).

(6) In this section "course of further or higher education" means-

(a) in England and Wales, a course of a description referred to in Schedule 6 to the Education Reform Act 1988 or Schedule 2 to the Further and Higher Education Act 1992;

(b) in Scotland, a course or programme of a description mentioned in or falling within section 6(1) or 38 of the Further and Higher Education (Scotland) Act 1992;

(c) in Northern Ireland, a course of a description referred to in Schedule 1 to the Further Education (Northern Ireland) Order 1997 or a course providing further education within the meaning of Article 3 of that Order."

s.22 – *Amends the National Minimum Wage Act 1998 to exempt residential members of religious or other similar communities thereby implementing recommendation by the Low Pay Commission Report (Cm 4321 March 1999) and a commitment by the Secretary of State in the House of Commons on 31 March 1999 (Commons Hansard WA cols 812-813). The exemption will apply to individuals if, the community of which they are a member is a charity or is established by a charity (but is not an independent school or a community which provides a course of Further or Higher Education); a purpose of the community is to practise or advance a religious or similar belief; and all or some of the members live together for that purpose.*

Commencement – *This section came into force on 25 October 1999 under Commencement Order No.2*

23.– (1) This section applies to any right conferred on an individual against an employer (however defined) under or by virtue of any of the following-

(a) the Trade Union and Labour Relations (Consolidation) Act 1992;

(b) the Employment Rights Act 1996;

(c) this Act;

(d) any instrument made under section 2(2) of the European Communities Act 1972.

(2) The Secretary of State may by order make provision which has the effect of conferring any such right on individuals who are of a specified description.

(3) The reference in subsection (2) to individuals includes a reference to individuals expressly excluded from exercising the right.

(4) An order under this section may-

(a) provide that individuals are to be treated as parties to workers' contracts or contracts of employment;

(b) make provision as to who are to be regarded as the employers of individuals;

(c) make provision which has the effect of modifying the operation of any right as conferred on individuals by the order;

(d) include such consequential, incidental or supplementary provisions as the Secretary of State thinks fit.

(5) An order under this section may make provision in such way as the Secretary of State thinks fit, whether by amending Acts or instruments or otherwise.

(6) Section 209(7) of the Employment Rights Act 1996 (which is superseded by this section) shall be omitted.

(7) Any order made or having effect as if made under section 209(7), so far as effective immediately before the commencement of this section, shall have effect as if made under this section.

s.23 – This section gives the Secretary of State power to extend statutory employment rights to individuals who do not currently have such rights under the 1992, 1996 and 1999 Acts and any Instrument made under s.2(2) of the European Communities Act 1972. Much of the employment rights legislation applies at present to a relatively narrow band of employees *i.e. those engaged under a contract of employment, while some of the rights are extended to a wider category of* worker. *There are many individuals with atypical work relationships who either fall outside the definition of* employee *or* worker *or whose status under such definitions is unclear. The Government propose to use s.23 to ensure that all workers other than the genuinely self-employed are covered by the statutory regime of minimum standards of protection regardless of the technicalities or whether their working relationship is typical or atypical. The Secretary of State's power to confer rights on individuals is exercisable by Order requiring affirmative resolution. The Order must be laid in draft, and approved by resolution of each House of Parliament, by virtue of s.42.*

Commencement – This section came into force on 25 October 1999 under Commencement Order No. 2, the power of the Secretary of State to make an Order exercisable by statutory instrument having come into force on 30 September 1999 under Commencement Order No. 1. No proposals for the implementation of this section have yet been made public.

CAC, ACAS, Commissioners and Certification Officer

24. In section 260 of the Trade Union and Labour Relations (Consolidation) Act 1992 (members of the Committee) these subsections shall be substituted for subsections (1) to (3)-

"(1) The Central Arbitration Committee shall consist of members appointed by the Secretary of State.

(2) The Secretary of State shall appoint a member as chairman, and may appoint a member as deputy chairman or members as deputy chairmen.

(3) The Secretary of State may appoint as members only persons experienced in industrial relations, and they shall include some persons whose experience is as representatives of employers and some whose experience is as representatives of workers.

(3A) Before making an appointment under subsection (1) or (2) the Secretary of State shall consult ACAS and may consult other persons."

s.24 – This section amends the procedures for the appointment of members to the CAC and contains new provisions amending s.260 of the 1992 Act. In short, the Secretary of State has power to appoint all members of the CAC, the Chairman and one or more Deputy Chairmen, after consulting ACAS and others as he sees fit. The appointees must be experienced in industrial relations and the Secretary of State must ensure that membership includes experienced individuals from both sides of industry.

Commencement - At the time of publication, no Commencement Order has been made specifying the date on which this section comes into force.

25.– (1) The Trade Union and Labour Relations (Consolidation) Act 1992 shall be amended as follows.

(2) In section 263 (proceedings of the Committee) this subsection shall be inserted after subsection (6)-

"(7) In relation to the discharge of the Committee's functions under Schedule A1-

(a) section 263A and subsection (6) above shall apply, and

(b) subsections (1) to (5) above shall not apply."

(3) This section shall be inserted after section 263-

"**263A.**– (1) For the purpose of discharging its functions under Schedule A1 in any particular case, the Central Arbitration Committee shall consist of a panel established under this section.

(2) The chairman of the Committee shall establish a panel or panels, and a panel shall consist of these three persons appointed by him-

(a) the chairman or a deputy chairman of the Committee, who shall be chairman of the panel;

(b) a member of the Committee whose experience is as a representative of employers;

(c) a member of the Committee whose experience is as a representative of workers.

(3) The chairman of the Committee shall decide which panel is to deal with a particular case.

(4) A panel may at the discretion of its chairman sit in private where it appears expedient to do so.

(5) If-

(a) a panel cannot reach a unanimous decision on a question arising before it, and

(b) a majority of the panel have the same opinion,

the question shall be decided according to that opinion.

(6) If-

(a) a panel cannot reach a unanimous decision on a question arising before it, and

(b) a majority of the panel do not have the same opinion,

the chairman of the panel shall decide the question acting with the full powers of an umpire or, in Scotland, an oversman.

(7) Subject to the above provisions, a panel shall determine its own procedure."

(4) In section 264 (awards of the Committee)-

(a) in subsection (1) after "award" there shall be inserted ", or in any decision or declaration of the Committee under Schedule A1,";

(b) in subsection (2) after "of the Committee," there shall be inserted "or of a decision or declaration of the Committee under Schedule A1,".

> **s.25** - *This section extends s.263 of the 1992 Act to establish the composition of the CAC' and how it conducts its proceeding when discharging its function in relation to recognition and derecognition issues under s.1 of the Act.*
>
> Commencement - *At the time of publication, no Commencement Order has been made specifying the date on which this section comes into force.*

26. In section 209 of the Trade Union and Labour Relations (Consolidation) Act 1992 (ACAS' general duty) the words from ", in particular" to the end shall be omitted.

> **s.26** – *The general duty of ACAS set out in s.209 of the 1992 Act is amended by deleting the requirement on ACAS to give priority to dispute resolution. S.209 now reads* "it is the general duty of ACAS to promote the improvement of industrial relations".
>
> Commencement – *This section came into force on 25 October 1999 under Commencement Order No.2*

27.– (1) In section 253(1) of the Trade Union and Labour Relations (Consolidation) Act 1992 (ACAS: annual report) for "calendar year" there shall be substituted "financial year".

(2) In section 265(1) of that Act (ACAS: report about CAC) for "calendar year" there shall be substituted "financial year".

> **s.27** – *The reporting arrangements for ACAS and the CAC are amended by changing the period covered by the Annual Report from a calendar year to a financial year. This means that the periods covered by the ACAS Annual Report and its accounts will be the same. Similarly the periods covered by the CAC's Report and Financial Account will be the same.*
>
> Commencement – *This section came into force on 25 October 1999 under Commencement Order No.2*

28.– (1) These offices shall cease to exist-

    (a) the office of Commissioner for the Rights of Trade Union Members;
    (b) the office of Commissioner for Protection Against Unlawful Industrial Action.

(2) In the Trade Union and Labour Relations (Consolidation) Act 1992 these provisions shall cease to have effect-

(a) Chapter VIII of Part I (provision by Commissioner for the Rights of Trade Union Members of assistance in relation to certain proceedings);

(b) sections 235B and 235C (provision of assistance by Commissioner for Protection Against Unlawful Industrial Action of assistance in relation to certain proceedings);

(c) section 266 (and the heading immediately preceding it) and sections 267 to 271 (Commissioners' appointment, remuneration, staff, reports, accounts, etc.).

(3) In section 32A of that Act (statement to members of union following annual return) in the third paragraph of subsection (6)(a) (application for assistance from Commissioner for the Rights of Trade Union Members) for the words from "may" to "case," there shall be substituted "should".

s.28 – *Two public offices are abolished; the Commissioner for the Rights of Trade Union Members and the Commissioner for Protection against Unlawful Industrial Action, with consequential amendments. Both posts were part-time appointments held by the same individual. The workload of the Commission for the Rights of Trade Union Members was on average ten applications a year. The Commissioner for Protection against Unlawful Industrial Action provided assistance with only one application.*

Commencement – *This section came into force on 25 October 1999 under Commencement Order No.2, subject to the Commissioner having power to continue to act in cases where an application for assistance had been made before that date.*

29. Schedule 6 shall have effect.

s.29 – *Gives effect to Schedule 6 which amends the Certification Officer's statutory powers in the 1992 Act. The Certification Officer is an independent statutory officer established under the Employment Protection Act 1975 whose current functions include the maintenance of lists of Trade Unions and Employers' Associations; monitoring compliance with statutory memberships and accounting requirements; auditing accounts; monitoring annual return, financial affairs and political funds; and procedures for amalgamations and transfers of engagement. The detailed and important provisions are set out in Schedule 6 and summarised in the notes to the Schedule.*

Commencement – *This section came into force on 25 October 1999 under Commencement Order No. 2*

Miscellaneous

30.– (1) The Secretary of State may spend money or provide money to other persons for the purpose of encouraging and helping employers (or their representatives) and employees (or their representatives) to improve the way they work together.

(2) Money may be provided in such way as the Secretary of State thinks fit (whether as grants or otherwise) and on such terms as he thinks fit (whether as to repayment or otherwise).

s.30 – *This section authorises the Secretary of State to provide funding to assist and develop partnerships at work and to establish and communicate examples of good practice. Illustrative insight to the Government's purpose is set out in Chapter 2 of* Fairness at Work.

Commencement – *This section came into force on 25 October 1999 under Commencement Order No.2*

31. Schedule 7 shall have effect.

s.31 – *Gives effect to Schedule 7 which amends the Employment Agencies Act 1973. The effect is to give the Secretary of State wider powers of regulation to secure the proper conduct of Employment Agencies and Employment businesses and to protect the interests of persons using such Agencies and businesses e.g. prohibitions on charging fees to prospective employees. The principal provisions are summarised in the notes to Schedule 7.*

Commencement – *This section came into force in part on 25 October 1999 under Commencement Order No. 2*

32.– (1) In section 285(1) of the Trade Union and Labour Relations (Consolidation) Act 1992 (employment outside Great Britain) for "Chapter II (procedure for handling redundancies)" there shall be substituted "sections 193 and 194 (duty to notify Secretary of State of certain redundancies)".

(2) After section 287(3) of that Act (offshore employment) there shall be inserted-

"(3A) An Order in Council under this section shall be subject to annulment in pursuance of a resolution of either House of Parliament.".

(3) Section 196 of the Employment Rights Act 1996 (employment outside Great Britain) shall cease to have effect; and in section 5(1) for "sections 196 and" there shall be substituted "section".

(4) After section 199(6) of that Act (mariners) there shall be inserted-

"(7) The provisions mentioned in subsection (8) apply to employment on board a ship registered in the register maintained under section 8 of the Merchant Shipping Act 1995 if and only if-

(a) the ship's entry in the register specifies a port in Great Britain as the port to which the vessel is to be treated as belonging,

(b) under his contract of employment the person employed does not work wholly outside Great Britain, and

(c) the person employed is ordinarily resident in Great Britain.

(8) The provisions are-

(a) sections 8 to 10,

(b) Parts II, III and V,

(c) Part VI, apart from sections 58 to 60,

(d) Parts VII and VIII,

(e) sections 92 and 93, and

(f) Part X."

s.32 – *This section repeals the statutory provisions in the 1992 and 1996 Acts which limit the application of certain employment rights generally to those who ordinarily work in Great Britain. Its effect will include for example providing employment rights to airline crew, based in Great Britain, employed by a foreign airline where their work is ordinarily outside Great Britain. There are two technical provisions; an amendment to s.199 of the 1996 Act means that Seafarers will be eligible for certain employment rights under the 1996 Act if and only if the ship on which they are employed is registered as reporting to a Port in Great Britain, they are ordinarily resident in Great Britain and the work is not wholly outside Great Britain; and s.287 of the 1992 Act is amended to provide that where employment rights are extended by Order in Council to offshore employees (primarily oil and gas rigs in the North Sea), such Order is subject to negative resolution procedure. At present no procedure is specified for making such Orders.*

Commencement – *This section came into force on 25 October 1999 under Commencement Order No. 2.*

33.– (1) The following provisions (which require, or relate to, the making of special awards by employment tribunals in unfair dismissal cases) shall cease to have effect-

(a) sections 117(4)(b), 118(2) and (3) and 125 of the Employment Rights Act 1996 (and the word "or" before section 117(4)(b));

(b) sections 157 and 158 of the Trade Union and Labour Relations (Consolidation) Act 1992.

(2) In section 117(3)(b) of the Employment Rights Act 1996 (amount of additional award) for "the appropriate amount" there shall be substituted "an amount not less than twenty-six nor more than fifty-two weeks' pay"; and subsections (5) and (6) of section 117 shall cease to have effect.

(3) In section 14 of the Employment Rights (Dispute Resolution) Act 1998-

(a) subsection (1) shall cease to have effect, and

(b) in subsection (2) for "that Act" substitute "the Employment Rights Act 1996".

> **s.33** – *Replaces special awards in unfair dismissal cases with additional awards. If a Tribunal makes an Order for reinstatement or re-engagement of an employee who has been unfairly dismissed and the employer fails to comply with the Order, the Tribunal will assess the basic and compensatory awards and consider making an* additional award *of between 13 to 26 weeks pay or between 26 and 52 weeks pay if a dismissal involves unlawful discrimination (sex, race or disability). Where the employee has been unfairly dismissed because of membership or non-membership of a Trade Union activities, certain activities as an employee representative or Occupational Pension Scheme Trustee or for having taken certain types of action on health and safety grounds, the Tribunal may award, as an* alternative *to an* additional award, a *special award of 104 weeks pay. This may be awarded even if re-employment is not ordered. S.33 repeals the special award provisions, replacing them with additional awards and provides that the additional award will consist of between 26 and 52 weeks pay.*
>
> Commencement – *This section came into force on 25 October 1999 under Commencement Order No. 2.*

34.– (1) This section applies to the sums specified in the following provisions-

(a) section 31(1) of the Employment Rights Act 1996 (guarantee payments: limits);

(b) section 120(1) of that Act (unfair dismissal: minimum amount of basic award);

(c) section 124(1) of that Act (unfair dismissal: limit of compensatory award);

(d) section 186(1)(a) and (b) of that Act (employee's rights on insolvency of employer: maximum amount payable);

(e) section 227(1) of that Act (maximum amount of a week's pay for purposes of certain calculations);

(f) section 156(1) of the Trade Union and Labour Relations (Consolidation) Act 1992 (unfair dismissal: minimum basic award);

(g) section 176(6) of that Act (right to membership of trade union: remedies).

> **s.34** – *This section provides that limits on certain payments and Employment Tribunal awards should be indexed linked rather than subject to annual or discretionary review. The types of payment or award are set out in s.34(1), e.g. the limits on guaranteed payments, compensatory award, employee's rights on the employer's insolvency. These payments and awards will be linked to the retail prices index using the September index as the reference point. An Order must be made by statutory instrument and laid before Parliament.*

(2) If the retail prices index for September of a year is higher or lower than the index for the previous September, the Secretary of State shall as soon as practicable make an order in relation to each sum mentioned in subsection (1)-

    (a) increasing each sum, if the new index is higher, or
    (b) decreasing each sum, if the new index is lower,

> **s.34(2)** – *See the note to s.34(6)*

by the same percentage as the amount of the increase or decrease of the index.

(3) In making the calculation required by subsection (2) the Secretary of State shall-

    (a) in the case of the sum mentioned in subsection (1)(a), round the result up to the nearest 10 pence,
    (b) in the case of the sums mentioned in subsection (1)(b), (c), (f) and (g), round the result up to the nearest £100, and
    (c) in the case of the sums mentioned in subsection (1)(d) and (e), round the result up to the nearest £10.

(4) For the sum specified in section 124(1) of the Employment Rights Act 1996 (unfair dismissal: limit of compensatory award) there shall be substituted the sum of £50,000 (subject to subsection (2) above).

s34(4) – *Raises the former limit of £12,000 on the compensatory award to a maximum limit of £50,000 subject to future adjustment under the indexation provisions. Although he vast majority of compensatory awards have been well below the £12,000 limit, the limit has operated in a number of cases to prevent full compensation for the employee's loss. As there is no limit on the potential compensation in discrimination cases this may have resulted in a number discrimination claims being pursued against the merits of such complaint, in order to gain potentially higher compensation. For the immediate future there should be less need to resort to such a device.* Fairness at Work *proposed the abolition of the upper limit altogether but the views expressed through the consultation process resulted in the substitution of a higher cap which broadly restores the original value of the maximum award in 1972 adjusted for subsequent pay inflation.*

Commencement – *s.34(4), the increase in the limit of the compensatory award to £50,000 came into force on 25 October 1999 under Commencement Order No. 2. The increase in the compensatory award applies if the effective date of termination (as defined in s.97 of the 1996 Act) was on or after the commencement date. All the remaining subsections came into force on 17 December 1999 under Commencement Order No. 3.*

(5) In this section "the retail prices index" means-

  (a) the general index of retail prices (for all items) published by the Office for National Statistics, or
  (b) where that index is not published for a month, any substituted index or figures published by that Office.

(6) An order under this section-

  (a) shall be made by statutory instrument,
  (b) may include transitional provision, and
  (c) shall be laid before Parliament after being made.

s.34(6) – *In relation to the first order under s.34(6), when it is made, the reference in s.34(2) to "the previous September" shall be treated as if it were "September 1997 – Article 3 of Commencement Order No. 3."*

35. For section 31(7) of the Employment Rights Act 1996 (guarantee payments: limits) there shall be substituted-

  "(7) The Secretary of State may by order vary-

  (a) the length of the period specified in subsection (2);

(b) a limit specified in subsection (3) or (4)."

> **s.35** – *The effect of this section is that there will no longer be annual reviews of the time periods in respect of guaranteed payments. Subject to meeting a number of conditions, guaranteed payments are made to employees for up to five days of layoff in any three month period and are subject to annual review. The time periods may be varied under s.35 by Order of the Secretary of State subject to the negative resolution procedure.*
>
> Commencement – *This section came into force in part on 25 October 1999 under Commencement Order No. 2*

36.– (1) The following provisions (which confer power to increase sums) shall cease to have effect-

  (a) sections 120(2), 124(2), 186(2) and 227(2) to (4) of the Employment Rights Act 1996;

  (b) sections 159 and 176(7) and (8) of the Trade Union and Labour Relations (Consolidation) Act 1992.

(2) Section 208 of the Employment Rights Act 1996 (review of limits) shall cease to have effect.

(3) An increase effected, before section 34 comes into force, by virtue of a provision repealed by this section shall continue to have effect notwithstanding this section (but subject to section 34(2) and (4)).

> **s.36** *These are technical provisions consequential on s.33-s.35, repealing existing powers for increasing certain limits, annual review requirements and transitional arrangements prior to s.34 coming force. The repeal of s.159(1)(b) of the 1992 Act came into effect on 25·10·99 under Commencement Order No. 2. All other provisions of s.36 came into effect on 17·12·99 under Commencement Order No. 3.*

37.– (1) After section 124(1) of the Employment Rights Act 1996 (limit of compensatory award etc) there shall be inserted-

"(1A) Subsection (1) shall not apply to compensation awarded, or a compensatory award made, to a person in a case where he is regarded as unfairly dismissed by virtue of section 100, 103A, 105(3) or 105(6A)."

(2) Section 127B of that Act (power to specify method of calculation of compensation where dismissal a result of protected disclosure) shall cease to have effect.

s.37 – *This section removes the upper limit on compensation where an employee is unfairly dismissed or selected for redundancy for reasons connected with health and safety matters, under s.100(1) of the 1996 Act or for whistle-blowing under the Public Interests Disclosure Act 1998 ("the 1998 Act") which came into force on 2 July 1999. Accordingly s.127B of the 1996 Act and the Regulation (SI 1999/1548) made under that power for calculating compensation in whistle blowing cases, cease to have effect.*

Commencement – *This section came into force in part on 25 October 1999 under Commencement Order No. 2*

38.– (1) This section applies where regulations under section 2(2) of the European Communities Act 1972 (general implementation of Treaties) make provision for the purpose of implementing, or for a purpose concerning, a Community obligation of the United Kingdom which relates to the treatment of employees on the transfer of an undertaking or business or part of an undertaking or business.

(2) The Secretary of State may by regulations make the same or similar provision in relation to the treatment of employees in circumstances other than those to which the Community obligation applies (including circumstances in which there is no transfer, or no transfer to which the Community obligation applies).

(3) Regulations under this section shall be subject to annulment in pursuance of a resolution of either House of Parliament.

s.38 – *This section gives the Secretary of State power to make provision by statutory instrument, subject to the negative resolution procedure, for employees to be given the same or similar treatment in specified circumstances falling outside the scope for the EC Acquired Rights Directive 77/187/EEC as they are given under the Transfer of Undertakings (Protection of Employment) Regulations 1981 as amended in circumstances falling within the scope of that Directive. The DTI has said this power may be used to ensure the equivalent of TUPE protection for all contracting-out of services.*

Commencement – *Commencement Order No. 1 empowered the Secretary of State with effect from 30 September 1999 to make Regulations under this section. At the time of publication no Regulations have been made. Regulations relating to the transfer of Rent Officers were made in September 1999.*

39.– (1) Information obtained by a revenue official in the course of carrying out a function of the Commissioners of Inland Revenue may be-

(a) supplied by the Commissioners of Inland Revenue to the Secretary of State for any purpose relating to the National Minimum Wage Act 1998;

(b) supplied by the Secretary of State with the authority of the Commissioners of Inland Revenue to any person acting under section 13(1)(b) of that Act;

(c) supplied by the Secretary of State with the authority of the Commissioners of Inland Revenue to an officer acting for the purposes of any of the agricultural wages legislation.

(2) In this section-

"revenue official" means an officer of the Commissioners of Inland Revenue appointed under section 4 of the Inland Revenue Regulation Act 1890 (appointment of collectors, officers and other persons), and

"the agricultural wages legislation" has the same meaning as in section 16 of the National Minimum Wage Act 1998 (agricultural wages officers).

s.39 – *This section allows Inland Revenue Officials to pass information obtained in respect of tax and national insurance contributions to their colleagues in the Inland Revenue's NMW (National Minimum Wage) Compliance Teams and to others where this will assist in NMW enforcement. Inland Revenue safeguards on confidentiality and disclosure remain intact. This is the only section in the 1999 Act which applies to Northern Ireland.*

Commencement – *This section came into force on 25 October 1999 under Commencement Order No. 2*

40.– (1) In paragraph 27(3)(b) of Schedule 16 to the School Standards and Framework Act 1998 (dismissal of staff: representations and appeal) for "for a period of two years or more (within the meaning of the Rights Act 1996)" there shall be substituted ", within the meaning of the Employment Rights Act 1996, for a period at least as long as the period for the time being specified in section 108(1) of that Act (unfair dismissal: qualifying period)".

(2) In paragraph 24(4)(b) of Schedule 17 to the School Standards and Framework Act 1998 (dismissal of staff: representations and appeal) for "for a period of two years or more (within the meaning of the Employment Rights Act 1996)" there shall be substituted ", within the meaning of the Employment Rights Act 1996, for a period at least as long as the period for the time being specified in section 108(1) of that Act (unfair dismissal: qualifying period)".

s.40 – *Contains technical provisions of interest to those concerned with compliance with the School Standards and Framework Act 1998. The effect of the Act is to require schools to give staff facing dismissal the right to make representations and the right to appeal. This right is disapplied to staff with less than two years continuous employment, linked to the qualifying period for protection against unfair dismissal. As the service requirement for unfair dismissal was reduced to one year on 1 June 1999 under SI 1999/1436, s.40 amends the School Standards and Framework Act 1998 to link it with whatever qualifying period is in force from time to time under the 1996 Act.*

Commencement – *This section came into force on 25 October 1999 under Commencement Order No. 2*

41. Schedule 8 shall have effect.

s.41 – *This section gives effect to Schedule 8 which will allow certain Crown servants, including staff of Security and Intelligence Agencies, access to a range of statutory employment rights and the right to make claims in respect of them to an Employment Tribunal and restrains the powers of Ministers to impose restrictions on Tribunal hearings in the interests of National Security.*

Commencement – *at the time of publication, no Commencement Order has been made specifying the date on which this section comes into force.*

General

42.– (1) Any power to make an order or regulations under this Act shall be exercised by statutory instrument.

(2) No order or regulations shall be made under section 3, 17, 19 or 23 unless a draft has been laid before, and approved by resolution of, each House of Parliament.

s.42 – *Any power in the 1999 Act given to the Secretary of State to make an Order or Regulation is exercisable by statutory instrument. In four cases such secondary legislation requires affirmative resolution by each House of Parliament i.e. Regulations prohibiting blacklisting Trade Union members (s.3); Regulations about cases where a worker is subjected to a detriment or is dismissed because of a refusal to enter into an individual contract which differs from the terms of a collective agreement (s.17); Regulations to prevent discrimination against part-time workers (s.19); and an order broadening the application of employment protection rights to those in atypical work relationships (s.23). Schedule 4 inserts regulation-making provisions to the 1996 Act which also require affirmative resolution, but s.42 does not deal with these because they are part of the 1996 Act.*

Commencement – *This section came into force on 30 September 1999 under Commencement Order No. 1*

43. There shall be paid out of money provided by Parliament-

   (a) any increase attributable to this Act in the sums so payable under any other enactment;

   (b) any other expenditure of the Secretary of State under this Act.

s.43 – *This section provides for Parliament to fund the costs arising from the 1999 Act.*

Commencement – *This section came into force in part on 25 October 1999 under Commencement Order No. 2*

44. The provisions mentioned in Schedule 9 are repealed (or revoked) to the extent specified in column 3.

s.44 – *This section provides a Table of Repeals set out in Schedule 9. The repeals specified in column 3 of Schedule 9 came into force on 17 December 1999 under Commencement Order No. 3 but only to the extent set out in the Schedule to Commencement Order No. 3 (column 3).*

45.– (1) The preceding provisions of this Act shall come into force in accordance with provision made by the Secretary of State by order made by statutory instrument.

(2) An order under this section-

   (a) may make different provision for different purposes;

(b) may include supplementary, incidental, saving or transitional provisions.

> **s.45** – *This section gives the Secretary of State the power to introduce provisions of the Act by Order made by statutory instrument and for such Orders to make different provisions for different purposes and to include supplementary incidental saving or transitional provisions.*

46.– (1) Any amendment or repeal in this Act has the same extent as the provision amended or repealed.

(2) An Order in Council under paragraph 1(1)(b) of Schedule 1 to the Northern Ireland Act 1974 (legislation for Northern Ireland in the interim period) which contains a statement that it is made only for purposes corresponding to any of the purposes of this Act-

   (a) shall not be subject to paragraph 1(4) and (5) of that Schedule (affirmative resolution of both Houses of Parliament), but
   (b) shall be subject to annulment in pursuance of a resolution of either House of Parliament.

(3) Apart from sections 39 and 45 and subject to subsection (1), the preceding sections of this Act shall not extend to Northern Ireland.

> **s.46** – *Provides that any amendment or appeal is coextensive with the provision amended or repealed. Except for s.39, permitting the provision of information by Inland Revenue Officials for the purpose of The National Minimum Wage legislation, the 1999 Act does not apply to Northern Ireland. An Employment Relations (NI) Order was made on 12 October 1999 in substantially the same terms as the 1999 Act.*

47. This Act may be cited as the Employment Relations Act 1999.

> **s.47** – *This section provides for the 1999 Act to be cited as the Employment Relations Act 1999.*
>
> Commencement – 27 July 1999

SCHEDULES

SCHEDULE 1

SECTION 1

COLLECTIVE BARGAINING: RECOGNITION

The Schedule to be inserted immediately before Schedule 1 to the Trade Union and Labour Relations (Consolidation) Act 1992 is as follows-

"SCHEDULE A1

COLLECTIVE BARGAINING: RECOGNITION

PART I

RECOGNITION

SCHEDULE 1 – Part I

Contains:

Procedures for the recognition of an independent Trade Union to conduct collective bargaining on behalf of a bargaining unit i.e a specific group of workers. Part I sets out:

- *The means of establishing the bargaining unit*
- *Whether the Union has the right to be recognised*
- *How collective bargaining should be undertaken*

The main elements and progression through the recognition procedure and the process of establishing the method of collective bargaining are helpfully summarised in the two flowcharts in the DTI's Explanatory Notes at http://www.dti.gov.uk

Introduction

1. A trade union (or trade unions) seeking recognition to be entitled to conduct collective bargaining on behalf of a group or groups of workers may make a request in accordance with this Part of this Schedule.

2.– (1) This paragraph applies for the purposes of this Part of this Schedule.

(2) References to the bargaining unit are to the group of workers concerned (or the groups taken together).

(3) References to the proposed bargaining unit are to the bargaining unit proposed in the request for recognition.

(4) References to the employer are to the employer of the workers constituting the bargaining unit concerned.

(5) References to the parties are to the union (or unions) and the employer.

3.– (1) This paragraph applies for the purposes of this Part of this Schedule.

(2) The meaning of collective bargaining given by section 178(1) shall not apply.

(3) References to collective bargaining are to negotiations relating to pay, hours and holidays; but this has effect subject to sub-paragraph (4).

> **Part I - Recognition**
> **Introduction:**
> *Paras 1-3 - Provides a recognition application to be made by a single Union or a group of Unions and contains definitions of the following terms, Bargaining Unit, Proposed Bargaining Unit, Employer, Parties, Collective Bargaining and the scope of that term for the purpose of the Schedule. Briefly these are that the requesting Union must be independent, the request must be in writing and contain the information specified in paras 8(b) and (c), and para 7 below. (The Secretary of State has power to prescribe a mandatory form of request by statutory instrument. Para 9 will be helpful if a model is made available by this means to minimise the risk of technical challenges).*

(4) If the parties agree matters as the subject of collective bargaining, references to collective bargaining are to negotiations relating to the agreed matters; and this is the case whether the agreement is made before or after the time when the CAC issues a declaration, or the parties agree, that the union is (or unions are) entitled to conduct collective bargaining on behalf of a bargaining unit.

(5) Sub-paragraph (4) does not apply in construing paragraph 31(3).

(6) Sub-paragraphs (2) to (5) do not apply in construing paragraph 35 or 44.

Request for recognition

4.– (1) The union or unions seeking recognition must make a request for recognition to the employer.

(2) Paragraphs 5 to 9 apply to the request.

5.   The request is not valid unless it is received by the employer.

6.   The request is not valid unless the union (or each of the unions) has a certificate under section 6 that it is independent.

7.– (1) The request is not valid unless the employer, taken with any associated employer or employers, employs-

(a) at least 21 workers on the day the employer receives the request, or
(b) an average of at least 21 workers in the 13 weeks ending with that day.

(2) To find the average under sub-paragraph (1)(b)-

(a) take the number of workers employed in each of the 13 weeks (including workers not employed for the whole of the week);
(b) aggregate the 13 numbers;
(c) divide the aggregate by 13.

(3) For the purposes of sub-paragraph (1)(a) any worker employed by an associated company incorporated outside Great Britain must be ignored unless the day the request was made fell within a period during which he ordinarily worked in Great Britain.

(4) For the purposes of sub-paragraph (1)(b) any worker employed by an associated company incorporated outside Great Britain must be ignored in relation to a week unless the whole or any part of that week fell within a period during which he ordinarily worked in Great Britain.

(5) For the purposes of sub-paragraphs (3) and (4) a worker who is employed on board a ship registered in the register maintained under section 8 of the Merchant Shipping Act 1995 shall be treated as ordinarily working in Great Britain unless-

(a) the ship's entry in the register specifies a port outside Great Britain as the port to which the vessel is to be treated as belonging,
(b) the employment is wholly outside Great Britain, or
(c) the worker is not ordinarily resident in Great Britain.

(6) The Secretary of State may by order-

(a) provide that sub-paragraphs (1) to (5) are not to apply, or are not to apply in specified circumstances, or
(b) vary the number of workers for the time being specified in sub-paragraph (1);

and different provision may be made for different circumstances.

(7) An order under sub-paragraph (6)-

(a) shall be made by statutory instrument, and
(b) may include supplementary, incidental, saving or transitional provisions.

(8) No such order shall be made unless a draft of it has been laid before Parliament and approved by a resolution of each House of Parliament.

8.   The request is not valid unless it-

(a) is in writing,
(b) identifies the union or unions and the bargaining unit, and
(c) states that it is made under this Schedule.

9. The Secretary of State may by order made by statutory instrument prescribe the form of requests and the procedure for making them; and if he does so the request is not valid unless it complies with the order.

> **Request for Recognition:**
> *Paras 4-9 - Provides that the recognition process commences with a formal request from the Union which in order to be valid has to meet the criteria set out in paragraphs 5-9. To be independent the Union must have a Certificate of Independence from the Certification Officer (see ss.2-9 of the 1992 Act). In particular para 7 exempts small employers with fewer than 21 workers. The Secretary of State may vary the exemption threshold by statutory instrument. There are detailed provisions regarding associated employers and the inclusion/exclusion of those who work for associated employers incorporated outside Great Britain and who do not ordinarily work in Great Britain. Workers employed on UK registered ships by associated employers, as defined, count in calculating the number of relevant workers. The method of making a formal request, its form and the information contained, is also covered.*

Parties agree

10.– (1) If before the end of the first period the parties agree a bargaining unit and that the union is (or unions are) to be recognised as entitled to conduct collective bargaining on behalf of the unit, no further steps are to be taken under this Part of this Schedule.

(2) If before the end of the first period the employer informs the union (or unions) that the employer does not accept the request but is willing to negotiate, sub-paragraph (3) applies.

(3) The parties may conduct negotiations with a view to agreeing a bargaining unit and that the union is (or unions are) to be recognised as entitled to conduct collective bargaining on behalf of the unit.

(4) If such an agreement is made before the end of the second period no further steps are to be taken under this Part of this Schedule.

(5) The employer and the union (or unions) may request ACAS to assist in conducting the negotiations.

(6) The first period is the period of 10 working days starting with the day after that on which the employer receives the request for recognition.

(7) The second period is-

(a) the period of 20 working days starting with the day after that on which the first period ends, or

(b) such longer period (so starting) as the parties may from time to time agree.

> **Parties Agree:**
> *Para 10 - The statutory recognition procedure ends automatically if within ten working days the Union and employer reach agreement on the appropriate bargaining unit and on collective bargaining by the Union. The parties have any balance of the ten working plus a further twenty working days to conduct negotiations and can extend the period by agreement.*

Employer rejects request

11.– (1) This paragraph applies if-

   (a) before the end of the first period the employer fails to respond to the request, or
   (b) before the end of the first period the employer informs the union (or unions) that the employer does not accept the request (without indicating a willingness to negotiate).

(2) The union (or unions) may apply to the CAC to decide both these questions-

   (a) whether the proposed bargaining unit is appropriate or some other bargaining unit is appropriate;
   (b) whether the union has (or unions have) the support of a majority of the workers constituting the appropriate bargaining unit.

> **Employer Rejects Request:**
> *Para 11 - If the employer rejects the Union's request within the ten working day period, or fails to respond, the Union may apply to the CAC to rule on the appropriate bargaining unit and recognition.*

Negotiations fail

12.– (1) Sub-paragraph (2) applies if-

   (a) the employer informs the union (or unions) under paragraph 10(2), and
   (b) no agreement is made before the end of the second period.

(2) The union (or unions) may apply to the CAC to decide both these questions-

   (a) whether the proposed bargaining unit is appropriate or some other bargaining unit is appropriate;
   (b) whether the union has (or unions have) the support of a majority of the workers constituting the appropriate bargaining unit.

(3) Sub-paragraph (4) applies if-

   (a) the employer informs the union (or unions) under paragraph 10(2), and

   (b) before the end of the second period the parties agree a bargaining unit but not that the union is (or unions are) to be recognised as entitled to conduct collective bargaining on behalf of the unit.

(4) The union (or unions) may apply to the CAC to decide the question whether the union has (or unions have) the support of a majority of the workers constituting the bargaining unit.

(5) But no application may be made under this paragraph if within the period of 10 working days starting with the day after that on which the employer informs the union (or unions) under paragraph 10(2) the employer proposes that ACAS be requested to assist in conducting the negotiations and-

   (a) the union rejects (or unions reject) the proposal, or

   (b) the union fails (or unions fail) to accept the proposal within the period of 10 working days starting with the day after that on which the employer makes the proposal.

Negotiations Fail:
Para 12 – If the employer has initially agreed but the parties subsequently during the second period of twenty days cannot reach agreement the Union can apply to the CAC to decide the appropriate bargaining unit. The Union cannot apply to the CAC if it has rejected or failed to respond to the employer's proposal to involve ACAS in the negotiations.

Acceptance of applications

13. The CAC must give notice to the parties of receipt of an application under paragraph 11 or 12.

14.– (1) This paragraph applies if-

   (a) two or more relevant applications are made,

   (b) at least one worker falling within one of the relevant bargaining units also falls within the other relevant bargaining unit (or units), and

   (c) the CAC has not accepted any of the applications.

(2) A relevant application is an application under paragraph 11 or 12.

(3) In relation to a relevant application, the relevant bargaining unit is-

   (a) the proposed bargaining unit, where the application is under paragraph 11(2) or 12(2);

   (b) the agreed bargaining unit, where the application is under paragraph 12(4).

(4) Within the acceptance period the CAC must decide, with regard to each relevant application, whether the 10 per cent test is satisfied.

(5) The 10 per cent test is satisfied if members of the union (or unions) constitute at least 10 per cent of the workers constituting the relevant bargaining unit.

(6) The acceptance period is-

(a) the period of 10 working days starting with the day after that on which the CAC receives the last relevant application, or

(b) such longer period (so starting) as the CAC may specify to the parties by notice containing reasons for the extension.

(7) If the CAC decides that-

(a) the 10 per cent test is satisfied with regard to more than one of the relevant applications, or

(b) the 10 per cent test is satisfied with regard to none of the relevant applications,

the CAC must not accept any of the relevant applications.

(8) If the CAC decides that the 10 per cent test is satisfied with regard to one only of the relevant applications the CAC-

(a) must proceed under paragraph 15 with regard to that application, and

(b) must not accept any of the other relevant applications.

(9) The CAC must give notice of its decision to the parties.

(10) If by virtue of this paragraph the CAC does not accept an application, no further steps are to be taken under this Part of this Schedule in relation to that application.

15.– (1) This paragraph applies to these applications-

(a) any application with regard to which no decision has to be made under paragraph 14;

(b) any application with regard to which the CAC must proceed under this paragraph by virtue of paragraph 14.

(2) Within the acceptance period the CAC must decide whether-

(a) the request for recognition to which the application relates is valid within the terms of paragraphs 5 to 9, and

(b) the application is made in accordance with paragraph 11 or 12 and admissible within the terms of paragraphs 33 to 42.

(3) In deciding those questions the CAC must consider any evidence which it has been given by the employer or the union (or unions).

(4) If the CAC decides that the request is not valid or the application is not made in accordance with paragraph 11 or 12 or is not admissible-

(a) the CAC must give notice of its decision to the parties,

(b) the CAC must not accept the application, and

(c) no further steps are to be taken under this Part of this Schedule.

(5) If the CAC decides that the request is valid and the application is made in accordance with paragraph 11 or 12 and is admissible it must-

(a) accept the application, and

(b) give notice of the acceptance to the parties.

(6) The acceptance period is-

(a) the period of 10 working days starting with the day after that on which the CAC receives the application, or

(b) such longer period (so starting) as the CAC may specify to the parties by notice containing reasons for the extension.

Acceptance of Qualifications:

Paras 14-15 - The CAC must give notice to the parties of receipt of an application and be satisfied that it is valid and admissible. If the CAC receives two or more applications with overlapping bargaining units (i.e. at least one worker is a member of both or all the bargaining units), the applications are subject to a 10% test. Only those applications which pass the test may proceed. If more than one applicant union has 10% or more members within the bargaining unit, or all have less than 10%, all the applications must be rejected. Recognition applications must be valid *in terms of paras 5-9 and* admissible *in terms of paras 33-42. If the application is valid and admissible the CAC then decides the appropriate bargaining unit and whether the Union has sufficient support unless the parties are agreed on the bargaining unit in which case the CAC simply determines the level of support.*

Withdrawal of application

16.– (1) If an application under paragraph 11 or 12 is accepted by the CAC, the union (or unions) may not withdraw the application-

(a) after the CAC issues a declaration under paragraph 22(2), or

(b) after the union (or the last of the unions) receives notice under paragraph 22(3) or 23(2).

(2) If an application is withdrawn by the union (or unions)-

(a) the CAC must give notice of the withdrawal to the employer, and

(b) no further steps are to be taken under this Part of this Schedule.

Withdrawal of Application:
Para 16 - The Union may withdraw its application before the CAC awards automatic recognition under para 22(2) or within ten working days of the CAC announcing its intention to hold a ballot. If the Union withdraws it may reformulate the application and resubmit it. However, if the Union withdraws after its application has been accepted by the CAC under para 15 or cancels a ballot, the Union will be unable to reapply for recognition for three years in respect of the same or similar bargaining unit.

Notice to cease consideration of application

17.– (1) This paragraph applies if the CAC has received an application under paragraph 11 or 12 and-

   (a) it has not decided whether the application is admissible, or

   (b) it has decided that the application is admissible.

(2) No further steps are to be taken under this Part of this Schedule if, before the final event occurs, the parties give notice to the CAC that they want no further steps to be taken.

(3) The final event occurs when the first of the following occurs-

   (a) the CAC issues a declaration under paragraph 22(2) in consequence of the application,

   (b) the last day of the notification period ends;

and the notification period is that defined by paragraph 24(5) and arising from the application.

Notice to Cease Consideration of Application:
Para 17 - The Union and employer can make a joint application before the CAC formally determines recognition requesting that the CAC stops work on the application e.g. because have reached an agreement themselves.

Appropriate bargaining unit

18.– (1) If the CAC accepts an application under paragraph 11(2) or 12(2) it must try to help the parties to reach within the appropriate period an agreement as to what the appropriate bargaining unit is.

(2) The appropriate period is-

(a) the period of 20 working days starting with the day after that on which the CAC gives notice of acceptance of the application, or

(b) such longer period (so starting) as the CAC may specify to the parties by notice containing reasons for the extension.

19.– (1) This paragraph applies if-

(a) the CAC accepts an application under paragraph 11(2) or 12(2), and

(b) the parties have not agreed an appropriate bargaining unit at the end of the appropriate period.

(2) The CAC must decide the appropriate bargaining unit within-

(a) the period of 10 working days starting with the day after that on which the appropriate period ends, or

(b) such longer period (so starting) as the CAC may specify to the parties by notice containing reasons for the extension.

(3) In deciding the appropriate bargaining unit the CAC must take these matters into account-

(a) the need for the unit to be compatible with effective management;

(b) the matters listed in sub-paragraph (4), so far as they do not conflict with that need.

(4) The matters are-

(a) the views of the employer and of the union (or unions);

(b) existing national and local bargaining arrangements;

(c) the desirability of avoiding small fragmented bargaining units within an undertaking;

(d) the characteristics of workers falling within the proposed bargaining unit and of any other employees of the employer whom the CAC considers relevant;

(e) the location of workers.

(5) The CAC must give notice of its decision to the parties.

Appropriate Bargaining Unit:
Paras 18-19 - The CAC has twenty working days to help the Union and employer to reach agreement on an appropriate bargaining unit. If this is unsuccessful the CAC will determine the appropriate bargaining unit within ten working days afterwards. It must take into account the need for the bargaining unit to be compatible with effective management and, consistently with that, the factors listed in para 19(4).

The CAC is required by para 20 to apply a number of tests equivalent to those applied under para 15. If the tests are satisfied or the bargaining unit has not changed, the CAC must proceed with the application as required by para 21.

Union recognition

20.– (1) This paragraph applies if-

(a) the CAC accepts an application under paragraph 11(2) or 12(2),

(b) the parties have agreed an appropriate bargaining unit at the end of the appropriate period, or the CAC has decided an appropriate bargaining unit, and

(c) that bargaining unit differs from the proposed bargaining unit.

(2) Within the decision period the CAC must decide whether the application is invalid within the terms of paragraphs 43 to 50.

(3) In deciding whether the application is invalid, the CAC must consider any evidence which it has been given by the employer or the union (or unions).

(4) If the CAC decides that the application is invalid-

(a) the CAC must give notice of its decision to the parties,

(b) the CAC must not proceed with the application, and

(c) no further steps are to be taken under this Part of this Schedule.

(5) If the CAC decides that the application is not invalid it must-

(a) proceed with the application, and

(b) give notice to the parties that it is so proceeding.

(6) The decision period is-

(a) the period of 10 working days starting with the day after that on which the parties agree an appropriate bargaining unit or the CAC decides an appropriate bargaining unit, or

(b) such longer period (so starting) as the CAC may specify to the parties by notice containing reasons for the extension.

21.– (1) This paragraph applies if-

(a) the CAC accepts an application under paragraph 11(2) or 12(2),

(b) the parties have agreed an appropriate bargaining unit at the end of the appropriate period, or the CAC has decided an appropriate bargaining unit, and

(c) that bargaining unit is the same as the proposed bargaining unit.

(2) This paragraph also applies if the CAC accepts an application under paragraph 12(4).

(3) The CAC must proceed with the application.

22.– (1) This paragraph applies if-

(a) the CAC proceeds with an application in accordance with paragraph 20 or 21, and

(b) the CAC is satisfied that a majority of the workers constituting the bargaining unit are members of the union (or unions).

(2) The CAC must issue a declaration that the union is (or unions are) recognised as entitled to conduct collective bargaining on behalf of the workers constituting the bargaining unit.

(3) But if any of the three qualifying conditions is fulfilled, instead of issuing a declaration under sub-paragraph (2) the CAC must give notice to the parties that it intends to arrange for the holding of a secret ballot in which the workers constituting the bargaining unit are asked whether they want the union (or unions) to conduct collective bargaining on their behalf.

(4) These are the three qualifying conditions-

    (a) the CAC is satisfied that a ballot should be held in the interests of good industrial relations;

    (b) a significant number of the union members within the bargaining unit inform the CAC that they do not want the union (or unions) to conduct collective bargaining on their behalf;

    (c) membership evidence is produced which leads the CAC to conclude that there are doubts whether a significant number of the union members within the bargaining unit want the union (or unions) to conduct collective bargaining on their behalf.

(5) For the purposes of sub-paragraph (4)(c) membership evidence is-

    (a) evidence about the circumstances in which union members became members;

    (b) evidence about the length of time for which union members have been members, in a case where the CAC is satisfied that such evidence should be taken into account.

23.– (1) This paragraph applies if-

    (a) the CAC proceeds with an application in accordance with paragraph 20 or 21, and

    (b) the CAC is not satisfied that a majority of the workers constituting the bargaining unit are members of the union (or unions).

(2) The CAC must give notice to the parties that it intends to arrange for the holding of a secret ballot in which the workers constituting the bargaining unit are asked whether they want the union (or unions) to conduct collective bargaining on their behalf.

24.– (1) This paragraph applies if the CAC gives notice under paragraph 22(3) or 23(2).

(2) Within the notification period-

    (a) the union (or unions), or

    (b) the union (or unions) and the employer,

may notify the CAC that the party making the notification does not (or the parties making the notification do not) want the CAC to arrange for the holding of the ballot.

(3) If the CAC is so notified-

    (a) it must not arrange for the holding of the ballot,

    (b) it must inform the parties that it will not arrange for the holding of the ballot, and why, and

    (c) no further steps are to be taken under this Part of this Schedule.

(4) If the CAC is not so notified it must arrange for the holding of the ballot.

(5) The notification period is the period of 10 working days starting-

    (a) for the purposes of sub-paragraph (2)(a), with the day on which the union (or last of the unions) receives the CAC's notice under paragraph 22(3) or 23(2), or

    (b) for the purposes of sub-paragraph (2)(b), with that day or (if later) the day on which the employer receives the CAC's notice under paragraph 22(3) or 23(2).

25.– (1) This paragraph applies if the CAC arranges under paragraph 24 for the holding of a ballot.

(2) The ballot must be conducted by a qualified independent person appointed by the CAC.

(3) The ballot must be conducted within-

    (a) the period of 20 working days starting with the day after that on which the qualified independent person is appointed, or

    (b) such longer period (so starting) as the CAC may decide.

(4) The ballot must be conducted-

    (a) at a workplace or workplaces decided by the CAC,

    (b) by post, or

    (c) by a combination of the methods described in sub-paragraphs (a) and (b),

depending on the CAC's preference.

(5) In deciding how the ballot is to be conducted the CAC must take into account-

    (a) the likelihood of the ballot being affected by unfairness or malpractice if it were conducted at a workplace or workplaces;

    (b) costs and practicality;

    (c) such other matters as the CAC considers appropriate.

(6) The CAC may not decide that the ballot is to be conducted as mentioned in sub-paragraph (4)(c) unless there are special factors making such a decision appropriate; and special factors include-

    (a) factors arising from the location of workers or the nature of their employment;

    (b) factors put to the CAC by the employer or the union (or unions).

(7) A person is a qualified independent person if-

    (a) he satisfies such conditions as may be specified for the purposes of this paragraph by order of the Secretary of State or is himself so specified, and

(b) there are no grounds for believing either that he will carry out any functions conferred on him in relation to the ballot otherwise than competently or that his independence in relation to the ballot might reasonably be called into question.

(8) An order under sub-paragraph (7)(a) shall be made by statutory instrument subject to annulment in pursuance of a resolution of either House of Parliament.

(9) As soon as is reasonably practicable after the CAC is required under paragraph 24 to arrange for the holding of a ballot it must inform the parties-

(a) that it is so required;
(b) of the name of the person appointed to conduct the ballot and the date of his appointment;
(c) of the period within which the ballot must be conducted;
(d) whether the ballot is to be conducted by post or at a workplace or workplaces;
(e) of the workplace or workplaces concerned (if the ballot is to be conducted at a workplace or workplaces).

26.– (1) An employer who is informed by the CAC under paragraph 25(9) must comply with the following three duties.

(2) The first duty is to co-operate generally, in connection with the ballot, with the union (or unions) and the person appointed to conduct the ballot; and the second and third duties are not to prejudice the generality of this.

(3) The second duty is to give to the union (or unions) such access to the workers constituting the bargaining unit as is reasonable to enable the union (or unions) to inform the workers of the object of the ballot and to seek their support and their opinions on the issues involved.

(4) The third duty is to do the following (so far as it is reasonable to expect the employer to do so)-

(a) to give to the CAC, within the period of 10 working days starting with the day after that on which the employer is informed under paragraph 25(9), the names and home addresses of the workers constituting the bargaining unit;
(b) to give to the CAC, as soon as is reasonably practicable, the name and home address of any worker who joins the unit after the employer has complied with paragraph (a);
(c) to inform the CAC, as soon as is reasonably practicable, of any worker whose name has been given to the CAC under paragraph (a) or (b) but who ceases to be within the unit.

(5) As soon as is reasonably practicable after the CAC receives any information under sub-paragraph (4) it must pass it on to the person appointed to conduct the ballot.

(6) If asked to do so by the union (or unions) the person appointed to conduct the ballot must send to any worker-

(a) whose name and home address have been given under sub-paragraph (5), and

(b) who is still within the unit (so far as the person so appointed is aware),

any information supplied by the union (or unions) to the person so appointed.

(7) The duty under sub-paragraph (6) does not apply unless the union bears (or unions bear) the cost of sending the information.

(8) Each of the following powers shall be taken to include power to issue Codes of Practice about reasonable access for the purposes of sub-paragraph (3)-

(a) the power of ACAS under section 199(1);

(b) the power of the Secretary of State under section 203(1)(a).

27.– (1) If the CAC is satisfied that the employer has failed to fulfil any of the three duties imposed by paragraph 26, and the ballot has not been held, the CAC may order the employer-

(a) to take such steps to remedy the failure as the CAC considers reasonable and specifies in the order, and

(b) to do so within such period as the CAC considers reasonable and specifies in the order.

(2) If the CAC is satisfied that the employer has failed to comply with an order under sub-paragraph (1), and the ballot has not been held, the CAC may issue a declaration that the union is (or unions are) recognised as entitled to conduct collective bargaining on behalf of the bargaining unit.

(3) If the CAC issues a declaration under sub-paragraph (2) it shall take steps to cancel the holding of the ballot; and if the ballot is held it shall have no effect.

28.– (1) This paragraph applies if the holding of a ballot has been arranged under paragraph 24 whether or not it has been cancelled.

(2) The gross costs of the ballot shall be borne-

(a) as to half, by the employer, and

(b) as to half, by the union (or unions).

(3) If there is more than one union they shall bear their half of the gross costs-

(a) in such proportions as they jointly indicate to the person appointed to conduct the ballot, or

(b) in the absence of such an indication, in equal shares.

(4) The person appointed to conduct the ballot may send to the employer and the union (or each of the unions) a demand stating-

(a) the gross costs of the ballot, and

(b) the amount of the gross costs to be borne by the recipient.

(5) In such a case the recipient must pay the amount stated to the person sending the demand, and must do so within the period of 15 working days starting with the day after that on which the demand is received.

(6) In England and Wales, if the amount stated is not paid in accordance with sub-paragraph (5) it shall, if a county court so orders, be recoverable by execution issued from that court or otherwise as if it were payable under an order of that court.

(7) References to the costs of the ballot are to-

(a) the costs wholly, exclusively and necessarily incurred in connection with the ballot by the person appointed to conduct it,

(b) such reasonable amount as the person appointed to conduct the ballot charges for his services, and

(c) such other costs as the employer and the union (or unions) agree.

29.– (1) As soon as is reasonably practicable after the CAC is informed of the result of a ballot by the person conducting it, the CAC must act under this paragraph.

(2) The CAC must inform the employer and the union (or unions) of the result of the ballot.

(3) If the result is that the union is (or unions are) supported by-

(a) a majority of the workers voting, and

(b) at least 40 per cent of the workers constituting the bargaining unit,

the CAC must issue a declaration that the union is (or unions are) recognised as entitled to conduct collective bargaining on behalf of the bargaining unit.

(4) If the result is otherwise the CAC must issue a declaration that the union is (or unions are) not entitled to be so recognised.

(5) The Secretary of State may by order amend sub-paragraph (3) so as to specify a different degree of support; and different provision may be made for different circumstances.

(6) An order under sub-paragraph (5) shall be made by statutory instrument.

(7) No such order shall be made unless a draft of it has been laid before Parliament and approved by a resolution of each House of Parliament.

Consequences of recognition

30.– (1) This paragraph applies if the CAC issues a declaration under this Part of this Schedule that the union is (or unions are) recognised as entitled to conduct collective bargaining on behalf of a bargaining unit.

(2) The parties may in the negotiation period conduct negotiations with a view to agreeing a method by which they will conduct collective bargaining.

(3) If no agreement is made in the negotiation period the employer or the union (or unions) may apply to the CAC for assistance.

(4) The negotiation period is-

(a) the period of 30 working days starting with the start day, or
(b) such longer period (so starting) as the parties may from time to time agree.

(5) The start day is the day after that on which the parties are notified of the declaration.

31.– (1) This paragraph applies if an application for assistance is made to the CAC under paragraph 30.

(2) The CAC must try to help the parties to reach in the agreement period an agreement on a method by which they will conduct collective bargaining.

(3) If at the end of the agreement period the parties have not made such an agreement the CAC must specify to the parties the method by which they are to conduct collective bargaining.

(4) Any method specified under sub-paragraph (3) is to have effect as if it were contained in a legally enforceable contract made by the parties.

(5) But if the parties agree in writing-

(a) that sub-paragraph (4) shall not apply, or shall not apply to particular parts of the method specified by the CAC, or
(b) to vary or replace the method specified by the CAC,

the written agreement shall have effect as a legally enforceable contract made by the parties.

(6) Specific performance shall be the only remedy available for breach of anything which is a legally enforceable contract by virtue of this paragraph.

(7) If at any time before a specification is made under sub-paragraph (3) the parties jointly apply to the CAC requesting it to stop taking steps under this paragraph, the CAC must comply with the request.

(8) The agreement period is-

(a) the period of 20 working days starting with the day after that on which the CAC receives the application under paragraph 30, or
(b) such longer period (so starting) as the CAC may decide with the consent of the parties.

Union Recognition:

Paras 20-31 - The provisions for the conduct of recognition ballot is set out in para 25 and the employer's obligations to cooperate with the ballot in para 26. The CAC may order under para 27 the employer to take specific steps to remedy its non-cooperation. The sanction for non-compliance is that the CAC may declare the Union recognised and cancel the ballot. Para 28 provides that the cost of the ballot is borne equally between the employer and the Union, other than the cost of providing information to workers incurred by the Union or the employer. Para 29 requires the CAC to notify the parties of the ballot outcome as soon as possible. If the ballot result is confirmed support for recognition by a majority of those who voted and at least 40% of the workers constituting the bargaining unit, Union recognition must be declared by the CAC. If those two criteria are not met, the CAC must declare that the Union is not recognised. The Secretary of State is empowered by order to amend the recognition conditions from time to time subject to the affirmative resolution procedure.

Where the CAC make a Union Recognition Declaration but the parties cannot agree on the method of conducting collective bargaining, either party can seek assistance from the CAC. The detailed mechanism is helpfully illustrated in figure 2 on the DTI's Explanatory Notes at http://www.dti.gov.uk. *There is a similar process to that for recognition itself including an initial thirty working days to attempt voluntary agreement after which the CAC actively intervenes to assist the parties reach an agreement. This period is twenty working days after which the CAC will impose a method for collective bargaining. The imposed method is legally binding as if it were contractual i.e. the remedy of specific performance is available through Court proceedings. Non-compliance with such Court Order would amount to contempt of Court. The parties can subsequently vary in writing the imposed method including its legally binding status, by agreement.*

Method not carried out

32.– (1) This paragraph applies if-

    (a) the CAC issues a declaration under this Part of this Schedule that the union is (or unions are) recognised as entitled to conduct collective bargaining on behalf of a bargaining unit,

    (b) the parties agree a method by which they will conduct collective bargaining, and

    (c) one or more of the parties fails to carry out the agreement.

(2) The parties may apply to the CAC for assistance.

(3) Paragraph 31 applies as if "paragraph 30" (in each place) read "paragraph 30 or paragraph 32".

Method not Carried Out:
Para 32 - If a party complains that an agreed method, rather than an imposed method, has not been followed, the CAC will tell the parties to reach another agreement or if they cannot, the CAC will use its powers to introduce an imposed method.

General provisions about admissibility

33. An application under paragraph 11 or 12 is not admissible unless-

(a) it is made in such form as the CAC specifies, and
(b) it is supported by such documents as the CAC specifies.

34. An application under paragraph 11 or 12 is not admissible unless the union gives (or unions give) to the employer-

(a) notice of the application, and
(b) a copy of the application and any documents supporting it.

35.– (1) An application under paragraph 11 or 12 is not admissible if the CAC is satisfied that there is already in force a collective agreement under which a union is (or unions are) recognised as entitled to conduct collective bargaining on behalf of any workers falling within the relevant bargaining unit.

(2) But sub-paragraph (1) does not apply to an application under paragraph 11 or 12 if-

(a) the union (or unions) recognised under the collective agreement and the union (or unions) making the application under paragraph 11 or 12 are the same, and
(b) the matters in respect of which the union is (or unions are) entitled to conduct collective bargaining do not include pay, hours or holidays.

(3) A declaration of recognition which is the subject of a declaration under paragraph 83(2) must for the purposes of sub-paragraph (1) be treated as ceasing to have effect to the extent specified in paragraph 83(2) on the making of the declaration under paragraph 83(2).

(4) In applying sub-paragraph (1) an agreement for recognition (the agreement in question) must be ignored if-

(a) the union does not have (or none of the unions has) a certificate under section 6 that it is independent,
(b) at some time there was an agreement (the old agreement) between the employer and the union under which the union (whether alone or with other unions) was recognised as entitled to conduct collective bargaining on behalf of a group of workers which was the same or substantially the same as the group covered by the agreement in question, and

(c) the old agreement ceased to have effect in the period of three years ending with the date of the agreement in question.

(5) It is for the CAC to decide whether one group of workers is the same or substantially the same as another, but in deciding the CAC may take account of the views of any person it believes has an interest in the matter.

(6) The relevant bargaining unit is-

(a) the proposed bargaining unit, where the application is under paragraph 11(2) or 12(2);

(b) the agreed bargaining unit, where the application is under paragraph 12(4).

36.– (1) An application under paragraph 11 or 12 is not admissible unless the CAC decides that-

(a) members of the union (or unions) constitute at least 10 per cent of the workers constituting the relevant bargaining unit, and

(b) a majority of the workers constituting the relevant bargaining unit would be likely to favour recognition of the union (or unions) as entitled to conduct collective bargaining on behalf of the bargaining unit.

(2) The relevant bargaining unit is-

(a) the proposed bargaining unit, where the application is under paragraph 11(2) or 12(2);

(b) the agreed bargaining unit, where the application is under paragraph 12(4).

(3) The CAC must give reasons for the decision.

37.– (1) This paragraph applies to an application made by more than one union under paragraph 11 or 12.

(2) The application is not admissible unless-

(a) the unions show that they will co-operate with each other in a manner likely to secure and maintain stable and effective collective bargaining arrangements, and

(b) the unions show that, if the employer wishes, they will enter into arrangements under which collective bargaining is conducted by the unions acting together on behalf of the workers constituting the relevant bargaining unit.

(3) The relevant bargaining unit is-

(a) the proposed bargaining unit, where the application is under paragraph 11(2) or 12(2);

(b) the agreed bargaining unit, where the application is under paragraph 11(4).

38.– (1) This paragraph applies if-

(a) the CAC accepts a relevant application relating to a bargaining unit or proceeds under paragraph 20 with an application relating to a bargaining unit,

(b) the application has not been withdrawn,

(c) no notice has been given under paragraph 17(2),

(d) the CAC has not issued a declaration under paragraph 22(2), 27(2), 29(3) or 29(4) in relation to that bargaining unit, and

(e) no notification has been made under paragraph 24(2).

(2) Another relevant application is not admissible if-

(a) at least one worker falling within the relevant bargaining unit also falls within the bargaining unit referred to in sub-paragraph (1), and

(b) the application is made by a union (or unions) other than the union (or unions) which made the application referred to in sub-paragraph (1).

(3) A relevant application is an application under paragraph 11 or 12.

(4) The relevant bargaining unit is-

(a) the proposed bargaining unit, where the application is under paragraph 11(2) or 12(2);

(b) the agreed bargaining unit, where the application is under paragraph 12(4).

39.– (1) This paragraph applies if the CAC accepts a relevant application relating to a bargaining unit or proceeds under paragraph 20 with an application relating to a bargaining unit.

(2) Another relevant application is not admissible if-

(a) the application is made within the period of 3 years starting with the day after that on which the CAC gave notice of acceptance of the application mentioned in sub-paragraph (1),

(b) the relevant bargaining unit is the same or substantially the same as the bargaining unit mentioned in sub-paragraph (1), and

(c) the application is made by the union (or unions) which made the application mentioned in sub-paragraph (1).

(3) A relevant application is an application under paragraph 11 or 12.

(4) The relevant bargaining unit is-

(a) the proposed bargaining unit, where the application is under paragraph 11(2) or 12(2);

(b) the agreed bargaining unit, where the application is under paragraph 12(4).

(5) This paragraph does not apply if paragraph 40 or 41 applies.

40.– (1) This paragraph applies if the CAC issues a declaration under paragraph 29(4) that a union is (or unions are) not entitled to be recognised as entitled to conduct collective bargaining on behalf of a bargaining unit; and this is so whether the ballot concerned is held under this Part or Part III of this Schedule.

(2) An application under paragraph 11 or 12 is not admissible if-

(a) the application is made within the period of 3 years starting with the day after that on which the declaration was issued,

(b) the relevant bargaining unit is the same or substantially the same as the bargaining unit mentioned in sub-paragraph (1), and

(c) the application is made by the union (or unions) which made the application leading to the declaration.

(3) The relevant bargaining unit is-

(a) the proposed bargaining unit, where the application is under paragraph 11(2) or 12(2);

(b) the agreed bargaining unit, where the application is under paragraph 12(4).

41.– (1) This paragraph applies if the CAC issues a declaration under paragraph 121(3) that bargaining arrangements are to cease to have effect; and this is so whether the ballot concerned is held under Part IV or Part V of this Schedule.

(2) An application under paragraph 11 or 12 is not admissible if-

(a) the application is made within the period of 3 years starting with the day after that on which the declaration was issued,

(b) the relevant bargaining unit is the same or substantially the same as the bargaining unit to which the bargaining arrangements mentioned in sub-paragraph (1) relate, and

(c) the application is made by the union which was a party (or unions which were parties) to the proceedings leading to the declaration.

(3) The relevant bargaining unit is-

(a) the proposed bargaining unit, where the application is under paragraph 11(2) or 12(2);

(b) the agreed bargaining unit, where the application is under paragraph 12(4).

42.– (1) This paragraph applies for the purposes of paragraphs 39 to 41.

(2) It is for the CAC to decide whether one bargaining unit is the same or substantially the same as another, but in deciding the CAC may take account of the views of any person it believes has an interest in the matter.

General Provisions of Admissibility:
Paras 33-42 - These provisions should be read in conjunction with the terms of paras 5-9 which have to be satisfied for an application to be valid. The admissibility requirements include the following:

- *Must be made in proper form*

- *Must be copied to the employer along with any supporting documents*

- *Must not cover any worker for whom there is already a recognised Union (unless the application is made by the same Union, and recognition does not extend to pay, hours or holidays or there has been a change in status regarding the application is made by the same Union, and its certification of independence)*

- *The CAC must be satisfied that at least 10% of workers in the proposed bargaining unit are members of the Union and that a majority would be likely to favour recognition*

- *In multi-Union applications, evidence that the Unions will cooperate effectively and if required by the employer, conduct single-table bargaining*

- *The bargaining unit must not overlap with any other unit where the CAC has accepted an application*

- *Not be substantially the same as an application accepted by the CAC within the preceding three years*

- *Not be made within three years of a CAC declaration that the Union is not entitled to recognition*

- *Not be made within three years of the Union being derecognised by the CAC in respect of that bargaining unit*

The general purpose is to implement the principle that following a recognition decision by the CAC it should not be re-opened for at least three years.

General provisions about validity

43.– (1) Paragraphs 44 to 50 apply if the CAC has to decide under paragraph 20 whether an application is valid.

(2) In those paragraphs-

  (a) references to the application in question are to that application, and
  (b) references to the relevant bargaining unit are to the bargaining unit agreed by the parties or decided by the CAC.

44.– (1) The application in question is invalid if the CAC is satisfied that there is already in force a collective agreement under which a union is (or unions are) recognised as entitled to conduct collective bargaining on behalf of any workers falling within the relevant bargaining unit.

(2) But sub-paragraph (1) does not apply to the application in question if-

  (a) the union (or unions) recognised under the collective agreement and the union (or unions) making the application in question are the same, and

(b) the matters in respect of which the union is (or unions are) entitled to conduct collective bargaining do not include pay, hours or holidays.

(3) A declaration of recognition which is the subject of a declaration under paragraph 83(2) must for the purposes of sub-paragraph (1) be treated as ceasing to have effect to the extent specified in paragraph 83(2) on the making of the declaration under paragraph 83(2).

(4) In applying sub-paragraph (1) an agreement for recognition (the agreement in question) must be ignored if-

(a) the union does not have (or none of the unions has) a certificate under section 6 that it is independent,

(b) at some time there was an agreement (the old agreement) between the employer and the union under which the union (whether alone or with other unions) was recognised as entitled to conduct collective bargaining on behalf of a group of workers which was the same or substantially the same as the group covered by the agreement in question, and

(c) the old agreement ceased to have effect in the period of three years ending with the date of the agreement in question.

(5) It is for the CAC to decide whether one group of workers is the same or substantially the same an another, but in deciding the CAC may take account of the views of any person it believes has an interest in the matter.

45. The application in question is invalid unless the CAC decides that-

(a) members of the union (or unions) constitute at least 10 per cent of the workers constituting the relevant bargaining unit, and

(b) a majority of the workers constituting the relevant bargaining unit would be likely to favour recognition of the union (or unions) as entitled to conduct collective bargaining on behalf of the bargaining unit.

46.– (1) This paragraph applies if-

(a) the CAC accepts an application under paragraph 11 or 12 relating to a bargaining unit or proceeds under paragraph 20 with an application relating to a bargaining unit,

(b) the application has not been withdrawn,

(c) no notice has been given under paragraph 17(2),

(d) the CAC has not issued a declaration under paragraph 22(2), 27(2), 29(3) or 29(4) in relation to that bargaining unit, and

(e) no notification has been made under paragraph 24(2).

(2) The application in question is invalid if-

(a) at least one worker falling within the relevant bargaining unit also falls within the bargaining unit referred to in sub-paragraph (1), and

(b) the application in question is made by a union (or unions) other than the union (or unions) which made the application referred to in sub-paragraph (1).

47.– (1) This paragraph applies if the CAC accepts an application under paragraph 11 or 12 relating to a bargaining unit or proceeds under paragraph 20 with an application relating to a bargaining unit.

(2) The application in question is invalid if-

   (a) the application is made within the period of 3 years starting with the day after that on which the CAC gave notice of acceptance of the application mentioned in sub-paragraph (1),

   (b) the relevant bargaining unit is the same or substantially the same as the bargaining unit mentioned in sub-paragraph (1), and

   (c) the application is made by the union (or unions) which made the application mentioned in sub-paragraph (1).

(3) This paragraph does not apply if paragraph 48 or 49 applies.

48.– (1) This paragraph applies if the CAC issues a declaration under paragraph 29(4) that a union is (or unions are) not entitled to be recognised as entitled to conduct collective bargaining on behalf of a bargaining unit; and this is so whether the ballot concerned is held under this Part or Part III of this Schedule.

(2) The application in question is invalid if-

   (a) the application is made within the period of 3 years starting with the date of the declaration,

   (b) the relevant bargaining unit is the same or substantially the same as the bargaining unit mentioned in sub-paragraph (1), and

   (c) the application is made by the union (or unions) which made the application leading to the declaration.

49.– (1) This paragraph applies if the CAC issues a declaration under paragraph 121(3) that bargaining arrangements are to cease to have effect; and this is so whether the ballot concerned is held under Part IV or Part V of this Schedule.

(2) The application in question is invalid if-

   (a) the application is made within the period of 3 years starting with the day after that on which the declaration was issued,

   (b) the relevant bargaining unit is the same or substantially the same as the bargaining unit to which the bargaining arrangements mentioned in sub-paragraph (1) relate, and

   (c) the application is made by the union which was a party (or unions which were parties) to the proceedings leading to the declaration.

50.– (1) This paragraph applies for the purposes of paragraphs 47 to 49.

(2) It is for the CAC to decide whether one bargaining unit is the same or substantially the same as another, but in deciding the CAC may take account of the views of any person it believes has an interest in the matter.

Competing applications

51.– (1) For the purposes of this paragraph-

    (a) the original application is the application referred to in paragraph 38(1) or 46(1), and

    (b) the competing application is the other application referred to in paragraph 38(2) or the application in question referred to in paragraph 46(2);

but an application cannot be an original application unless it was made under paragraph 11(2) or 12(2).

(2) This paragraph applies if-

    (a) the CAC decides that the competing application is not admissible by reason of paragraph 38 or is invalid by reason of paragraph 46,

    (b) at the time the decision is made the parties to the original application have not agreed the appropriate bargaining unit under paragraph 18, and the CAC has not decided the appropriate bargaining unit under paragraph 19, in relation to the application, and

    (c) the 10 per cent test (within the meaning given by paragraph 14) is satisfied with regard to the competing application.

(3) In such a case-

    (a) the CAC must cancel the original application,

    (b) the CAC must give notice to the parties to the application that it has been cancelled,

    (c) no further steps are to be taken under this Part of this Schedule in relation to the application, and

    (d) the application shall be treated as if it had never been admissible.

Competing Applications:
Para 51 - Applies if an application is accepted, and there is a later application for recognition in a bargaining unit which includes at least one worker in the original application's bargaining unit. Para 38 provides that the new application will always be rejected. Para 51 provides that if the Union making the new application has at least 10% membership and no bargaining unit has been determined under the original application, the CAC must stop working on the original application and treat it as if it has never been admissible.

PART II

VOLUNTARY RECOGNITION

Agreements for recognition

52.– (1) This paragraph applies for the purposes of this Part of this Schedule.

(2) An agreement is an agreement for recognition if the following conditions are fulfilled in relation to it-

(a) the agreement is made in the permitted period between a union (or unions) and an employer in consequence of a request made under paragraph 4 and valid within the terms of paragraphs 5 to 9;

(b) under the agreement the union is (or unions are) recognised as entitled to conduct collective bargaining on behalf of a group or groups of workers employed by the employer;

(c) if sub-paragraph (5) applies to the agreement, it is satisfied.

(3) The permitted period is the period which begins with the day on which the employer receives the request and ends when the first of the following occurs-

(a) the union withdraws (or unions withdraw) the request;

(b) the union withdraws (or unions withdraw) any application under paragraph 11 or 12 made in consequence of the request;

(c) the CAC gives notice of a decision under paragraph 14(7) which precludes it from accepting such an application under paragraph 11 or 12;

(d) the CAC gives notice under paragraph 15(4)(a) or 20(4)(a) in relation to such an application under paragraph 11 or 12;

(e) the parties give notice to the CAC under paragraph 17(2) in relation to such an application under paragraph 11 or 12;

(f) the CAC issues a declaration under paragraph 22(2) in consequence of such an application under paragraph 11 or 12;

(g) the CAC is notified under paragraph 24(2) in relation to such an application under paragraph 11 or 12;

(h) the last day of the notification period ends (the notification period being that defined by paragraph 24(5) and arising from such an application under paragraph 11 or 12);

(i) the CAC is required under paragraph 51(3) to cancel such an application under paragraph 11 or 12.

(4) Sub-paragraph (5) applies to an agreement if-

(a) at the time it is made the CAC has received an application under paragraph 11 or 12 in consequence of the request mentioned in sub-paragraph (2), and

(b) the CAC has not decided whether the application is admissible or it has decided that it is admissible.

(5) This sub-paragraph is satisfied if, in relation to the application under paragraph 11 or 12, the parties give notice to the CAC under paragraph 17 before the final event (as defined in paragraph 17) occurs.

Other interpretation

53.– (1) This paragraph applies for the purposes of this Part of this Schedule.

(2) In relation to an agreement for recognition, references to the bargaining unit are to the group of workers (or the groups taken together) to which the agreement for recognition relates.

(3) In relation to an agreement for recognition, references to the parties are to the union (or unions) and the employer who are parties to the agreement.

54.– (1) This paragraph applies for the purposes of this Part of this Schedule.

(2) The meaning of collective bargaining given by section 178(1) shall not apply.

(3) Except in paragraph 63(2), in relation to an agreement for recognition references to collective bargaining are to negotiations relating to the matters in respect of which the union is (or unions are) recognised as entitled to conduct negotiations under the agreement for recognition.

(4) In paragraph 63(2) the reference to collective bargaining is to negotiations relating to pay, hours and holidays.

**Part II – Voluntary Recognition
Agreements for Recognition:**
*Paras 52-54 - Part II of Schedule A1 deals with agreements for recognition which
are made as a result of an application under Part I but without a formal CAC
declaration that the Union is recognised. Part II does not deal with entirely
voluntary agreements. A Part II agreement will require an employer to maintain an*
agreement for recognition *for three years and if either party fails to follow the
agreed bargaining process the Union or the employer may apply to the CAC to
impose a bargaining method. Para 52 provides the conditions for an agreement to
amount to an* agreement for recognition. *Paras 53 and 54 contain definitions
including bargaining unit, the parties, collective bargaining and* agreement for
recognition.

Determination of type of agreement

55.– (1) This paragraph applies if one or more of the parties to an agreement applies to
the CAC for a decision whether or not the agreement is an agreement for
recognition.

(2) The CAC must give notice of receipt of an application under sub-paragraph (1) to
any parties to the agreement who are not parties to the application.

(3) The CAC must within the decision period decide whether the agreement is an
agreement for recognition.

(4) If the CAC decides that the agreement is an agreement for recognition it must
issue a declaration to that effect.

(5) If the CAC decides that the agreement is not an agreement for recognition it must
issue a declaration to that effect.

(6) The decision period is-

(a) the period of 10 working days starting with the day after that on which the
CAC receives the application under sub-paragraph (1), or
(b) such longer period (so starting) as the CAC may specify to the parties to the
agreement by notice containing reasons for the extension.

Determination of Type of Agreement:
*Para 55 permits an application to the CAC for a ruling on whether an agreement is
an agreement for recognition.*

Termination of agreement for recognition

56.– (1) The employer may not terminate an agreement for recognition before the relevant period ends.

(2) After that period ends the employer may terminate the agreement, with or without the consent of the union (or unions).

(3) The union (or unions) may terminate an agreement for recognition at any time, with or without the consent of the employer.

(4) Sub-paragraphs (1) to (3) have effect subject to the terms of the agreement or any other agreement of the parties.

(5) The relevant period is the period of three years starting with the day after the date of the agreement.

57.– (1) If an agreement for recognition is terminated, as from the termination the agreement and any provisions relating to the collective bargaining method shall cease to have effect.

(2) For this purpose provisions relating to the collective bargaining method are-

(a) any agreement between the parties as to the method by which collective bargaining is to be conducted with regard to the bargaining unit, or
(b) anything effective as, or as if contained in, a legally enforceable contract and relating to the method by which collective bargaining is to be conducted with regard to the bargaining unit.

Termination of Agreement for Recognition

Paras 56-57 - An employer is prevented from ending an agreement for recognition within three years of it being made whilst a Union can end the agreement at any time subject to compliance with the terms of the agreement. Para 57 makes it clear that if the agreement for recognition is terminated the bargaining method also ceases.

Application to CAC to specify method

58.– (1) This paragraph applies if the parties make an agreement for recognition.

(2) The parties may in the negotiation period conduct negotiations with a view to agreeing a method by which they will conduct collective bargaining.

(3) If no agreement is made in the negotiation period the employer or the union (or unions) may apply to the CAC for assistance.

(4) The negotiation period is-

(a) the period of 30 working days starting with the start day, or
(b) such longer period (so starting) as the parties may from time to time agree.

(5) The start day is the day after that on which the agreement is made.

59.– (1) This paragraph applies if-

    (a) the parties to an agreement for recognition agree a method by which they will conduct collective bargaining, and

    (b) one or more of the parties fails to carry out the agreement as to a method.

(2) The employer or the union (or unions) may apply to the CAC for assistance.

60.– (1) This paragraph applies if an application for assistance is made to the CAC under paragraph 58 or 59.

(2) The application is not admissible unless the conditions in sub-paragraphs (3) and (4) are satisfied.

(3) The condition is that the employer, taken with any associated employer or employers, must-

    (a) employ at least 21 workers on the day the application is made, or

    (b) employ an average of at least 21 workers in the 13 weeks ending with that day.

(4) The condition is that the union (or every union) has a certificate under section 6 that it is independent.

(5) To find the average under sub-paragraph (3)(b)-

    (a) take the number of workers employed in each of the 13 weeks (including workers not employed for the whole of the week);

    (b) aggregate the 13 numbers;

    (c) divide the aggregate by 13.

(6) For the purposes of sub-paragraph (3)(a) any worker employed by an associated company incorporated outside Great Britain must be ignored unless the day the application was made fell within a period during which he ordinarily worked in Great Britain.

(7) For the purposes of sub-paragraph (3)(b) any worker employed by an associated company incorporated outside Great Britain must be ignored in relation to a week unless the whole or any part of that week fell within a period during which he ordinarily worked in Great Britain.

(8) For the purposes of sub-paragraphs (6) and (7) a worker who is employed on board a ship registered in the register maintained under section 8 of the Merchant Shipping Act 1995 shall be treated as ordinarily working in Great Britain unless-

    (a) the ship's entry in the register specifies a port outside Great Britain as the port to which the vessel is to be treated as belonging,

    (b) the employment is wholly outside Great Britain, or

    (c) the worker is not ordinarily resident in Great Britain.

(9) An order made under paragraph 7(6) may also-

    (a) provide that sub-paragraphs (2), (3) and (5) to (8) of this paragraph are not to apply, or are not to apply in specified circumstances, or

    (b) vary the number of workers for the time being specified in sub-paragraph (3).

61.– (1) An application to the CAC is not admissible unless-

    (a) it is made in such form as the CAC specifies, and

    (b) it is supported by such documents as the CAC specifies.

(2) An application which is made by a union (or unions) to the CAC is not admissible unless the union gives (or unions give) to the employer-

    (a) notice of the application, and

    (b) a copy of the application and any documents supporting it.

(3) An application which is made by an employer to the CAC is not admissible unless the employer gives to the union (or each of the unions)-

    (a) notice of the application, and

    (b) a copy of the application and any documents supporting it.

> **Application to CAC to Specify Method:**
> *Paras 58-61 - If the Union and employer enter into an agreement for recognition they then have thirty working days in which to agree a bargaining method, otherwise either party may apply to the CAC for assistance para 58 or 59. The smaller employer exemption applies by virtue of para 60 and para 61 sets out all the other requirements which must be satisfied for the CAC to be able to accept the application.*

CAC's response to application

62.– (1) The CAC must give notice to the parties of receipt of an application under paragraph 58 or 59.

(2) Within the acceptance period the CAC must decide whether the application is admissible within the terms of paragraphs 60 and 61.

(3) In deciding whether an application is admissible the CAC must consider any evidence which it has been given by the employer or the union (or unions).

(4) If the CAC decides that the application is not admissible-

    (a) the CAC must give notice of its decision to the parties,

    (b) the CAC must not accept the application, and

    (c) no further steps are to be taken under this Part of this Schedule.

(5) If the CAC decides that the application is admissible it must-

    (a) accept the application, and

    (b) give notice of the acceptance to the parties.

(6) The acceptance period is-

    (a) the period of 10 working days starting with the day after that on which the CAC receives the application, or

    (b) such longer period (so starting) as the CAC may specify to the parties by notice containing reasons for the extension.

63.– (1) If the CAC accepts an application it must try to help the parties to reach in the agreement period an agreement on a method by which they will conduct collective bargaining.

(2) If at the end of the agreement period the parties have not made such an agreement the CAC must specify to the parties the method by which they are to conduct collective bargaining.

(3) Any method specified under sub-paragraph (2) is to have effect as if it were contained in a legally enforceable contract made by the parties.

(4) But if the parties agree in writing-

    (a) that sub-paragraph (3) shall not apply, or shall not apply to particular parts of the method specified by the CAC, or

    (b) to vary or replace the method specified by the CAC,

the written agreement shall have effect as a legally enforceable contract made by the parties.

(5) Specific performance shall be the only remedy available for breach of anything which is a legally enforceable contract by virtue of this paragraph.

(6) If the CAC accepts an application, the applicant may not withdraw it after the end of the agreement period.

(7) If at any time before a specification is made under sub-paragraph (2) the parties jointly apply to the CAC requesting it to stop taking steps under this paragraph, the CAC must comply with the request.

(8) The agreement period is-

    (a) the period of 20 working days starting with the day after that on which the CAC gives notice of acceptance of the application, or

    (b) such longer period (so starting) as the parties may from time to time agree.

CAC's Response to Application:
Paras 62-63 - If the CAC accepts the application under para 62 it must help the parties to try and agree a bargaining method within twenty working days otherwise the CAC must specify the method for collective bargaining unless the parties otherwise jointly request. The method specified y the CAC will be legally enforceable, by order of specific performance in the same way as methods specified after an award of recognition. Under s.168 the Secretary of State may specify a model collective bargaining method.

PART III

CHANGES AFFECTING BARGAINING UNIT

Introduction

64.– (1) This Part of this Schedule applies if-

(a) the CAC has issued a declaration that a union is (or unions are) recognised as entitled to conduct collective bargaining on behalf of a bargaining unit, and

(b) provisions relating to the collective bargaining method apply in relation to the unit.

(2) In such a case, in this Part of this Schedule-

(a) references to the original unit are to the bargaining unit on whose behalf the union is (or unions are) recognised as entitled to conduct collective bargaining, and

(b) references to the bargaining arrangements are to the declaration and to the provisions relating to the collective bargaining method which apply in relation to the original unit.

(3) For this purpose provisions relating to the collective bargaining method are-

(a) the parties' agreement as to the method by which collective bargaining is to be conducted with regard to the original unit,

(b) anything effective as, or as if contained in, a legally enforceable contract and relating to the method by which collective bargaining is to be conducted with regard to the original unit, or

(c) any provision of this Part of this Schedule that a method of collective bargaining is to have effect with regard to the original unit.

65. References in this Part of this Schedule to the parties are to the employer and the union (or unions) concerned.

Part III – Changes Affecting Bargaining Unit
Introduction:
*Paras 64-65 - In a rapidly changing business world, organisations can change
radically and significantly. Those changes may require more appropriate collective
bargaining arrangements (e.g. the original bargaining unit may changed or split into
several different bargaining units). Part III provides a procedure for responding to
such change after recognition has been imposed under Part I. The main steps are set
out in figure 3 on the DTI's Explanatory Notes at* http://www.dti.gov.uk.

Either party believes unit no longer appropriate

66.– (1) This paragraph applies if the employer believes or the union believes (or
unions believe) that the original unit is no longer an appropriate bargaining unit.

(2) The employer or union (or unions) may apply to the CAC to make a decision as to
what is an appropriate bargaining unit.

67.– (1) An application under paragraph 66 is not admissible unless the CAC decides
that it is likely that the original unit is no longer appropriate by reason of any of
the matters specified in sub-paragraph (2).

(2) The matters are-

    (a) a change in the organisation or structure of the business carried on by the
employer;
    (b) a change in the activities pursued by the employer in the course of the business
carried on by him;
    (c) a substantial change in the number of workers employed in the original unit.

68.– (1) The CAC must give notice to the parties of receipt of an application under
paragraph 66.

(2) Within the acceptance period the CAC must decide whether the application is
admissible within the terms of paragraphs 67 and 92.

(3) In deciding whether the application is admissible the CAC must consider any
evidence which it has been given by the employer or the union (or unions).

(4) If the CAC decides that the application is not admissible -

    (a) the CAC must give notice of its decision to the parties,
    (b) the CAC must not accept the application, and
    (c) no further steps are to be taken under this Part of this Schedule.

(5) If the CAC decides that the application is admissible it must-

    (a) accept the application, and
    (b) give notice of the acceptance to the parties.

(6) The acceptance period is-

(a) the period of 10 working days starting with the day after that on which the CAC receives the application, or

(b) such longer period (so starting) as the CAC may specify to the parties by notice containing reasons for the extension.

69.– (1) This paragraph applies if-

(a) the CAC gives notice of acceptance of the application, and

(b) before the end of the first period the parties agree a bargaining unit or units (the new unit or units) differing from the original unit and inform the CAC of their agreement.

(2) If in the CAC's opinion the new unit (or any of the new units) contains at least one worker falling within an outside bargaining unit no further steps are to be taken under this Part of this Schedule.

(3) If sub-paragraph (2) does not apply-

(a) the CAC must issue a declaration that the union is (or unions are) recognised as entitled to conduct collective bargaining on behalf of the new unit or units;

(b) so far as it affects workers in the new unit (or units) who fall within the original unit, the declaration shall have effect in place of any declaration that the union is (or unions are) recognised as entitled to conduct collective bargaining on behalf of the original unit;

(c) the method of collective bargaining relating to the original unit shall have effect in relation to the new unit or units, with any modifications which the CAC considers necessary to take account of the change of bargaining unit and specifies in the declaration.

(4) The first period is-

(a) the period of 10 working days starting with the day after that on which the CAC gives notice of acceptance of the application, or

(b) such longer period (so starting) as the parties may from time to time agree and notify to the CAC.

(5) An outside bargaining unit is a bargaining unit which fulfils these conditions-

(a) it is not the original unit;

(b) a union is (or unions are) recognised as entitled to conduct collective bargaining on its behalf;

(c) the union (or at least one of the unions) is not a party referred to in paragraph 64.

70.– (1) This paragraph applies if-

(a) the CAC gives notice of acceptance of the application, and

(b) the parties do not inform the CAC before the end of the first period that they have agreed a bargaining unit or units differing from the original unit.

(2) During the second period-

- (a) the CAC must decide whether or not the original unit continues to be an appropriate bargaining unit;
- (b) if the CAC decides that the original unit does not so continue, it must decide what other bargaining unit is or units are appropriate;
- (c) the CAC must give notice to the parties of its decision or decisions under paragraphs (a) and (b).

(3) In deciding whether or not the original unit continues to be an appropriate bargaining unit the CAC must take into account only these matters-

- (a) any change in the organisation or structure of the business carried on by the employer;
- (b) any change in the activities pursued by the employer in the course of the business carried on by him;
- (c) any substantial change in the number of workers employed in the original unit.

(4) In deciding what other bargaining unit is or units are appropriate the CAC must take these matters into account-

- (a) the need for the unit or units to be compatible with effective management;
- (b) the matters listed in sub-paragraph (5), so far as they do not conflict with that need.

(5) The matters are-

- (a) the views of the employer and of the union (or unions);
- (b) existing national and local bargaining arrangements;
- (c) the desirability of avoiding small fragmented bargaining units within an undertaking;
- (d) the characteristics of workers falling within the original unit and of any other employees of the employer whom the CAC considers relevant;
- (e) the location of workers.

(6) If the CAC decides that two or more bargaining units are appropriate its decision must be such that no worker falls within more than one of them.

(7) The second period is-

- (a) the period of 10 working days starting with the day after that on which the first period ends, or
- (b) such longer period (so starting) as the CAC may specify to the parties by notice containing reasons for the extension.

71. If the CAC gives notice under paragraph 70 of a decision that the original unit continues to be an appropriate bargaining unit no further steps are to be taken under this Part of this Schedule.

72. Paragraph 82 applies if the CAC gives notice under paragraph 70 of-

(a) a decision that the original unit is no longer an appropriate bargaining unit, and

(b) a decision as to the bargaining unit which is (or units which are) appropriate.

73.– (1) This paragraph applies if-

(a) the parties agree under paragraph 69 a bargaining unit or units differing from the original unit,

(b) paragraph 69(2) does not apply, and

(c) at least one worker falling within the original unit does not fall within the new unit (or any of the new units).

(2) In such a case-

(a) the CAC must issue a declaration that the bargaining arrangements, so far as relating to the worker or workers mentioned in sub-paragraph (1)(c), are to cease to have effect on a date specified by the CAC in the declaration, and

(b) the bargaining arrangements shall cease to have effect accordingly.

Either Party Believes Unit no Longer Appropriate:
Paras 66-73 - The employer or the Union may apply to the CAC. The effect of para 67 is that supporting evidence must be lodged with the CAC. Para 67 states that an application is inadmissible unless the CAC decides that it is likely that the original unit is no longer appropriate by reason of a change in the business organisation or structure, the business activity or a substantial change in the number of workers.

Para 68 requires the CAC to reject the application unless there is evidence, the application is made in proper form and as the applying party has provided the other party with supporting documents. Para 69 provides ten working days for the employer and the Union to reach agreement on the new bargaining unit or units. If they achieve this, the CAC must decide whether the new unit or units contain workers covered by a collective agreement with another Union. If they do the CAC takes no further action. If not, the CAC must declare the Union recognised for the new unit. The original method of collective bargaining will apply unless adapted by the CAC as it thinks necessary. If the Union and employer do not agree, the CAC under para 70 has ten working days in which to decide whether to preserve the original unit or whether another unit is appropriate. It takes no action in the former case but otherwise it will determine the appropriate new unit in accordance with the criteria in para 70; effectively the same criteria for a Part I application plus a requirement that if there are several new units created they must not overlap. The CAC must then determine whether the Union should be recognised for the new unit and does so in accordance with the provisions in paras 82-89. Para 73 provides that where there are workers from the original unit who no longer fall within the new unit, the Union will lose its recognition rights in respect of them.

Employer believes unit has ceased to exist

74.– (1) If the employer-

   (a) believes that the original unit has ceased to exist, and
   (b) wishes the bargaining arrangements to cease to have effect,

he must give the union (or each of the unions) a notice complying with sub-paragraph (2) and must give a copy of the notice to the CAC.

(2) A notice complies with this sub-paragraph if it-

   (a) identifies the unit and the bargaining arrangements,
   (b) states the date on which the notice is given,
   (c) states that the unit has ceased to exist, and
   (d) states that the bargaining arrangements are to cease to have effect on a date which is specified in the notice and which falls after the end of the period of 35 working days starting with the day after that on which the notice is given.

(3) Within the validation period the CAC must decide whether the notice complies with sub-paragraph (2).

(4) If the CAC decides that the notice does not comply with sub-paragraph (2)-

   (a) the CAC must give the parties notice of its decision, and
   (b) the employer's notice shall be treated as not having been given.

(5) If the CAC decides that the notice complies with sub-paragraph (2) it must give the parties notice of the decision.

(6) The bargaining arrangements shall cease to have effect on the date specified under sub-paragraph (2)(d) if-

   (a) the CAC gives notice under sub-paragraph (5), and
   (b) the union does not (or unions do not) apply to the CAC under paragraph 75.

(7) The validation period is-

   (a) the period of 10 working days starting with the day after that on which the CAC receives the copy of the notice, or
   (b) such longer period (so starting) as the CAC may specify to the parties by notice containing reasons for the extension.

75.– (1) Paragraph 76 applies if-

   (a) the CAC gives notice under paragraph 74(5), and
   (b) within the period of 10 working days starting with the day after that on which the notice is given the union makes (or unions make) an application to the CAC for a decision on the questions specified in sub-paragraph (2).

(2) The questions are-

   (a) whether the original unit has ceased to exist;

(b) whether the original unit is no longer appropriate by reason of any of the matters specified in sub-paragraph (3).

(3) The matters are-

(a) a change in the organisation or structure of the business carried on by the employer;
(b) a change in the activities pursued by the employer in the course of the business carried on by him;
(c) a substantial change in the number of workers employed in the original unit.

76.– (1) The CAC must give notice to the parties of receipt of an application under paragraph 75.

(2) Within the acceptance period the CAC must decide whether the application is admissible within the terms of paragraph 92.

(3) In deciding whether the application is admissible the CAC must consider any evidence which it has been given by the employer or the union (or unions).

(4) If the CAC decides that the application is not admissible-

(a) the CAC must give notice of its decision to the parties,
(b) the CAC must not accept the application, and
(c) no further steps are to be taken under this Part of this Schedule.

(5) If the CAC decides that the application is admissible it must-

(a) accept the application, and
(b) give notice of the acceptance to the parties.

(6) The acceptance period is-

(a) the period of 10 working days starting with the day after that on which the CAC receives the application, or
(b) such longer period (so starting) as the CAC may specify to the parties by notice containing reasons for the extension.

77.– (1) If the CAC accepts an application it-

(a) must give the employer and the union (or unions) an opportunity to put their views on the questions in relation to which the application was made;
(b) must decide the questions before the end of the decision period.

(2) If the CAC decides that the original unit has ceased to exist-

(a) the CAC must give the parties notice of its decision, and
(b) the bargaining arrangements shall cease to have effect on the termination date.

(3) If the CAC decides that the original unit has not ceased to exist, and that it is not the case that the original unit is no longer appropriate by reason of any of the matters specified in paragraph 75(3)-

(a) the CAC must give the parties notice of its decision, and

(b) the employer's notice shall be treated as not having been given.

(4) If the CAC decides that the original unit has not ceased to exist, and that the original unit is no longer appropriate by reason of any of the matters specified in paragraph 75(3), the CAC must give the parties notice of its decision.

(5) The decision period is-

(a) the period of 10 working days starting with the day after that on which the CAC gives notice of acceptance of the application, or

(b) such longer period (so starting) as the CAC may specify to the parties by notice containing reasons for the extension.

(6) The termination date is the later of-

(a) the date specified under paragraph 74(2)(d), and

(b) the day after the last day of the decision period.

78.– (1) This paragraph applies if-

(a) the CAC gives notice under paragraph 77(4), and

(b) before the end of the first period the parties agree a bargaining unit or units (the new unit or units) differing from the original unit and inform the CAC of their agreement.

(2) If in the CAC's opinion the new unit (or any of the new units) contains at least one worker falling within an outside bargaining unit no further steps are to be taken under this Part of this Schedule.

(3) If sub-paragraph (2) does not apply-

(a) the CAC must issue a declaration that the union is (or unions are) recognised as entitled to conduct collective bargaining on behalf of the new unit or units;

(b) so far as it affects workers in the new unit (or units) who fall within the original unit, the declaration shall have effect in place of any declaration that the union is (or unions are) recognised as entitled to conduct collective bargaining on behalf of the original unit;

(c) the method of collective bargaining relating to the original unit shall have effect in relation to the new unit or units, with any modifications which the CAC considers necessary to take account of the change of bargaining unit and specifies in the declaration.

(4) The first period is-

(a) the period of 10 working days starting with the day after that on which the CAC gives notice under paragraph 77(4), or

(b) such longer period (so starting) as the parties may from time to time agree and notify to the CAC.

(5) An outside bargaining unit is a bargaining unit which fulfils these conditions-

(a) it is not the original unit;

(b) a union is (or unions are) recognised as entitled to conduct collective bargaining on its behalf;

(c) the union (or at least one of the unions) is not a party referred to in paragraph 64.

79.– (1) This paragraph applies if-

(a) the CAC gives notice under paragraph 77(4), and

(b) the parties do not inform the CAC before the end of the first period that they have agreed a bargaining unit or units differing from the original unit.

(2) During the second period the CAC-

(a) must decide what other bargaining unit is or units are appropriate;

(b) must give notice of its decision to the parties.

(3) In deciding what other bargaining unit is or units are appropriate, the CAC must take these matters into account-

(a) the need for the unit or units to be compatible with effective management;

(b) the matters listed in sub-paragraph (4), so far as they do not conflict with that need.

(4) The matters are-

(a) the views of the employer and of the union (or unions);

(b) existing national and local bargaining arrangements;

(c) the desirability of avoiding small fragmented bargaining units within an undertaking;

(d) the characteristics of workers falling within the original unit and of any other employees of the employer whom the CAC considers relevant;

(e) the location of workers.

(5) If the CAC decides that two or more bargaining units are appropriate its decision must be such that no worker falls within more than one of them.

(6) The second period is-

(a) the period of 10 working days starting with the day after that on which the first period ends, or

(b) such longer period (so starting) as the CAC may specify to the parties by notice containing reasons for the extension.

80. Paragraph 82 applies if the CAC gives notice under paragraph 79 of a decision as to the bargaining unit which is (or units which are) appropriate.

81.– (1) This paragraph applies if-

(a) the parties agree under paragraph 78 a bargaining unit or units differing from the original unit,

(b) paragraph 78(2) does not apply, and

(c) at least one worker falling within the original unit does not fall within the new unit (or any of the new units).

(2) In such a case -

(a) the CAC must issue a declaration that the bargaining arrangements, so far as relating to the worker or workers mentioned in sub-paragraph (1)(c), are to cease to have effect on a date specified by the CAC in the declaration, and

(b) the bargaining arrangements shall cease to have effect accordingly.

Employer Believes Unit has Ceased to Exist:
Paras 74-81 - A situation in which in an employer may seek derecognition is where the bargaining unit has ceased to exist. An employer must give details to the Union under para 74 and the CAC must determine whether the notice is valid. The Union has ten working days under para 75 to require the CAC to determine whether the original unit has ceased to exist or is no longer appropriate. Failure to apply will result in derecognition. If a Union's application under para 75 is defective in terms of para 92 the CAC must under para 76 reject the application. If the CAC accepts the application para 77 requires that both parties be given an opportunity to present evidence. The CAC will then decide whether the original unit remains appropriate in which case the employer's notice has no effect. If the employer establishes that the original bargaining unit is no longer appropriate the CAC must give notice accordingly which triggers para 78. The parties then have ten working days to agree a new bargaining unit. The CAC will declare the Union recognised for that unit and the original collective bargaining method will apply to the new unit. If the parties disagree, the CAC under para 79 has ten working days in which to decide whether the original unit is appropriate using the para 62 criteria and if not, what other unit is appropriate.

The procedure is similar to the procedure adopted where the CAC is invited to consider whether a unit is no longer appropriate under paras 70-73.

Position where CAC decides new unit

Position Where CAC Decides New Unit:
Paras 82-89 - The decision is taken under para 82 by reference to the factors set out in para 79(3)-(5). The procedure to be followed is at figure 4 on the DTI's Explanatory Notes at http://www.dti.gov.uk. *It applies where the CAC decides that one or more new bargaining units are appropriate under para 70 or para 79. The detailed procedure is contained in para 83-89 and has to be applied to each new unit where there is more than one.*

82.– (1) This paragraph applies if the CAC gives notice under paragraph 70 of-

(a) a decision that the original unit is no longer an appropriate bargaining unit, and

(b) a decision as to the bargaining unit which is (or units which are) appropriate.

(2) This paragraph also applies if the CAC gives notice under paragraph 79 of a decision as to the bargaining unit which is (or units which are) appropriate.

(3) The CAC-

(a) must proceed as stated in paragraphs 83 to 89 with regard to the appropriate unit (if there is one only), or

(b) must proceed as stated in paragraphs 83 to 89 with regard to each appropriate unit separately (if there are two or more).

(4) References in those paragraphs to the new unit are to the appropriate unit under consideration.

83.– (1) This paragraph applies if in the CAC's opinion the new unit contains at least one worker falling within a statutory outside bargaining unit.

(2) In such a case-

(a) the CAC must issue a declaration that the relevant bargaining arrangements, so far as relating to workers falling within the new unit, are to cease to have effect on a date specified by the CAC in the declaration, and

(b) the relevant bargaining arrangements shall cease to have effect accordingly.

(3) The relevant bargaining arrangements are-

(a) the bargaining arrangements relating to the original unit, and

(b) the bargaining arrangements relating to each statutory outside bargaining unit containing workers who fall within the new unit.

(4) The bargaining arrangements relating to the original unit are the bargaining arrangements as defined in paragraph 64.

(5) The bargaining arrangements relating to an outside unit are-

(a) the declaration recognising a union (or unions) as entitled to conduct collective bargaining on behalf of the workers constituting the outside unit, and

(b) the provisions relating to the collective bargaining method.

(6) For this purpose the provisions relating to the collective bargaining method are-

(a) any agreement by the employer and the union (or unions) as to the method by which collective bargaining is to be conducted with regard to the outside unit,

(b) anything effective as, or as if contained in, a legally enforceable contract and relating to the method by which collective bargaining is to be conducted with regard to the outside unit, or

(c) any provision of this Part of this Schedule that a method of collective bargaining is to have effect with regard to the outside unit.

(7) A statutory outside bargaining unit is a bargaining unit which fulfils these conditions-

(a) it is not the original unit;

(b) a union is (or unions are) recognised as entitled to conduct collective bargaining on its behalf by virtue of a declaration of the CAC;

(c) the union (or at least one of the unions) is not a party referred to in paragraph 64.

(8) The date specified under sub-paragraph (1)(a) must be-

(a) the date on which the relevant period expires, or

(b) if the CAC believes that to maintain the relevant bargaining arrangements would be impracticable or contrary to the interests of good industrial relations, the date after the date on which the declaration is issued;

and the relevant period is the period of 65 working days starting with the day after that on which the declaration is issued.

Para 83 deals within the situation where a new unit contains at least one worker who is part of another bargaining unit which the Union has recognition under Part I or Part III i.e. an overlap. The collective bargaining arrangements cease in respect of workers in the new unit who were in the original unit or in a statutory outside unit. The CAC takes no further action but the Union could seek recognition under Part I Schedule A1 for the new unit. There are further provisions in para 91 to ensure that recognition continues for the workers in the statutory outside unit not affected by the overlap.

84.– (1) This paragraph applies if in the CAC's opinion the new unit contains-

(a) at least one worker falling within a voluntary outside bargaining unit, but

(b) no worker falling within a statutory outside bargaining unit.

(2) In such a case-

(a) the CAC must issue a declaration that the original bargaining arrangements, so far as relating to workers falling within the new unit, are to cease to have effect on a date specified by the CAC in the declaration, and

(b) the original bargaining arrangements shall cease to have effect accordingly.

(3) The original bargaining arrangements are the bargaining arrangements as defined in paragraph 64.

(4) A voluntary outside bargaining unit is a bargaining unit which fulfils these conditions-

(a) it is not the original unit;

(b) a union is (or unions are) recognised as entitled to conduct collective bargaining on its behalf by virtue of an agreement with the employer;

(c) the union (or at least one of the unions) is not a party referred to in paragraph 64.

(5) The date specified under sub-paragraph (2)(a) must be-

(a) the date on which the relevant period expires, or

(b) if the CAC believes that to maintain the original bargaining arrangements would be impracticable or contrary to the interests of good industrial relations, the date after the date on which the declaration is issued;

and the relevant period is the period of 65 working days starting with the day after that on which the declaration is issued.

> *Para 84 deals with the situation when a new unit overlaps with a* voluntary *outside bargaining unit. The collective bargaining arrangements cease in respect of the workers in the new unit who were in the original unit. Those in the outside unit are not affected and the CAC takes no further action.*

85.– (1) If the CAC's opinion is not that mentioned in paragraph 83(1) or 84(1) it must-

(a) decide whether the difference between the original unit and the new unit is such that the support of the union (or unions) within the new unit needs to be assessed, and

(b) inform the parties of its decision.

(2) If the CAC's decision is that such support does not need to be assessed-

(a) the CAC must issue a declaration that the union is (or unions are) recognised as entitled to conduct collective bargaining on behalf of the new unit;

(b) so far as it affects workers in the new unit who fall within the original unit, the declaration shall have effect in place of any declaration that the union is (or unions are) recognised as entitled to conduct collective bargaining on behalf of the original unit;

(c) the method of collective bargaining relating to the original unit shall have effect in relation to the new unit, with any modifications which the CAC considers necessary to take account of the change of bargaining unit and specifies in the declaration.

> *Para 85 requires the CAC to decide whether the support for recognition needs to be reassessed where the new unit contains no workers covered by other collective agreements. If the changes to the bargaining unit are sufficiently minor, the CAC must declare the Union recognised for the new unit and the collective bargaining method will apply with any changes instituted by the CAC. If support does not reassessment the approach in Part I is adopted. See paras 86-88 (e.g. 10% Union membership; recognition likely to have majority support, balloting and the implications of 50%+ membership).*

86.– (1) This paragraph applies if the CAC decides under paragraph 85(1) that the support of the union (or unions) within the new unit needs to be assessed.

(2) The CAC must decide these questions-

   (a) whether members of the union (or unions) constitute at least 10 per cent of the workers constituting the new unit;

   (b) whether a majority of the workers constituting the new unit would be likely to favour recognition of the union (or unions) as entitled to conduct collective bargaining on behalf of the new unit.

(3) If the CAC decides one or both of the questions in the negative-

   (a) the CAC must issue a declaration that the bargaining arrangements, so far as relating to workers falling within the new unit, are to cease to have effect on a date specified by the CAC in the declaration, and

   (b) the bargaining arrangements shall cease to have effect accordingly.

87.– (1) This paragraph applies if-

   (a) the CAC decides both the questions in paragraph 86(2) in the affirmative, and

   (b) the CAC is satisfied that a majority of the workers constituting the new unit are members of the union (or unions).

(2) The CAC must issue a declaration that the union is (or unions are) recognised as entitled to conduct collective bargaining on behalf of the workers constituting the new unit.

(3) But if any of the three qualifying conditions is fulfilled, instead of issuing a declaration under sub-paragraph (2) the CAC must give notice to the parties that it intends to arrange for the holding of a secret ballot in which the workers constituting the new unit are asked whether they want the union (or unions) to conduct collective bargaining on their behalf.

(4) These are the three qualifying conditions-

   (a) the CAC is satisfied that a ballot should be held in the interests of good industrial relations;

   (b) a significant number of the union members within the new unit inform the CAC that they do not want the union (or unions) to conduct collective bargaining on their behalf;

   (c) membership evidence is produced which leads the CAC to conclude that there are doubts whether a significant number of the union members within the new unit want the union (or unions) to conduct collective bargaining on their behalf.

(5) For the purposes of sub-paragraph (4)(c) membership evidence is-

   (a) evidence about the circumstances in which union members became members;

   (b) evidence about the length of time for which union members have been members, in a case where the CAC is satisfied that such evidence should be taken into account.

(6) If the CAC issues a declaration under sub-paragraph (2)-

   (a) so far as it affects workers in the new unit who fall within the original unit, the declaration shall have effect in place of any declaration that the union is (or unions are) recognised as entitled to conduct collective bargaining on behalf of the original unit;

   (b) the method of collective bargaining relating to the original unit shall have effect in relation to the new unit, with any modifications which the CAC considers necessary to take account of the change of bargaining unit and specifies in the declaration.

88.– (1) This paragraph applies if-

   (a) the CAC decides both the questions in paragraph 86(2) in the affirmative, and

   (b) the CAC is not satisfied that a majority of the workers constituting the new unit are members of the union (or unions).

(2) The CAC must give notice to the parties that it intends to arrange for the holding of a secret ballot in which the workers constituting the new unit are asked whether they want the union (or unions) to conduct collective bargaining on their behalf.

89.– (1) If the CAC gives notice under paragraph 87(3) or 88(2) the union (or unions) may within the notification period notify the CAC that the union does not (or unions do not) want the CAC to arrange for the holding of the ballot; and the notification period is the period of 10 working days starting with the day after that on which the union (or last of the unions) receives the CAC's notice.

(2) If the CAC is so notified-

   (a) it must not arrange for the holding of the ballot,

   (b) it must inform the parties that it will not arrange for the holding of the ballot, and why,

(c) it must issue a declaration that the bargaining arrangements, so far as relating to workers falling within the new unit, are to cease to have effect on a date specified by it in the declaration, and

(d) the bargaining arrangements shall cease to have effect accordingly.

(3) If the CAC is not so notified it must arrange for the holding of the ballot.

(4) Paragraph 25 applies if the CAC arranges under this paragraph for the holding of a ballot (as well as if the CAC arranges under paragraph 24 for the holding of a ballot).

(5) Paragraphs 26 to 29 apply accordingly, but as if references to the bargaining unit were references to the new unit.

(6) If as a result of the ballot the CAC issues a declaration that the union is (or unions are) recognised as entitled to conduct collective bargaining on behalf of the new unit-

(a) so far as it affects workers in the new unit who fall within the original unit, the declaration shall have effect in place of any declaration that the union is (or unions are) recognised as entitled to conduct collective bargaining on behalf of the original unit;

(b) the method of collective bargaining relating to the original unit shall have effect in relation to the new unit, with any modifications which the CAC considers necessary to take account of the change of bargaining unit and specifies in the declaration.

(7) If as a result of the ballot the CAC issues a declaration that the union is (or unions are) not entitled to be recognised as entitled to conduct collective bargaining on behalf of the new unit-

(a) the CAC must state in the declaration the date on which the bargaining arrangements, so far as relating to workers falling within the new unit, are to cease to have effect, and

(b) the bargaining arrangements shall cease to have effect accordingly.

(8) Paragraphs (a) and (b) of sub-paragraph (6) also apply if the CAC issues a declaration under paragraph 27(2).

Para 89 provides for a ballot to be held unless the Union cancels it. If the ballot is held it operates in the same way as under Part I (paras 25-29) and if the result is against recognition, the Union is derecognised.

Residual workers

90.– (1) This paragraph applies if-

(a) the CAC decides an appropriate bargaining unit or units under paragraph 70 or 79, and

(b) at least one worker falling within the original unit does not fall within the new unit (or any of the new units).

(2) In such a case -

(a) the CAC must issue a declaration that the bargaining arrangements, so far as relating to the worker or workers mentioned in sub-paragraph (1)(b), are to cease to have effect on a date specified by the CAC in the declaration, and

(b) the bargaining arrangements shall cease to have effect accordingly.

91.– (1) This paragraph applies if-

(a) the CAC has proceeded as stated in paragraphs 83 to 89 with regard to the new unit (if there is one only) or with regard to each new unit (if there are two or more), and

(b) in so doing the CAC has issued one or more declarations under paragraph 83.

(2) The CAC must-

(a) consider each declaration issued under paragraph 83, and

(b) in relation to each declaration, identify each statutory outside bargaining unit which contains at least one worker who also falls within the new unit to which the declaration relates;

and in this paragraph each statutory outside bargaining unit so identified is referred to as a parent unit.

(3) The CAC must then-

(a) consider each parent unit, and

(b) in relation to each parent unit, identify any workers who fall within the parent unit but who do not fall within the new unit (or any of the new units);

and in this paragraph the workers so identified in relation to a parent unit are referred to as a residual unit.

(4) In relation to each residual unit, the CAC must issue a declaration that the outside union is (or outside unions are) recognised as entitled to conduct collective bargaining on its behalf.

(5) But no such declaration shall be issued in relation to a residual unit if the CAC has received an application under paragraph 66 or 75 in relation to its parent unit.

(6) In this paragraph references to the outside union (or to outside unions) in relation to a residual unit are to the union which is (or unions which are) recognised as entitled to conduct collective bargaining on behalf of its parent unit.

(7) If the CAC issues a declaration under sub-paragraph (4)-

(a) the declaration shall have effect in place of the existing declaration that the outside union is (or outside unions are) recognised as entitled to conduct collective bargaining on behalf of the parent unit, so far as the existing declaration relates to the residual unit;

(b) if there is a method of collective bargaining relating to the parent unit, it shall have effect in relation to the residual unit with any modifications which the CAC considers necessary to take account of the change of bargaining unit and specifies in the declaration.

Residual Workers:
Paras 90-91 - The effect of para 90 is that the Union ceases to be recognised in respect of any worker in the original unit who falls outside the new unit or all of the new units. Para 91 removes workers in the new unit from any statutory outside bargaining unit but requires the CAC, where the statutory method of collective bargaining but applies to issue a declaration containing statutory recognition for the outside bargaining unit, excluding workers who fall within the new unit.

Applications under this Part

92.– (1) An application to the CAC under this Part of this Schedule is not admissible unless-

(a) it is made in such form as the CAC specifies, and

(b) it is supported by such documents as the CAC specifies.

(2) An application which is made by a union (or unions) to the CAC under this Part of this Schedule is not admissible unless the union gives (or unions give) to the employer-

(a) notice of the application, and

(b) a copy of the application and any documents supporting it.

(3) An application which is made by an employer to the CAC under this Part of this Schedule is not admissible unless the employer gives to the union (or each of the unions)-

(a) notice of the application, and

(b) a copy of the application and any documents supporting it.

Applications under this Part:
Para 92 - Sets out the formalities required for an application under this Part to the CAC.

Withdrawal of application

93.– (1) If an application under paragraph 66 or 75 is accepted by the CAC, the applicant (or applicants) may not withdraw the application-

    (a) after the CAC issues a declaration under paragraph 69(3) or 78(3),

    (b) after the CAC decides under paragraph 77(2) or 77(3),

    (c) after the CAC issues a declaration under paragraph 83(1), 85(2), 86(3) or 87(2) in relation to the new unit (where there is only one) or a declaration under any of those paragraphs in relation to any of the new units (where there is more than one),

    (d) after the union has (or unions have) notified the CAC under paragraph 89(1) in relation to the new unit (where there is only one) or any of the new units (where there is more than one), or

    (e) after the end of the notification period referred to in paragraph 89(1) and relating to the new unit (where there is only one) or any of the new units (where there is more than one).

(2) If an application is withdrawn by the applicant (or applicants)-

    (a) the CAC must give notice of the withdrawal to the other party (or parties), and

    (b) no further steps are to be taken under this Part of this Schedule.

> **Withdrawal of Application:**
> *Para 93 - Provides that applications to the CAC cannot be withdrawn after it makes a decision or declaration that recognition should continue or should cease or after a recognition ballot is cancelled by the Union.*

Meaning of collective bargaining

94.– (1) This paragraph applies for the purposes of this Part of this Schedule.

(2) Except in relation to paragraphs 69(5), 78(5) and 83(6), the meaning of collective bargaining given by section 178(1) shall not apply.

(3) In relation to a new unit references to collective bargaining are to negotiations relating to the matters which were the subject of collective bargaining in relation to the corresponding original unit; and the corresponding original unit is the unit which was the subject of an application under paragraph 66 or 75 in consequence of which the new unit was agreed by the parties or decided by the CAC.

(4) But if the parties agree matters as the subject of collective bargaining in relation to the new unit, references to collective bargaining in relation to that unit are to negotiations relating to the agreed matters; and this is the case whether the agreement is made before or after the time when the CAC issues a declaration that

the union is (or unions are) recognised as entitled to conduct collective bargaining on behalf of the new unit.

(5) In relation to a residual unit in relation to which a declaration is issued under paragraph 91, references to collective bargaining are to negotiations relating to the matters which were the subject of collective bargaining in relation to the corresponding parent unit.

(6) In construing paragraphs 69(3)(c), 78(3)(c), 85(2)(c), 87(6)(b) and 89(6)(b)-

(a) sub-paragraphs (3) and (4) do not apply, and
(b) references to collective bargaining are to negotiations relating to pay, hours and holidays.

Meaning of Collective Bargaining:
Para 94 - Defines collective bargaining according to where the term is used.

Method of collective bargaining

95.– (1) This paragraph applies for the purposes of this Part of this Schedule.

(2) Where a method of collective bargaining has effect in relation to a new unit, that method shall have effect as if it were contained in a legally enforceable contract made by the parties.

(3) But if the parties agree in writing-

(a) that sub-paragraph (2) shall not apply, or shall not apply to particular parts of the method, or
(b) to vary or replace the method,

the written agreement shall have effect as a legally enforceable contract made by the parties.

(4) Specific performance shall be the only remedy available for breach of anything which is a legally enforceable contract by virtue of this paragraph.

Method of Collective Bargaining:
Para 95 - Allows the Union and the employer to vary a statutory bargaining method by agreement.

PART IV

DERECOGNITION: GENERAL

Introduction

96.– (1) This Part of this Schedule applies if the CAC has issued a declaration that a union is (or unions are) recognised as entitled to conduct collective bargaining on behalf of a bargaining unit.

(2) In such a case references in this Part of this Schedule to the bargaining arrangements are to the declaration and to the provisions relating to the collective bargaining method.

(3) For this purpose the provisions relating to the collective bargaining method are-

   (a) the parties' agreement as to the method by which collective bargaining is to be conducted,

   (b) anything effective as, or as if contained in, a legally enforceable contract and relating to the method by which collective bargaining is to be conducted, or

   (c) any provision of Part III of this Schedule that a method of collective bargaining is to have effect.

97. For the purposes of this Part of this Schedule the relevant date is the date of the expiry of the period of 3 years starting with the date of the CAC's declaration.

98. References in this Part of this Schedule to the parties are to the employer and the union (or unions) concerned.

Part IV – Derecognition : General
Introduction:
Paras 96-98 - Derecognition procedure for a Union recognised through a CAC declaration is set out in para 96. Para 97 makes it clear that an application for derecognition may not be made until three or more years after the CAC declaration was made.

Employer employs fewer than 21 workers

Employer Employs Fewer than 21 Workers:
Paras 99-103 - Provides, adopting the definition in para 7 that if the employer employs an average of fewer than 21 workers over a period of thirteen weeks the employer may at the end of that period give notice to the Union setting out the manning levels and state that the bargaining arrangements will not apply from a specified date which must not be sooner than 35 working days after notifying the Union. This acts as an application for derecognition, and must be notified to the CAC accordingly.

99.– (1) This paragraph applies if-

    (a) the employer believes that he, taken with any associated employer or employers, employed an average of fewer than 21 workers in any period of 13 weeks, and

    (b) that period ends on or after the relevant date.

(2) If the employer wishes the bargaining arrangements to cease to have effect, he must give the union (or each of the unions) a notice complying with sub-paragraph (3) and must give a copy of the notice to the CAC.

(3) A notice complies with this sub-paragraph if it-

    (a) identifies the bargaining arrangements,

    (b) specifies the period of 13 weeks in question,

    (c) states the date on which the notice is given,

    (d) is given within the period of 5 working days starting with the day after the last day of the specified period of 13 weeks,

    (e) states that the employer, taken with any associated employer or employers, employed an average of fewer than 21 workers in the specified period of 13 weeks, and

    (f) states that the bargaining arrangements are to cease to have effect on a date which is specified in the notice and which falls after the end of the period of 35 working days starting with the day after that on which the notice is given.

(4) To find the average number of workers employed by the employer, taken with any associated employer or employers, in the specified period of 13 weeks-

    (a) take the number of workers employed in each of the 13 weeks (including workers not employed for the whole of the week);

    (b) aggregate the 13 numbers;

    (c) divide the aggregate by 13.

(5) For the purposes of sub-paragraph (1)(a) any worker employed by an associated company incorporated outside Great Britain must be ignored in relation to a week unless the whole or any part of that week fell within a period during which he ordinarily worked in Great Britain.

(6) For the purposes of sub-paragraph (5) a worker who is employed on board a ship registered in the register maintained under section 8 of the Merchant Shipping Act 1995 shall be treated as ordinarily working in Great Britain unless-

    (a) the ship's entry in the register specifies a port outside Great Britain as the port to which the vessel is to be treated as belonging,

    (b) the employment is wholly outside Great Britain, or

    (c) the worker is not ordinarily resident in Great Britain.

(7) An order made under paragraph 7(6) may also-

    (a) provide that sub-paragraphs (1) to (6) of this paragraph and paragraphs 100 to 103 are not to apply, or are not to apply in specified circumstances, or

    (b) vary the number of workers for the time being specified in sub-paragraphs (1)(a) and (3)(e).

100.– (1) Within the validation period the CAC must decide whether the notice complies with paragraph 99(3).

(2) If the CAC decides that the notice does not comply with paragraph 99(3)-

    (a) the CAC must give the parties notice of its decision, and

    (b) the employer's notice shall be treated as not having been given.

(3) If the CAC decides that the notice complies with paragraph 99(3) it must give the parties notice of the decision.

(4) The bargaining arrangements shall cease to have effect on the date specified under paragraph 99(3)(f) if-

    (a) the CAC gives notice under sub-paragraph (3), and

    (b) the union does not (or unions do not) apply to the CAC under paragraph 101.

(5) The validation period is-

    (a) the period of 10 working days starting with the day after that on which the CAC receives the copy of the notice, or

    (b) such longer period (so starting) as the CAC may specify to the parties by notice containing reasons for the extension.

Para 100 gives the CAC ten working days from the date it receives an application from an employer under para 99 in which to decide on its validity. If it holds the notification invalid, the collective bargaining arrangements remain in place. If the notice is valid, the CAC must inform the Union and the employer. The Union then has ten working days in which to make an application of the CAC disputing the employer's claim on the grounds either that less than three years has elapsed by the date of the application or that the average number of workers employed during the reference period was not fewer than 21. If the claim goes unchallenged or the challenge is unsuccessful the notice takes effect and the bargaining arrangements end on the specified date. If the CAC rules under para 102 that the Union's application is well-founded, recognition will continue.

101.– (1) This paragraph applies if-

(a) the CAC gives notice under paragraph 100(3), and
(b) within the period of 10 working days starting with the day after that on which the notice is given, the union makes (or unions make) an application to the CAC for a decision whether the period of 13 weeks specified under paragraph 99(3)(b) ends on or after the relevant date and whether the statement made under paragraph 99(3)(e) is correct.

(2) An application is not admissible unless-

(a) it is made in such form as the CAC specifies, and
(b) it is supported by such documents as the CAC specifies.

(3) An application is not admissible unless the union gives (or unions give) to the employer-

(a) notice of the application, and
(b) a copy of the application and any documents supporting it.

(4) An application is not admissible if-

(a) a relevant application was made within the period of 3 years prior to the date of the application,
(b) the relevant application and the application relate to the same bargaining unit, and
(c) the CAC accepted the relevant application.

(5) A relevant application is an application made to the CAC-

(a) by the union (or the unions) under this paragraph,
(b) by the employer under paragraph 106, 107 or 128, or
(c) by a worker (or workers) under paragraph 112.

102.– (1) The CAC must give notice to the parties of receipt of an application under paragraph 101.

(2) Within the acceptance period the CAC must decide whether the application is admissible within the terms of paragraph 101.

(3) In deciding whether an application is admissible the CAC must consider any evidence which it has been given by the employer or the union (or unions).

(4) If the CAC decides that the application is not admissible-

(a) the CAC must give notice of its decision to the parties,
(b) the CAC must not accept the application,
(c) no further steps are to be taken under this Part of this Schedule, and
(d) the bargaining arrangements shall cease to have effect on the date specified under paragraph 99(3)(f).

(5) If the CAC decides that the application is admissible it must-

(a) accept the application, and
(b) give notice of the acceptance to the parties.

(6) The acceptance period is-

(a) the period of 10 working days starting with the day after that on which the CAC receives the application, or
(b) such longer period (so starting) as the CAC may specify to the parties by notice containing reasons for the extension.

103.– (1) If the CAC accepts an application it-

(a) must give the employer and the union (or unions) an opportunity to put their views on the questions whether the period of 13 weeks specified under paragraph 99(3)(b) ends on or after the relevant date and whether the statement made under paragraph 99(3)(e) is correct;
(b) must decide the questions within the decision period and must give reasons for the decision.

(2) If the CAC decides that the period of 13 weeks specified under paragraph 99(3)(b) ends on or after the relevant date and that the statement made under paragraph 99(3)(e) is correct the bargaining arrangements shall cease to have effect on the termination date.

(3) If the CAC decides that the period of 13 weeks specified under paragraph 99(3)(b) does not end on or after the relevant date or that the statement made under paragraph 99(3)(e) is not correct, the notice under paragraph 99 shall be treated as not having been given.

(4) The decision period is-

(a) the period of 10 working days starting with the day after that on which the CAC gives notice of acceptance of the application, or
(b) such longer period (so starting) as the CAC may specify to the parties by notice containing reasons for the extension.

(5) The termination date is the later of-

(a) the date specified under paragraph 99(3)(f), and
(b) the day after the last day of the decision period.

Employer's request to end arrangements

104.– (1) This paragraph and paragraphs 105 to 111 apply if after the relevant date the employer requests the union (or each of the unions) to agree to end the bargaining arrangements.

(2) The request is not valid unless it-

(a) is in writing,
(b) is received by the union (or each of the unions),
(c) identifies the bargaining arrangements, and
(d) states that it is made under this Schedule.

105.– (1) If before the end of the first period the parties agree to end the bargaining arrangements no further steps are to be taken under this Part of this Schedule.

(2) Sub-paragraph (3) applies if before the end of the first period-

(a) the union informs the employer that the union does not accept the request but is willing to negotiate, or
(b) the unions inform the employer that the unions do not accept the request but are willing to negotiate.

(3) The parties may conduct negotiations with a view to agreeing to end the bargaining arrangements.

(4) If such an agreement is made before the end of the second period no further steps are to be taken under this Part of this Schedule.

(5) The employer and the union (or unions) may request ACAS to assist in conducting the negotiations.

(6) The first period is the period of 10 working days starting with the day after-

(a) the day on which the union receives the request, or
(b) the last day on which any of the unions receives the request.

(7) The second period is-

(a) the period of 20 working days starting with the day after that on which the first period ends, or
(b) such longer period (so starting) as the parties may from time to time agree.

106.– (1) This paragraph applies if-

(a) before the end of the first period the union fails (or unions fail) to respond to the request, or

(b) before the end of the first period the union informs the employer that it does not (or unions inform the employer that they do not) accept the request (without indicating a willingness to negotiate).

(2) The employer may apply to the CAC for the holding of a secret ballot to decide whether the bargaining arrangements should be ended.

107.– (1) This paragraph applies if -

(a) the union informs (or unions inform) the employer under paragraph 105(2), and

(b) no agreement is made before the end of the second period.

(2) The employer may apply to the CAC for the holding of a secret ballot to decide whether the bargaining arrangements should be ended.

(3) But no application may be made if within the period of 10 working days starting with the day after that on which the union informs (or unions inform) the employer under paragraph 105(2) the union proposes (or unions propose) that ACAS be requested to assist in conducting the negotiations and-

(a) the employer rejects the proposal, or

(b) the employer fails to accept the proposal within the period of 10 working days starting with the day after that on which the union makes (or unions make) the proposal.

108.– (1) An application under paragraph 106 or 107 is not admissible unless-

(a) it is made in such form as the CAC specifies, and

(b) it is supported by such documents as the CAC specifies.

(2) An application under paragraph 106 or 107 is not admissible unless the employer gives to the union (or each of the unions)-

(a) notice of the application, and

(b) a copy of the application and any documents supporting it.

109.– (1) An application under paragraph 106 or 107 is not admissible if-

(a) a relevant application was made within the period of 3 years prior to the date of the application under paragraph 106 or 107,

(b) the relevant application and the application under paragraph 106 or 107 relate to the same bargaining unit, and

(c) the CAC accepted the relevant application.

(2) A relevant application is an application made to the CAC-

(a) by the union (or the unions) under paragraph 101,

(b) by the employer under paragraph 106, 107 or 128, or

(c) by a worker (or workers) under paragraph 112.

110.– (1) An application under paragraph 106 or 107 is not admissible unless the CAC decides that-

(a) at least 10 per cent of the workers constituting the bargaining unit favour an end of the bargaining arrangements, and

(b) a majority of the workers constituting the bargaining unit would be likely to favour an end of the bargaining arrangements.

(2) The CAC must give reasons for the decision.

111.– (1) The CAC must give notice to the parties of receipt of an application under paragraph 106 or 107.

(2) Within the acceptance period the CAC must decide whether-

(a) the request is valid within the terms of paragraph 104, and

(b) the application is made in accordance with paragraph 106 or 107 and admissible within the terms of paragraphs 108 to 110.

(3) In deciding those questions the CAC must consider any evidence which it has been given by the employer or the union (or unions).

(4) If the CAC decides that the request is not valid or the application is not made in accordance with paragraph 106 or 107 or is not admissible-

(a) the CAC must give notice of its decision to the parties,

(b) the CAC must not accept the application, and

(c) no further steps are to be taken under this Part of this Schedule.

(5) If the CAC decides that the request is valid and the application is made in accordance with paragraph 106 or 107 and is admissible it must-

(a) accept the application, and

(b) give notice of the acceptance to the parties.

(6) The acceptance period is-

(a) the period of 10 working days starting with the day after that on which the CAC receives the application, or

(b) such longer period (so starting) as the CAC may specify to the parties by notice containing reasons for the extension.

Employer's Request to End Arrangements:
Paras 104-111 - Where the employer requests the Union to agree to end the bargaining arrangements, a process commences which is similar to the provisions in paras 10, 12 and 15 which deal with a Union's request for recognition. Paras 104-111 are not applicable to derecognition from a voluntary collective agreement. Such a request can only be made after three or more years have passed since the recognition was ordered. Under para 105 the derecognition procedure ends if the parties agree to end the bargaining arrangements within ten working days of the request. If alternatively the Union agrees to negotiate, the parties then have twenty working days plus any remainder of the initial ten working days, plus any further mutually agreed extension, in which to reach agreement. If they ultimately decide that the Union should remain recognised, no further action is required as the CAC would not be asked to reach a decision under paras 106 or 107. One or both parties may approach ACAS but their involvement is not obligatory.

Para 106 allows the employer, if the Union objects to the request but fails to respond before the end of the first period of ten days to seek a secret ballot from the CAC as to whether the majority of workers support derecognition. If the employer and Union fail to reach agreement by the end of the second period the employer can request the CAC to hold a secret ballot, such applications to be in the form set out in para 108. Such an application must be rejected if the CAC has accepted another application of derecognition under Part IV or Part V in the previous three years – para 109.

Where the CAC has to decide whether to hold a ballot to determine whether a Union should be derecognised, para 110 comes into play. The CAC must be satisfied there is sufficient support (i.e. at least 10%) for an end to collective bargaining and the majority of workers would be likely to vote in favour. This is broadly similar to the test considered under paras 20 and 36. If the tests are held to be satisfied the CAC orders a ballot.

Workers' application to end arrangements

Workers' Application to End Arrangements:
Paras 112-116 - Workers may apply for derecognition either alone or as a group. Such application cannot be considered if the CAC have accepted another derecognition application under Part IV or Part V in the previous three years and the 10% support and likely majority tests apply.

112.– (1) A worker or workers falling within the bargaining unit may after the relevant date apply to the CAC to have the bargaining arrangements ended.

(2) An application is not admissible unless-

  (a) it is made in such form as the CAC specifies, and
  (b) it is supported by such documents as the CAC specifies.

(3) An application is not admissible unless the worker gives (or workers give) to the employer and to the union (or each of the unions)-

  (a) notice of the application, and
  (b) a copy of the application and any documents supporting it.

113.– (1)   An application under paragraph 112 is not admissible if-

  (a) a relevant application was made within the period of 3 years prior to the date of the application under paragraph 112,
  (b) the relevant application and the application under paragraph 112 relate to the same bargaining unit, and
  (c) the CAC accepted the relevant application.

(2) A relevant application is an application made to the CAC-

  (a) by the union (or the unions) under paragraph 101,
  (b) by the employer under paragraph 106, 107 or 128, or
  (c) by a worker (or workers) under paragraph 112.

114.– (1) An application under paragraph 112 is not admissible unless the CAC decides that-

  (a) at least 10 per cent of the workers constituting the bargaining unit favour an end of the bargaining arrangements, and
  (b) a majority of the workers constituting the bargaining unit would be likely to favour an end of the bargaining arrangements.

(2) The CAC must give reasons for the decision.

115.– (1) The CAC must give notice to the worker (or workers), the employer and the union (or unions) of receipt of an application under paragraph 112.

(2) Within the acceptance period the CAC must decide whether the application is admissible within the terms of paragraphs 112 to 114.

(3) In deciding whether the application is admissible the CAC must consider any evidence which it has been given by the employer, the union (or unions) or any of the workers falling within the bargaining unit.

(4) If the CAC decides that the application is not admissible-

  (a) the CAC must give notice of its decision to the worker (or workers), the employer and the union (or unions),
  (b) the CAC must not accept the application, and
  (c) no further steps are to be taken under this Part of this Schedule.

(5) If the CAC decides that the application is admissible it must-

(a) accept the application, and

(b) give notice of the acceptance to the worker (or workers), the employer and the union (or unions).

(6) The acceptance period is-

(a) the period of 10 working days starting with the day after that on which the CAC receives the application, or

(b) such longer period (so starting) as the CAC may specify to the worker (or workers), the employer and the union (or unions) by notice containing reasons for the extension.

116.– (1) If the CAC accepts the application, in the negotiation period the CAC must help the employer, the union (or unions) and the worker (or workers) with a view to-

(a) the employer and the union (or unions) agreeing to end the bargaining arrangements, or

(b) the worker (or workers) withdrawing the application.

(2) The negotiation period is-

(a) the period of 20 working days starting with the day after that on which the CAC gives notice of acceptance of the application, or

(b) such longer period (so starting) as the CAC may decide with the consent of the worker (or workers), the employer and the union (or unions).

Para 116 requires the CAC to assist the three parties (employer, Union and workers) to find a consensus within twenty working days. It must then hold a ballot under paras 117-121 unless the parties reach agreement or the application is withdrawn.

Ballot on derecognition

117.– (1) This paragraph applies if the CAC accepts an application under paragraph 106 or 107.

(2) This paragraph also applies if-

(a) the CAC accepts an application under paragraph 112, and

(b) in the period mentioned in paragraph 116(1) there is no agreement or withdrawal as there described.

(3) The CAC must arrange for the holding of a secret ballot in which the workers constituting the bargaining unit are asked whether the bargaining arrangements should be ended.

(4) The ballot must be conducted by a qualified independent person appointed by the CAC.

(5) The ballot must be conducted within-

- (a) the period of 20 working days starting with the day after that on which the qualified independent person is appointed, or
- (b) such longer period (so starting) as the CAC may decide.

(6) The ballot must be conducted-

- (a) at a workplace or workplaces decided by the CAC,
- (b) by post, or
- (c) by a combination of the methods described in sub-paragraphs (a) and (b),

depending on the CAC's preference.

(7) In deciding how the ballot is to be conducted the CAC must take into account-

- (a) the likelihood of the ballot being affected by unfairness or malpractice if it were conducted at a workplace or workplaces;
- (b) costs and practicality;
- (c) such other matters as the CAC considers appropriate.

(8) The CAC may not decide that the ballot is to be conducted as mentioned in sub-paragraph (6)(c) unless there are special factors making such a decision appropriate; and special factors include-

- (a) factors arising from the location of workers or the nature of their employment;
- (b) factors put to the CAC by the employer or the union (or unions).

(9) A person is a qualified independent person if-

- (a) he satisfies such conditions as may be specified for the purposes of this paragraph by order of the Secretary of State or is himself so specified, and
- (b) there are no grounds for believing either that he will carry out any functions conferred on him in relation to the ballot otherwise than competently or that his independence in relation to the ballot might reasonably be called into question.

(10) An order under sub-paragraph (9)(a) shall be made by statutory instrument subject to annulment in pursuance of a resolution of either House of Parliament.

(11) As soon as is reasonably practicable after the CAC is required under sub-paragraph (3) to arrange for the holding of a ballot it must inform the employer and the union (or unions)-

- (a) that it is so required;
- (b) of the name of the person appointed to conduct the ballot and the date of his appointment;
- (c) of the period within which the ballot must be conducted;
- (d) whether the ballot is to be conducted by post or at a workplace or workplaces;
- (e) of the workplace or workplaces concerned (if the ballot is to be conducted at a workplace or workplaces).

118.– (1) An employer who is informed by the CAC under paragraph 117(11) must comply with the following three duties.

(2) The first duty is to co-operate generally, in connection with the ballot, with the union (or unions) and the person appointed to conduct the ballot; and the second and third duties are not to prejudice the generality of this.

(3) The second duty is to give to the union (or unions) such access to the workers constituting the bargaining unit as is reasonable to enable the union (or unions) to inform the workers of the object of the ballot and to seek their support and their opinions on the issues involved.

(4) The third duty is to do the following (so far as it is reasonable to expect the employer to do so)-

(a) to give to the CAC, within the period of 10 working days starting with the day after that on which the employer is informed under paragraph 117(11), the names and home addresses of the workers constituting the bargaining unit;

(b) to give to the CAC, as soon as is reasonably practicable, the name and home address of any worker who joins the unit after the employer has complied with paragraph (a);

(c) to inform the CAC, as soon as is reasonably practicable, of any worker whose name has been given to the CAC under paragraph (a) or (b) but who ceases to be within the unit.

(5) As soon as is reasonably practicable after the CAC receives any information under sub-paragraph (4) it must pass it on to the person appointed to conduct the ballot.

(6) If asked to do so by the union (or unions) the person appointed to conduct the ballot must send to any worker-

(a) whose name and home address have been given under sub-paragraph (5), and
(b) who is still within the unit (so far as the person so appointed is aware),

any information supplied by the union (or unions) to the person so appointed.

(7) The duty under sub-paragraph (6) does not apply unless the union bears (or unions bear) the cost of sending the information.

(8) Each of the following powers shall be taken to include power to issue Codes of Practice about reasonable access for the purposes of sub-paragraph (3)-

(a) the power of ACAS under section 199(1);
(b) the power of the Secretary of State under section 203(1)(a).

119.– (1) If the CAC is satisfied that the employer has failed to fulfil any of the three duties imposed by paragraph 118, and the ballot has not been held, the CAC may order the employer-

(a) to take such steps to remedy the failure as the CAC considers reasonable and specifies in the order, and

(b) to do so within such period as the CAC considers reasonable and specifies in the order.

(2) If-

(a) the ballot has been arranged in consequence of an application under paragraph 106 or 107,

(b) the CAC is satisfied that the employer has failed to comply with an order under sub-paragraph (1), and

(c) the ballot has not been held,

the CAC may refuse the application.

(3) If-

(a) the ballot has been arranged in consequence of an application under paragraph 112, and

(b) the ballot has not been held,

an order under sub-paragraph (1), on being recorded in the county court, may be enforced in the same way as an order of that court.

(4) If the CAC refuses an application under sub-paragraph (2) it shall take steps to cancel the holding of the ballot; and if the ballot is held it shall have no effect.

120.– (1) This paragraph applies if the holding of a ballot has been arranged under paragraph 117(3), whether or not it has been cancelled.

(2) The gross costs of the ballot shall be borne-

(a) as to half, by the employer, and

(b) as to half, by the union (or unions).

(3) If there is more than one union they shall bear their half of the gross costs-

(a) in such proportions as they jointly indicate to the person appointed to conduct the ballot, or

(b) in the absence of such an indication, in equal shares.

(4) The person appointed to conduct the ballot may send to the employer and the union (or each of the unions) a demand stating-

(a) the gross costs of the ballot, and

(b) the amount of the gross costs to be borne by the recipient.

(5) In such a case the recipient must pay the amount stated to the person sending the demand, and must do so within the period of 15 working days starting with the day after that on which the demand is received.

(6) In England and Wales, if the amount stated is not paid in accordance with sub-paragraph (5) it shall, if a county court so orders, be recoverable by execution issued from that court or otherwise as if it were payable under an order of that court.

(7) References to the costs of the ballot are to-

    (a) the costs wholly, exclusively and necessarily incurred in connection with the ballot by the person appointed to conduct it,

    (b) such reasonable amount as the person appointed to conduct the ballot charges for his services, and

    (c) such other costs as the employer and the union (or unions) agree.

121.– (1) As soon as is reasonably practicable after the CAC is informed of the result of a ballot by the person conducting it, the CAC must act under this paragraph.

(2) The CAC must inform the employer and the union (or unions) of the result of the ballot.

(3) If the result is that the proposition that the bargaining arrangements should be ended is supported by-

    (a) a majority of the workers voting, and

    (b) at least 40 per cent of the workers constituting the bargaining unit,

the CAC must issue a declaration that the bargaining arrangements are to cease to have effect on a date specified by the CAC in the declaration.

(4) If the result is otherwise the CAC must refuse the application under paragraph 106, 107 or 112.

(5) If a declaration is issued under sub-paragraph (3) the bargaining arrangements shall cease to have effect accordingly.

(6) The Secretary of State may by order amend sub-paragraph (3) so as to specify a different degree of support; and different provision may be made for different circumstances.

(7) An order under sub-paragraph (6) shall be made by statutory instrument.

(8) No such order shall be made unless a draft of it has been laid before Parliament and approved by a resolution of each House of Parliament.

Ballot on Derecognition:
Paras 117-121 - The procedures under paras 117-121 mirror recognition balloting procedure under paras 25-29. If ultimately the vote is supported by a majority of those who vote, and at least 40% of the workers eligible to vote, the CAC must declare an end to the bargaining arrangements on a specified date; otherwise the application must be refused and the Union remains recognised. The Secretary of State may by order change the percentage of derecognition support required subject to affirmative resolution.

PART V

DERECOGNITION WHERE RECOGNITION AUTOMATIC

Introduction

Part V – Derecognition where Recognition Automatic
Introduction:
Paras 122-126 - Part V provides for a different derecognition process in cases where Unions have been automatically recognised on the grounds of having greater than 50% membership, i.e. recognised without a ballot. Applications for derecognition of an automatically recognised Union will not be accepted by the CAC until three or more years after recognition. The derecognition procedure applies to Unions recognised as a result of a CAC declaration under paras 22 or 87, whether or not the method for collective bargaining is:

- *voluntarily agreed*

- *imposed by the CAC*

- *agreed as a variation on a CAC imposed method*

122.– (1) This Part of this Schedule applies if-

(a) the CAC has issued a declaration under paragraph 22(2) that a union is (or unions are) recognised as entitled to conduct collective bargaining on behalf of a bargaining unit, and
(b) the parties have agreed under paragraph 30 or 31 a method by which they will conduct collective bargaining.

(2) In such a case references in this Part of this Schedule to the bargaining arrangements are to-

(a) the declaration, and
(b) the parties' agreement.

123.– (1) This Part of this Schedule also applies if-

(a) the CAC has issued a declaration under paragraph 22(2) that a union is (or unions are) recognised as entitled to conduct collective bargaining on behalf of a bargaining unit, and
(b) the CAC has specified to the parties under paragraph 31(3) the method by which they are to conduct collective bargaining.

(2) In such a case references in this Part of this Schedule to the bargaining arrangements are to-

(a) the declaration, and

(b) anything effective as, or as if contained in, a legally enforceable contract by virtue of paragraph 31.

124.– (1) This Part of this Schedule also applies if the CAC has issued a declaration under paragraph 87(2) that a union is (or unions are) recognised as entitled to conduct collective bargaining on behalf of a bargaining unit.

(2) In such a case references in this Part of this Schedule to the bargaining arrangements are to -

(a) the declaration, and
(b) paragraph 87(6)(b).

125. For the purposes of this Part of this Schedule the relevant date is the date of the expiry of the period of 3 years starting with the date of the CAC's declaration.

> *Para 125 operates the three year principle i.e. that derecognition may not take place until three or more years after the CAC declaration of recognition was made.*

126. References in this Part of this Schedule to the parties are to the employer and the union (or unions) concerned.

Employer's request to end arrangements

127.– (1) The employer may after the relevant date request the union (or each of the unions) to agree to end the bargaining arrangements.

(2) The request is not valid unless it-

(a) is in writing,
(b) is received by the union (or each of the unions),
(c) identifies the bargaining arrangements,
(d) states that it is made under this Schedule, and
(e) states that fewer than half of the workers constituting the bargaining unit are members of the union (or unions).

128.– (1) If before the end of the negotiation period the parties agree to end the bargaining arrangements no further steps are to be taken under this Part of this Schedule.

(2) If no such agreement is made before the end of the negotiation period, the employer may apply to the CAC for the holding of a secret ballot to decide whether the bargaining arrangements should be ended.

(3) The negotiation period is the period of 10 working days starting with the day after-

(a) the day on which the union receives the request, or
(b) the last day on which any of the unions receives the request;

or such longer period (so starting) as the parties may from time to time agree.

Employer's Request to End Arrangements:

Paras 127-128 - Provides the procedure for derecognition under this Part. An employer may request the Union to terminate bargaining arrangements because fewer than half the workers in the bargaining unit are Union members. These paras are similar to paras 104-111 which deal with the standard request for derecognition. The general procedure is set out in paras 127 and 129. Again, the derecognition procedure ends if the parties agree to end the bargaining arrangements within ten working days of the request (para 128). The time can be extended for ten working days by mutual consent. If the outcome is that the parties agree to continued Union recognition no action is required by them. The bargaining arrangements remain in force and the CAC is not invited to hold a ballot under paras 106 or 107. However if the Union does not respond or rejects the request the employer may apply to the CAC for a secret ballot on derecognition. Before the CAC holds a ballot on derecognition it must be satisfied that a majority of the workers in the unit are not members of the recognised Union and that the CAC has not accepted an application for derecognition under Part IV or Part V in the previous three years. If a majority of the workers are Union members, the automatic recognition will remain in force and the CAC must decide within ten working days. The ballot procedure is the same as in Part IV.

129.– (1) An application under paragraph 128 is not admissible unless-

    (a) it is made in such form as the CAC specifies, and
    (b) it is supported by such documents as the CAC specifies.

(2) An application under paragraph 128 is not admissible unless the employer gives to the union (or each of the unions)-

    (a) notice of the application, and
    (b) a copy of the application and any documents supporting it.

130.– (1) An application under paragraph 128 is not admissible if-

    (a) a relevant application was made within the period of 3 years prior to the date of the application under paragraph 128,
    (b) the relevant application and the application under paragraph 128 relate to the same bargaining unit, and
    (c) the CAC accepted the relevant application.

(2) A relevant application is an application made to the CAC-

    (a) by the union (or the unions) under paragraph 101,
    (b) by the employer under paragraph 106, 107 or 128, or
    (c) by a worker (or workers) under paragraph 112.

131.– (1) An application under paragraph 128 is not admissible unless the CAC is satisfied that fewer than half of the workers constituting the bargaining unit are members of the union (or unions).

(2) The CAC must give reasons for the decision.

132.– (1) The CAC must give notice to the parties of receipt of an application under paragraph 128.

(2) Within the acceptance period the CAC must decide whether-

    (a) the request is valid within the terms of paragraph 127, and
    (b) the application is admissible within the terms of paragraphs 129 to 131.

(3) In deciding those questions the CAC must consider any evidence which it has been given by the parties.

(4) If the CAC decides that the request is not valid or the application is not admissible-

    (a) the CAC must give notice of its decision to the parties,
    (b) the CAC must not accept the application, and
    (c) no further steps are to be taken under this Part of this Schedule.

(5) If the CAC decides that the request is valid and the application is admissible it must-

    (a) accept the application, and
    (b) give notice of the acceptance to the parties.

(6) The acceptance period is-

    (a) the period of 10 working days starting with the day after that on which the CAC receives the application, or
    (b) such longer period (so starting) as the CAC may specify to the parties by notice containing reasons for the extension.

Ballot on derecognition

133.– (1) Paragraph 117 applies if the CAC accepts an application under paragraph 128 (as well as in the cases mentioned in paragraph 117(1) and (2)).

(2) Paragraphs 118 to 121 apply accordingly, but as if-

    (a) the reference in paragraph 119(2)(a) to paragraph 106 or 107 were to paragraph 106, 107 or 128;
    (b) the reference in paragraph 121(4) to paragraph 106, 107 or 112 were to paragraph 106, 107, 112 or 128.

Part VI

Derecognition where union not independent

Introduction

134.– (1) This Part of this Schedule applies if-

    (a) an employer and a union (or unions) have agreed that the union is (or unions are) recognised as entitled to conduct collective bargaining on behalf of a group or groups of workers, and

    (b) the union does not have (or none of the unions has) a certificate under section 6 that it is independent.

(2) In such a case references in this Part of this Schedule to the bargaining arrangements are to-

    (a) the parties' agreement mentioned in sub-paragraph (1)(a), and

    (b) any agreement between the parties as to the method by which they will conduct collective bargaining.

135. In this Part of this Schedule-

    (a) references to the parties are to the employer and the union (or unions);

    (b) references to the bargaining unit are to the group of workers referred to in paragraph 134(1)(a) (or the groups taken together).

136. The meaning of collective bargaining given by section 178(1) shall not apply in relation to this Part of this Schedule.

> **Part VI – Derecognition Where Union Not Independent**
> **Introduction:**
> *Paras 134-136 - Definitions for this part of Schedule A1 are contained in paras 135 and 136. Part VI allows a worker or a group of workers to apply to the CAC for derecognition of a Union which has been voluntarily recognised by an employer where the Union does not have a Certificate of Independence from the Certification Officer under the provisions of s.2-9 of the 1992 Act.*

Workers' application to end arrangements

Workers Application to End Arrangements:
Paras 137-146 - Under para 137 an application to the CAC to end the collective bargaining arrangements can be made at any time after a non-independent Union is recognised. Para 139 provides that an application is not admissible unless at least 10% of the bargaining unit favour an end to the collective bargaining arrangements and the majority of the bargaining unit are likely to do so. The CAC cannot admit an application for Part VI Derecognition if the Union already has, or has applied for, a Certificate of Independence under s.6 of the 1992 Act. In determining admissibility the CAC is required by para 141 to take evidence from the employer, Union and workers. Prior to a ballot being held under para 147 there is a twenty working day negotiation period in which the CAC is required to help the employer, Union and workers negotiate the issues to a resolution either by an agreement to end the bargaining arrangement or by the worker withdrawing the application. In this respect para 142(1) mirrors para 116(1).

137.– (1) A worker or workers falling within the bargaining unit may apply to the CAC to have the bargaining arrangements ended.

(2) An application is not admissible unless-

    (a) it is made in such form as the CAC specifies, and
    (b) it is supported by such documents as the CAC specifies.

(3) An application is not admissible unless the worker gives (or workers give) to the employer and to the union (or each of the unions)-

    (a) notice of the application, and
    (b) a copy of the application and any documents supporting it.

138. An application under paragraph 137 is not admissible if the CAC is satisfied that any of the unions has a certificate under section 6 that it is independent.

139.– (1) An application under paragraph 137 is not admissible unless the CAC decides that-

    (a) at least 10 per cent of the workers constituting the bargaining unit favour an end of the bargaining arrangements, and
    (b) a majority of the workers constituting the bargaining unit would be likely to favour an end of the bargaining arrangements.

(2) The CAC must give reasons for the decision.

140. An application under paragraph 137 is not admissible if the CAC is satisfied that-

    (a) the union (or any of the unions) has made an application to the Certification Officer under section 6 for a certificate that it is independent, and

(b) the Certification Officer has not come to a decision on the application (or each of the applications).

141.– (1) The CAC must give notice to the worker (or workers), the employer and the union (or unions) of receipt of an application under paragraph 137.

(2) Within the acceptance period the CAC must decide whether the application is admissible within the terms of paragraphs 137 to 140.

(3) In deciding whether the application is admissible the CAC must consider any evidence which it has been given by the employer, the union (or unions) or any of the workers falling within the bargaining unit.

(4) If the CAC decides that the application is not admissible-

(a) the CAC must give notice of its decision to the worker (or workers), the employer and the union (or unions),
(b) the CAC must not accept the application, and
(c) no further steps are to be taken under this Part of this Schedule.

(5) If the CAC decides that the application is admissible it must-

(a) accept the application, and
(b) give notice of the acceptance to the worker (or workers), the employer and the union (or unions).

(6) The acceptance period is-

(a) the period of 10 working days starting with the day after that on which the CAC receives the application, or
(b) such longer period (so starting) as the CAC may specify to the worker (or workers), the employer and the union (or unions) by notice containing reasons for the extension.

142.– (1) If the CAC accepts the application, in the negotiation period the CAC must help the employer, the union (or unions) and the worker (or workers) with a view to-

(a) the employer and the union (or unions) agreeing to end the bargaining arrangements, or
(b) the worker (or workers) withdrawing the application.

(2) The negotiation period is-

(a) the period of 20 working days starting with the day after that on which the CAC gives notice of acceptance of the application, or
(b) such longer period (so starting) as the CAC may decide with the consent of the worker (or workers), the employer and the union (or unions).

143.– (1) This paragraph applies if-

(a) the CAC accepts an application under paragraph 137,

(b) during the period mentioned in paragraph 142(1) or 145(3) the CAC is satisfied that the union (or each of the unions) has made an application to the Certification Officer under section 6 for a certificate that it is independent, that the application (or each of the applications) to the Certification Officer was made before the application under paragraph 137 and that the Certification Officer has not come to a decision on the application (or each of the applications), and

(c) at the time the CAC is so satisfied there has been no agreement or withdrawal as described in paragraph 142(1) or 145(3).

(2) In such a case paragraph 142(1) or 145(3) shall cease to apply from the time when the CAC is satisfied as mentioned in sub-paragraph (1)(b).

> *Para 143 requires the CAC to suspend its enquiries into the application if the CAC becomes aware that the Union applied for a Certificate of Independence before the derecognition application was made. The effect of para 144 is to automatically end the application if the Certification Officer rules that the Union is independent. If the ruling is that the Union is not independent the suspension is lifted and the application resumed with a fresh twenty working day negotiating period.*

144.– (1) This paragraph applies if the CAC is subsequently satisfied that-

(a) the Certification Officer has come to a decision on the application (or each of the applications) mentioned in paragraph 143(1)(b), and

(b) his decision is that the union (or any of the unions) which made an application under section 6 is independent.

(2) In such a case-

(a) the CAC must give the worker (or workers), the employer and the union (or unions) notice that it is so satisfied, and

(b) the application under paragraph 137 shall be treated as not having been made.

145.– (1) This paragraph applies if the CAC is subsequently satisfied that-

(a) the Certification Officer has come to a decision on the application (or each of the applications) mentioned in paragraph 143(1)(b), and

(b) his decision is that the union (or each of the unions) which made an application under section 6 is not independent.

(2) The CAC must give the worker (or workers), the employer and the union (or unions) notice that it is so satisfied.

(3) In the new negotiation period the CAC must help the employer, the union (or unions) and the worker (or workers) with a view to-

(a) the employer and the union (or unions) agreeing to end the bargaining arrangements, or

(b) the worker (or workers) withdrawing the application.

(4) The new negotiation period is-

(a) the period of 20 working days starting with the day after that on which the CAC gives notice under sub-paragraph (2), or

(b) such longer period (so starting) as the CAC may decide with the consent of the worker (or workers), the employer and the union (or unions).

146.– (1) This paragraph applies if-

(a) the CAC accepts an application under paragraph 137,

(b) paragraph 143 does not apply, and

(c) during the relevant period the CAC is satisfied that a certificate of independence has been issued to the union (or any of the unions) under section 6.

(2) In such a case the relevant period is the period starting with the first day of the negotiation period (as defined in paragraph 142(2)) and ending with the first of the following to occur-

(a) any agreement by the employer and the union (or unions) to end the bargaining arrangements;

(b) any withdrawal of the application by the worker (or workers);

(c) the CAC being informed of the result of a relevant ballot by the person conducting it;

and a relevant ballot is a ballot held by virtue of this Part of this Schedule.

(3) This paragraph also applies if-

(a) the CAC gives notice under paragraph 145(2), and

(b) during the relevant period the CAC is satisfied that a certificate of independence has been issued to the union (or any of the unions) under section 6.

(4) In such a case, the relevant period is the period starting with the first day of the new negotiation period (as defined in paragraph 145(4)) and ending with the first of the following to occur-

(a) any agreement by the employer and the union (or unions) to end the bargaining arrangements;

(b) any withdrawal of the application by the worker (or workers);

(c) the CAC being informed of the result of a relevant ballot by the person conducting it;

and a relevant ballot is a ballot held by virtue of this Part of this Schedule.

(5) If this paragraph applies-

(a) the CAC must give the worker (or workers), the employer and the union (or unions) notice that it is satisfied as mentioned in sub-paragraph (1)(c) or (3)(b), and

(b) the application under paragraph 137 shall be treated as not having been made.

Ballot on derecognition

147.– (1) Paragraph 117 applies if-

(a) the CAC accepts an application under paragraph 137, and

(b) in the period mentioned in paragraph 142(1) or 145(3) there is no agreement or withdrawal as there described,

(as well as in the cases mentioned in paragraph 117(1) and (2)).

(2) Paragraphs 118 to 121 apply accordingly, but as if-

(a) the reference in paragraph 119(3)(a) to paragraph 112 were to paragraph 112 or 137;

(b) the reference in paragraph 121(4) to paragraph 106, 107 or 112 were to paragraph 106, 107, 112 or 137.

(c) the reference in paragraph 119(4) to the CAC refusing an application under paragraph 119(2) included a reference to it being required to give notice under paragraph 146(5).

> **Ballot on Derecognition:**
> *Para 147 - If agreement cannot be reached the CAC is required to hold a ballot under para 147. If the status of the Union changes by an award of a Certificate of Independence at any time before the CAC is informed of the ballot results (e.g. because the Union successfully appeals the decision of the Certification Officer) para 146 requires the CAC to take no further action on a Part VI workers application for derecognition.*

Derecognition: other cases

148.– (1) This paragraph applies if as a result of a declaration by the CAC another union is (or other unions are) recognised as entitled to conduct collective bargaining on behalf of a group of workers at least one of whom falls within the bargaining unit.

(2) The CAC must issue a declaration that the bargaining arrangements are to cease to have effect on a date specified by the CAC in the declaration.

(3) If a declaration is issued under sub-paragraph (2) the bargaining arrangements shall cease to have effect accordingly.

(4) It is for the CAC to decide whether sub-paragraph (1) is fulfilled, but in deciding the CAC may take account of the views of any person it believes has an interest in the matter.

PART VII

LOSS OF INDEPENDENCE

Introduction

149.– (1) This Part of this Schedule applies if the CAC has issued a declaration that a union is (or unions are) recognised as entitled to conduct collective bargaining on behalf of a bargaining unit.

(2) In such a case references in this Part of this Schedule to the bargaining arrangements are to the declaration and to the provisions relating to the collective bargaining method.

(3) For this purpose the provisions relating to the collective bargaining method are-

    (a) the parties' agreement as to the method by which collective bargaining is to be conducted,

    (b) anything effective as, or as if contained in, a legally enforceable contract and relating to the method by which collective bargaining is to be conducted, or

    (c) any provision of Part III of this Schedule that a method of collective bargaining is to have effect.

150.– (1) This Part of this Schedule also applies if-

    (a) the parties have agreed that a union is (or unions are) recognised as entitled to conduct collective bargaining on behalf of a bargaining unit,

    (b) the CAC has specified to the parties under paragraph 63(2) the method by which they are to conduct collective bargaining, and

    (c) the parties have not agreed in writing to replace the method or that paragraph 63(3) shall not apply.

(2) In such a case references in this Part of this Schedule to the bargaining arrangements are to-

    (a) the parties' agreement mentioned in sub-paragraph (1)(a), and

    (b) anything effective as, or as if contained in, a legally enforceable contract by virtue of paragraph 63.

151. References in this Part of this Schedule to the parties are to the employer and the union (or unions) concerned.

> **Part VII – Loss of Independence**
> **Introduction:**
> *Paras 149-151 - Part VII deals with the situation where an independent Union recognised under Part I loses its Certificate of Independence. The Union is treated as voluntarily recognised by the employer without the statutory support for the bargaining arrangements. Part VII also deals with situations where there is an agreement for recognition between a Union and an employer and an imposed bargaining method under Part II. Where such a Union loses its Certificate of Independence the statutory support for the bargaining arrangements would also end.*

Loss of certificate

152.– (1) This paragraph applies if-

(a) only one union is a party, and
(b) under section 7 the Certification Officer withdraws the union's certificate of independence.

(2) This paragraph also applies if-

(a) more than one union is a party, and
(b) under section 7 the Certification Officer withdraws the certificate of independence of each union (whether different certificates are withdrawn on the same or on different days).

(3) Sub-paragraph (4) shall apply on the day after-

(a) the day on which the Certification Officer informs the union (or unions) of the withdrawal (or withdrawals), or
(b) if there is more than one union, and he informs them on different days, the last of those days.

(4) The bargaining arrangements shall cease to have effect; and the parties shall be taken to agree that the union is (or unions are) recognised as entitled to conduct collective bargaining on behalf of the bargaining unit concerned.

Loss of Certificate:

Para 152 - The effect of para 152 is that the bargaining arrangements cease if the Certification Officer withdraws the Certificate of Independence from the Union. Where there is more than one recognised Union the bargaining arrangements cease if the Certification Officer withdraws the Certificate of Independence from all the Unions.

Certificate re-issued

153.– (1) This paragraph applies if-

(a) only one union is a party,

(b) paragraph 152 applies, and

(c) as a result of an appeal under section 9 against the decision to withdraw the certificate, the Certification Officer issues a certificate that the union is independent.

(2) This paragraph also applies if-

(a) more than one union is a party,

(b) paragraph 152 applies, and

(c) as a result of an appeal under section 9 against a decision to withdraw a certificate, the Certification Officer issues a certificate that any of the unions concerned is independent.

(3) Sub-paragraph (4) shall apply, beginning with the day after-

(a) the day on which the Certification Officer issues the certificate, or

(b) if there is more than one union, the day on which he issues the first or only certificate.

(4) The bargaining arrangements shall have effect again; and paragraph 152 shall cease to apply.

Certificate Re-Issued:

Para 153 - The bargaining arrangements are restored under para 153 if the Certificate of Independence is reinstated e.g by a successful appeal against the Certification Officer's decision.

Miscellaneous

> **Miscellaneous:**
> *Paras 154-155 - The effect of para 154 is that if the bargaining arrangements cease to have effect under Part VII the employer can derecognise the Union without the need to undertake the procedures in Part IV or Part V. Alternatively, the employer can negotiate to change the bargaining unit without having to follow the Part III procedure. Again, if the Union successfully appeals against the loss of its Certificate of Independence, the statutory requirements will apply again.*

154. Parts III to VI of this Schedule shall not apply in the case of the parties at any time when, by virtue of this Part of this Schedule, the bargaining arrangements do not have effect.

155. If-

    (a) by virtue of paragraph 153 the bargaining arrangements have effect again beginning with a particular day, and

    (b) in consequence section 70B applies in relation to the bargaining unit concerned,

for the purposes of section 70B(3) that day shall be taken to be the day on which section 70B first applies in relation to the unit.

> *Para 155 relates to the obligation to consult a recognised Union on training issues in accordance with s.5 of the 1999 Act. Where the obligation lapses because the Union loses its Certificate of Independence but later resumes on restoring its certificate, the first subsequent consultation meeting must be held within six months of the day on which the bargaining arrangements take effect again.*

PART VIII

DETRIMENT

Detriment

156.– (1) A worker has a right not to be subjected to any detriment by any act, or any deliberate failure to act, by his employer if the act or failure takes place on any of the grounds set out in sub-paragraph (2).

(2) The grounds are that-

   (a) the worker acted with a view to obtaining or preventing recognition of a union (or unions) by the employer under this Schedule;

   (b) the worker indicated that he supported or did not support recognition of a union (or unions) by the employer under this Schedule;

   (c) the worker acted with a view to securing or preventing the ending under this Schedule of bargaining arrangements;

   (d) the worker indicated that he supported or did not support the ending under this Schedule of bargaining arrangements;

   (e) the worker influenced or sought to influence the way in which votes were to be cast by other workers in a ballot arranged under this Schedule;

   (f) the worker influenced or sought to influence other workers to vote or to abstain from voting in such a ballot;

   (g) the worker voted in such a ballot;

   (h) the worker proposed to do, failed to do, or proposed to decline to do, any of the things referred to in paragraphs (a) to (g).

(3) A ground does not fall within sub-paragraph (2) if it constitutes an unreasonable act or omission by the worker.

(4) This paragraph does not apply if the worker is an employee and the detriment amounts to dismissal within the meaning of the Employment Rights Act 1996.

(5) A worker may present a complaint to an employment tribunal on the ground that he has been subjected to a detriment in contravention of this paragraph.

(6) Apart from the remedy by way of complaint as mentioned in sub-paragraph (5), a worker has no remedy for infringement of the right conferred on him by this paragraph.

157.– (1) An employment tribunal shall not consider a complaint under paragraph 156 unless it is presented-

   (a) before the end of the period of 3 months starting with the date of the act or failure to which the complaint relates or, if that act or failure is part of a series of similar acts or failures (or both), the last of them, or

   (b) where the tribunal is satisfied that it was not reasonably practicable for the complaint to be presented before the end of that period, within such further period as it considers reasonable.

(2) For the purposes of sub-paragraph (1)-

   (a) where an act extends over a period, the reference to the date of the act is a reference to the last day of that period;

   (b) a failure to act shall be treated as done when it was decided on.

(3) For the purposes of sub-paragraph (2), in the absence of evidence establishing the contrary an employer must be taken to decide on a failure to act-

   (a) when he does an act inconsistent with doing the failed act, or

(b) if he has done no such inconsistent act, when the period expires within which he might reasonably have been expected to do the failed act if it was to be done.

158. On a complaint under paragraph 156 it shall be for the employer to show the ground on which he acted or failed to act.

159.– (1) If the employment tribunal finds that a complaint under paragraph 156 is well-founded it shall make a declaration to that effect and may make an award of compensation to be paid by the employer to the complainant in respect of the act or failure complained of.

(2) The amount of the compensation awarded shall be such as the tribunal considers just and equitable in all the circumstances having regard to the infringement complained of and to any loss sustained by the complainant which is attributable to the act or failure which infringed his right.

(3) The loss shall be taken to include-

(a) any expenses reasonably incurred by the complainant in consequence of the act or failure complained of, and

(b) loss of any benefit which he might reasonably be expected to have had but for that act or failure.

(4) In ascertaining the loss, the tribunal shall apply the same rule concerning the duty of a person to mitigate his loss as applies to damages recoverable under the common law of England and Wales or Scotland.

(5) If the tribunal finds that the act or failure complained of was to any extent caused or contributed to by action of the complainant, it shall reduce the amount of the compensation by such proportion as it considers just and equitable having regard to that finding.

160.– (1) If the employment tribunal finds that a complaint under paragraph 156 is well-founded and-

(a) the detriment of which the worker has complained is the termination of his worker's contract, but

(b) that contract was not a contract of employment,

any compensation awarded under paragraph 159 must not exceed the limit specified in sub-paragraph (2).

(2) The limit is the total of-

(a) the sum which would be the basic award for unfair dismissal, calculated in accordance with section 119 of the Employment Rights Act 1996, if the worker had been an employee and the contract terminated had been a contract of employment, and

(b) the sum for the time being specified in section 124(1) of that Act which is the limit for a compensatory award to a person calculated in accordance with section 123 of that Act.

Part VIII – Detriment
Detriment:
Paras 156-160 - Section 146 of the 1992 Act gives a worker the right not to suffer detriment on the grounds of membership, non-membership, or taking part in the activities, of a Trade Union. Detriment is an act or deliberate failure to act, by an employer which is damaging to the worker, other than dismissal – dismissing an employee for membership, non-membership or taking part in the activities of a Trade Union is protected separately.

Paras 156-160 - Prohibit detriment in respect of a worker on any of the eight grounds relating to recognition or derecognition of a Union set out in para 156(2). There is a right to complain in respect of detriment to an Employment Tribunal and paras 157-160 provide for procedural issues, time limits and calculation of awards.

Dismissal

161.– (1) For the purposes of Part X of the Employment Rights Act 1996 (unfair dismissal) the dismissal of an employee shall be regarded as unfair if the dismissal was made-

(a) for a reason set out in sub-paragraph (2), or
(b) for reasons the main one of which is one of those set out in sub-paragraph (2).

(2) The reasons are that-

(a) the employee acted with a view to obtaining or preventing recognition of a union (or unions) by the employer under this Schedule;
(b) the employee indicated that he supported or did not support recognition of a union (or unions) by the employer under this Schedule;
(c) the employee acted with a view to securing or preventing the ending under this Schedule of bargaining arrangements;
(d) the employee indicated that he supported or did not support the ending under this Schedule of bargaining arrangements ;
(e) the employee influenced or sought to influence the way in which votes were to be cast by other workers in a ballot arranged under this Schedule;
(f) the employee influenced or sought to influence other workers to vote or to abstain from voting in such a ballot;
(g) the employee voted in such a ballot;
(h) the employee proposed to do, failed to do, or proposed to decline to do, any of the things referred to in paragraphs (a) to (g).

(3) A reason does not fall within sub-paragraph (2) if it constitutes an unreasonable act or omission by the employee.

> **Dismissal:**
> *Para 161 - Provides that an employee's dismissal is automatically unfair if it is on the grounds relating to recognition or derecognition set out in para 161(2), the same eight grounds in para 156(2). Note that this protection only applies to employees; however in the case of a worker who is not an employee dismissal is included in the definition of detriment for para 156:para 156(4).*

Selection for redundancy

162. For the purposes of Part X of the Employment Rights Act 1996 (unfair dismissal) the dismissal of an employee shall be regarded as unfair if the reason or principal reason for the dismissal was that he was redundant but it is shown-

(a) that the circumstances constituting the redundancy applied equally to one or more other employees in the same undertaking who held positions similar to that held by him and who have not been dismissed by the employer, and

(b) that the reason (or, if more than one, the principal reason) why he was selected for dismissal was one falling within paragraph 161(2).

> **Selection for Redundancy:**
> *Para 162 - Makes similar provisions in respect of redundancy selection.*

Employees with fixed-term contracts

163. Section 197(1) of the Employment Rights Act 1996 (fixed-term contracts) does not prevent Part X of that Act from applying to a dismissal which is regarded as unfair by virtue of paragraph 161 or 162.

> **Employees with Fixed Term Contracts:**
> *Para 163 - As a precautionary measure, makes such dismissals automatically unfair if the reason for the non-extension of a fixed term contract, some of those listed in para 161(2), even though the employee may have lawfully waived the right to claim unfair dismissal under s.197(1) of the 1996 Act – precautionary because such waivers are prohibited by s.18 of the 1999 Act (but only for contracts or waivers entered into after 24.10.99).*

Exclusion of requirement as to qualifying period

164. Sections 108 and 109 of the Employment Rights Act 1996 (qualifying period and upper age limit for unfair dismissal protection) do not apply to a dismissal which by virtue of paragraph 161 or 162 is regarded as unfair for the purposes of Part X of that Act.

> **Exclusion of Requirement as to Qualifying Period:**
> *Para 164 - The protection against unfair dismissal applies even if the employee has not completed the normal qualifying period of protection against unfair dismissal, currently one year, and even if the statutory upper age limit, which protects against unfair dismissal is normally lost, has been passed.*

Meaning of worker's contract

165. References in this Part of this Schedule to a worker's contract are to the contract mentioned in paragraph (a) or (b) of section 296(1) or the arrangements for the employment mentioned in paragraph (c) of section 296(1).

PART IX

GENERAL

Power to amend

166.– (1) If the CAC represents to the Secretary of State that paragraph 22 or 87 has an unsatisfactory effect and should be amended, he may by order amend it with a view to rectifying that effect.

(2) He may amend it in such way as he thinks fit, and not necessarily in a way proposed by the CAC (if it proposes one).

(3) An order under this paragraph shall be made by statutory instrument.

(4) No such order shall be made unless a draft of it has been laid before Parliament and approved by a resolution of each House of Parliament.

> **Part IX – General**
> **Power to Amend:**
> *Para 166 - Under para 166 the Secretary of State is empowered to amend the automatic recognition procedure in paras 22 or 87 if the CAC represents to the Secretary of State that it has an unsatisfactory effect. The amendment must be made by statutory instrument subject to affirmative resolution.*

Paras 22 or 87 may be amended in such ways as the Secretary of State thinks fit and not necessarily as proposed by the CAC (if it has also made a proposal).

Guidance

167.– (1) The Secretary of State may issue guidance to the CAC on the way in which it is to exercise its functions under paragraph 22 or 87.

(2) The CAC must take into account any such guidance in exercising those functions.

(3) However, no guidance is to apply with regard to an application made to the CAC before the guidance in question was issued.

(4) The Secretary of State must-

    (a) lay before each House of Parliament any guidance issued under this paragraph, and

    (b) arrange for any such guidance to be published by such means as appear to him to be most appropriate for drawing it to the attention of persons likely to be affected by it.

Guidance:
Para 167 - Empowers the Secretary of State to issue guidance to the CAC on how to decide the three qualifying questions in para 22(4) and para 87(4) in order to exercise its functions under paras 22 and 87. The guidance must be laid before both Houses of Parliament and published.

Method of conducting collective bargaining

168.– (1) After consulting ACAS the Secretary of State may by order specify for the purposes of paragraphs 31(3) and 63(2) a method by which collective bargaining might be conducted.

(2) If such an order is made the CAC-

    (a) must take it into account under paragraphs 31(3) and 63(2), but

    (b) may depart from the method specified by the order to such extent as the CAC thinks it is appropriate to do so in the circumstances.

(3) An order under this paragraph shall be made by statutory instrument subject to annulment in pursuance of a resolution of either House of Parliament.

Method of Conducting Collective Bargaining:
Para 168 - Gives the Secretary of State power after consultation with ACAS to make an order specifying the statutory method of conducting collective bargaining to be taken into account by the CAC when it imposes a collective bargaining method under para 31(3) and para 63(2).

The CAC must take the method specified into account but may depart from it as it considers appropriate in the circumstances.

Directions about certain applications

169.– (1) The Secretary of State may make to the CAC directions as described in sub-paragraph (2) in relation to any case where-

(a) two or more applications are made to the CAC,
(b) each application is a relevant application,
(c) each application relates to the same bargaining unit, and
(d) the CAC has not accepted any of the applications.

(2) The directions are directions as to the order in which the CAC must consider the admissibility of the applications.

(3) The directions may include-

(a) provision to deal with a case where a relevant application is made while the CAC is still considering the admissibility of another one relating to the same bargaining unit;
(b) other incidental provisions.

(4) A relevant application is an application under paragraph 101, 106, 107, 112 or 128.

Directions About Certain Applications:
Para 169 - Empowers the Secretary of State to make directions to the CAC as to the order in which it must consider the admissibility of competing applications.

Notice of declarations

170.– (1) If the CAC issues a declaration under this Schedule it must notify the parties of the declaration and its contents.

(2) The reference here to the parties is to-

(a) the union (or unions) concerned and the employer concerned, and

(b) if the declaration is issued in consequence of an application by a worker or workers, the worker or workers making it.

Notice of Declaration:
Para 170 - Any declaration issued by the CAC must be notified to the Union (or Unions and employer) concerned and to the worker (or workers) where the declaration is issued in consequence of such application.

CAC's general duty

171. In exercising functions under this Schedule in any particular case the CAC must have regard to the object of encouraging and promoting fair and efficient practices and arrangements in the workplace, so far as having regard to that object is consistent with applying other provisions of this Schedule in the case concerned.

CAC's General Duty:
Para 171 - Succinctly states the CAC's generally duty namely, the object of encouraging and promoting fair and efficient practices and arrangements in the workplace. Undoubtedly a party disgruntled with the determination by the CAC will wish to assess the determination against the benchmark in para 171.

General interpretation

172.– (1) References in this Schedule to the CAC are to the Central Arbitration Committee.

(2) For the purposes of this Schedule in its application to a part of Great Britain a working day is a day other than-

(a) a Saturday or a Sunday,
(b) Christmas day or Good Friday, or
(c) a day which is a bank holiday under the Banking and Financial Dealings Act 1971 in that part of Great Britain."

General Interpretation:
Para 172 - Defines a working day as a day other than a Saturday or a Sunday, Christmas Day or Good Friday or a day which is a Bank Holiday under the Banking and Financial Dealings Act 1971.

SCHEDULE 2

UNION MEMBERSHIP: DETRIMENT

Introduction

1. The Trade Union and Labour Relations (Consolidation) Act 1992 shall be amended as provided in this Schedule.

Detriment

2.– (1) Section 146 (action short of dismissal on grounds related to union membership or activities) shall be amended as follows.

(2) In subsection (1) for "have action short of dismissal taken against him as an individual by his employer" substitute "be subjected to any detriment as an individual by any act, or any deliberate failure to act, by his employer if the act or failure takes place".

(3) In subsection (3) for "have action short of dismissal taken against him" substitute "be subjected to any detriment as an individual by any act, or any deliberate failure to act, by his employer if the act or failure takes place".

(4) In subsection (4) for "action short of dismissal taken against him" substitute "a detriment to which he has been subjected as an individual by an act of his employer taking place".

(5) In subsection (5) for "action has been taken against him" substitute "he has been subjected to a detriment".

(6) After subsection (5) insert-

"(6) For the purposes of this section detriment is detriment short of dismissal."

Time limit for proceedings

3.– (1) Section 147 shall be amended as follows.

(2) Before "An" insert "(1)".

(3) In paragraph (a) of subsection (1) (as created by sub-paragraph (2) above) for the words from "action to which" to "those actions" substitute "act or failure to which the complaint relates or, where that act or failure is part of a series of similar acts or failures (or both) the last of them".

(4) After subsection (1) (as created by sub-paragraph (2) above) insert-

"(2) For the purposes of subsection (1)-

(a) where an act extends over a period, the reference to the date of the act is a reference to the last day of that period;
(b) a failure to act shall be treated as done when it was decided on.

(3) For the purposes of subsection (2), in the absence of evidence establishing the contrary an employer shall be taken to decide on a failure to act-

(a) when he does an act inconsistent with doing the failed act, or

(b) if he has done no such inconsistent act, when the period expires within which he might reasonably have been expected to do the failed act if it was to be done."

Consideration of complaint

4.– (1) Section 148 shall be amended as follows.

(2) In subsection (1) for "action was taken against the complainant" substitute "he acted or failed to act".

(3) In subsection (2) for "action was taken by the employer or the purpose for which it was taken" substitute "the employer acted or failed to act, or the purpose for which he did so".

(4) In subsection (3)-

(a) for "action was taken by the employer against the complainant" substitute "the employer acted or failed to act";

(b) for the words from "took the action" to "would take" substitute "acted or failed to act, unless it considers that no reasonable employer would act or fail to act in the way concerned".

(5) For subsection (4) substitute-

"(4) Where the tribunal determines that-

(a) the complainant has been subjected to a detriment by an act or deliberate failure to act by his employer, and

(b) the act or failure took place in consequence of a previous act or deliberate failure to act by the employer,

paragraph (a) of subsection (3) is satisfied if the purpose mentioned in that paragraph was the purpose of the previous act or failure."

Remedies

5. In section 149 for "action" there shall be substituted "act or failure"-

(a) in subsections (1), (2) and (3)(a) and (b), and

(b) in subsection (6), in the first place where "action" occurs.

Awards against third parties

6. In section 150(1)-

(a) in paragraph (a) for "action has been taken against the complainant by his employer" there shall be substituted "the complainant has been subjected to detriment by an act or failure by his employer taking place";

(b) in paragraph (b) for "take the action" there shall be substituted "act or fail to act in the way".

Schedule 2

S.2 gives effect to Schedule 2, the purpose of which is to amend s.146-s.150 inclusive of the 1992 Act. These sections provide a remedy for action, and a deliberate failure to act, short of dismissal, taken by an employer on grounds related to Union membership or non-membership or activity. The amendments extend. Protection to deliberate failure to act. Consequential amendments are made to the 1992 Act to extend the scope of s.146-s.150 inclusive to provide a right not to be subjected, on grounds related to Trade Union membership, non-membership, or activities, to any detriment as an individual by an act or deliberate failure to act on the part of the employer for one of the prohibited purposes. The amendments include those affecting the ground on which an employee may present a complaint to an Employment Tribunal, time limits, the criteria to be applied by the Tribunal in determining the purpose of an employer's action or failure to act, remedies and awards against third parties.

Section 4.   SCHEDULE 3

BALLOTS AND NOTICES

Introduction

1. The Trade Union and Labour Relations (Consolidation) Act 1992 shall be amended as provided by this Schedule.

Schedule 3

Para 1 – S.4 gives effect to Schedule 3 which amends s.226-s.235 inclusive of the 1992 Act which set out the legal rules governing industrial action, ballots and notices.

Support of ballot

2.– (1) Section 226 (requirement of ballot before action by trade union) shall be amended as follows.

(2) In subsection (2) (industrial action to be regarded as having support of ballot only if certain conditions are fulfilled) in paragraph (a)(ii) for "231A" substitute "231",

omit the word "and" at the end of paragraph (b), and after paragraph (b) insert-

"(bb) section 232A does not prevent the industrial action from being regarded as having the support of the ballot; and".

(3) After subsection (3) insert-

"(3A) If the requirements of section 231A fall to be satisfied in relation to an employer, as respects that employer industrial action shall not be regarded as having the support of a ballot unless those requirements are satisfied in relation to that employer."

Support of Ballot:
Para 2 – A new s.231A is introduced requiring Unions to inform employers about the result of an industrial action ballot involving their employees. Each employer must be notified where the Union ballots its members employed by more than one employer. Provided an employer is informed of the result, and subject to the other statutory requirements for lawful industrial action it will be lawful for the Union to call on its members employed by that employer to take industrial action. This changes the current position where a failure to inform all the employers can make it unlawful for the Union to induce any of its balloted members to take action. It remains unlawful for a Union to induce its members to take industrial action if their employer has not been informed of the ballot result.

Documents for employers

3.– (1) Section 226A (notice of ballot and sample voting paper for employers) shall be amended as follows.

(2) In subsection (2)(c) (notice of ballot must describe employees entitled to vote) for "describing (so that he can readily ascertain them) the employees of the employer" substitute "containing such information in the union's possession as would help the employer to make plans and bring information to the attention of those of his employees".

(3) After subsection (3) insert-

"(3A) These rules apply for the purposes of paragraph (c) of subsection (2)-

(a) if the union possesses information as to the number, category or work-place of the employees concerned, a notice must contain that information (at least);

(b) if a notice does not name any employees, that fact shall not be a ground for holding that it does not comply with paragraph (c) of subsection (2).

(3B) In subsection (3) references to employees are to employees of the employer concerned."

Documents for Employers:
Para 3 – The effect of this paragraph is to amend the rule regarding properly conducted secret balloting without which immunity from legal liability is lost and in particular to remove the requirements for the Union to name the employees concerned in its notice to the employer. This alters the current law which has been interpreted by case law as requiring the Union in certain circumstances to provide the employer with the names of the employees being balloted or called upon to participate in industrial action (Blackpool and Fylde College v. National Association of Teachers in Further and Higher Education [1994] ICR 982). The statutory purpose of s.226A(2) is redefined as being to enable the employer to make plans to deal with the consequences of any industrial action and to provide information to employees being balloted. Further, the effect of the new section 266A(3)(B) is that Unions are no longer under an obligation to provide an employer with sample forms which are sent only to the employees of other employers.

Entitlement to vote

4. In section 227 (entitlement to vote in ballot) subsection (2) (position where member is denied entitlement to vote) shall be omitted.

Entitlement to Vote
Para 4 – S.227 of the 1992 Act is amended by repealing s.227(2). S.227(1) of the 1992 Act provides that entitlement to vote in a ballot must be accorded equally to all Union members who it is reasonable at the time of the ballot for the Union to believe will be induced to take part in the industrial action (i.e. other Trade Union members are not entitled to vote). S.227(2) expressly provides that the requirements of s.227(1) are not satisfied if a member who was denied a vote is subsequently induced by the Union to participate in the industrial action. The repeal of s.227(2) means that Unions will be free to induce new members, who join the Union after the ballot, to take industrial action. Those who were eligible to vote but were denied a vote, cannot be induced by the Unions to take industrial action.

Separate workplace ballots

5. The following shall be substituted for section 228 (separate workplace ballots)-

   "**228.**– (1) Subject to subsection (2), this section applies if the members entitled to vote in a ballot by virtue of section 227 do not all have the same workplace.

   (2) This section does not apply if the union reasonably believes that all those members have the same workplace.

(3) Subject to section 228A, a separate ballot shall be held for each workplace; and entitlement to vote in each ballot shall be accorded equally to, and restricted to, members of the union who-

(a) are entitled to vote by virtue of section 227, and
(b) have that workplace.

(4) In this section and section 228A "workplace" in relation to a person who is employed means-

(a) if the person works at or from a single set of premises, those premises, and
(b) in any other case, the premises with which the person's employment has the closest connection.

228A.– (1) Where section 228(3) would require separate ballots to be held for each workplace, a ballot may be held in place of some or all of the separate ballots if one of subsections (2) to (4) is satisfied in relation to it.

(2) This subsection is satisfied in relation to a ballot if the workplace of each member entitled to vote in the ballot is the workplace of at least one member of the union who is affected by the dispute.

(3) This subsection is satisfied in relation to a ballot if entitlement to vote is accorded to, and limited to, all the members of the union who-

(a) according to the union's reasonable belief have an occupation of a particular kind or have any of a number of particular kinds of occupation, and
(b) are employed by a particular employer, or by any of a number of particular employers, with whom the union is in dispute.

(4) This subsection is satisfied in relation to a ballot if entitlement to vote is accorded to, and limited to, all the members of the union who are employed by a particular employer, or by any of a number of particular employers, with whom the union is in dispute.

(5) For the purposes of subsection (2) the following are members of the union affected by a dispute-

(a) if the dispute relates (wholly or partly) to a decision which the union reasonably believes the employer has made or will make concerning a matter specified in subsection (1)(a), (b) or (c) of section 244 (meaning of "trade dispute"), members whom the decision directly affects,
(b) if the dispute relates (wholly or partly) to a matter specified in subsection (1)(d) of that section, members whom the matter directly affects,
(c) if the dispute relates (wholly or partly) to a matter specified in subsection (1)(e) of that section, persons whose membership or non-membership is in dispute,
(d) if the dispute relates (wholly or partly) to a matter specified in subsection (1)(f) of that section, officials of the union who have used or would use the facilities concerned in the dispute."

Separate Workplace Ballots

Para 5 – S.228 of the 1992 Act, which defines when a Union can hold an aggregate ballot across two or more separate workplaces, is replaced by a new s.228 and an additional s.228A. The new s.228 prohibits an aggregate ballot unless one or more of the circumstances set out in s.228A apply. Unless s.228A permits, the Trade Union balloting members at two or more workplaces must hold separate ballots at each workplace (as defined in s.228(4)).

Those circumstances, specified in s.228A in summary are:

- *If the workplace of each member entitled to vote in the ballot is the workplace of at least one member of the Union who is affected by the dispute*

- *Where the Union reasonably believes that it is balloting all its members in a particular occupational category employed by one or more of the employers with which it is in dispute*

- *Where the Union ballots all its members who are employed by one or more of the employers in dispute with the Union*

Voting paper

6.– (1) Section 229 (voting paper) shall be amended as follows.

(2) After subsection (2) (voting paper must ask whether voter is prepared to take part in a strike or industrial action short of a strike) insert-

"(2A) For the purposes of subsection (2) an overtime ban and a call-out ban constitute industrial action short of a strike."

(3) At the end of the statement in subsection (4) (statement that industrial action may be a breach of employment contract to be set out on every voting paper) insert-

"However, if you are dismissed for taking part in strike or other industrial action which is called officially and is otherwise lawful, the dismissal will be unfair if it takes place fewer than eight weeks after you started taking part in the action, and depending on the circumstances may be unfair if it takes place later."

(4) In the definition of "strike" in section 246 (interpretation) after "means" there shall be inserted "(except for the purposes of section 229(2))".

Voting Paper:

Para 6 – The obligatory statement required by s.229(4) of the 1992 Act on all ballot voting papers is extended by the following text in italics:

"If you take part in a strike or other industrial action you may be in breach of your contract of employment. *However, if you are dismissed for taking part in a strike or other industrial action which is called officially and is otherwise lawful, the dismissal will be unfair if it takes place fewer than eight weeks after you started taking part in the action, and depending on the circumstances, may be unfair if it takes place later".*

Conduct of ballot: merchant seamen

7. In section 230 (conduct of ballot) for subsections (2A) and (2B) there shall be substituted-

    "(2A) Subsection (2B) applies to a merchant seaman if the trade union reasonably believes that-

    (a) he will be employed in a ship either at sea or at a place outside Great Britain at some time in the period during which votes may be cast, and

    (b) it will be convenient for him to receive a voting paper and to vote while on the ship or while at a place where the ship is rather than in accordance with subsection (2).

    (2B) Where this subsection applies to a merchant seaman he shall, if it is reasonably practicable-

    (a) have a voting paper made available to him while on the ship or while at a place where the ship is, and

    (b) be given an opportunity to vote while on the ship or while at a place where the ship is."

Conduct of Ballot - Merchant Seamen:

Para 7 – This section addresses the practicalities of conducting a ballot among Trade Union members who are merchant seamen and who are on board a ship or at a port during the ballot period. S.230(2A) and s.230(2B) of the 1992 Act cater for the situation where the merchant seamen are at sea or at a foreign port for the entire period of the ballot. These sections are replaced by new s.230(2A) and s.230(2B) to cater also for the situation where the merchant seamen are at sea or at a foreign port for just part of the balloting period. The two new sections require a Union, if it is reasonably practicable, to ballot a member on board ship, or at a port where the ship is if:

> • *The member will be at sea, or at a foreign port where the ship is for all or part of the balloting period; and*
>
> • *It will be convenient for the member to receive the ballot paper and to vote in this way*

Inducement

8. After section 232 insert-

"**232A.** Industrial action shall not be regarded as having the support of a ballot if the following conditions apply in the case of any person-

(a) he was a member of the trade union at the time when the ballot was held,

(b) it was reasonable at that time for the trade union to believe he would be induced to take part or, as the case may be, to continue to take part in the industrial action,

(c) he was not accorded entitlement to vote in the ballot, and

(d) he was induced by the trade union to take part or, as the case may be, to continue to take part in the industrial action."

> **Inducement:**
> *Para 8 – A new section, s.232A, is inserted after s.232 of the 1992 Act. Its effect is that industrial action is not regarded as having the support of a ballot if in the case of any person who was a Trade Union member at the time of the ballot and who, it was reasonable for the Trade Union to believe, would participate in the industrial action, was not accorded entitlement to vote and was subsequently induced by the Trade Union to participate in the industrial action.*

Disregard of certain failures

9. After section 232A there shall be inserted-

"**232B.–** (1) If-

(a) in relation to a ballot there is a failure (or there are failures) to comply with a provision mentioned in subsection (2) or with more than one of those provisions, and

(b) the failure is accidental and on a scale which is unlikely to affect the result of the ballot or, as the case may be, the failures are accidental and taken together are on a scale which is unlikely to affect the result of the ballot,

the failure (or failures) shall be disregarded.

(2) The provisions are section 227(1), section 230(2) and section 230(2A)."

Disregard of Certain Failures:
Para 9 - A new s.232B is inserted after s.232A of the 1992 Act. Its purpose is to widen the extent to which small accidental failures in process can be disregarded. Managing a ballot can be logistically complex with perhaps thousands of members located on multiple sites and minor errors can invalidate the ballot on technical grounds. Under s.232B minor accidental failures to meet the requirements regarding entitlement to vote in a ballot (s.227(1)) and the conduct of a ballot (s.230) can be disregarded. Trade Unions should nevertheless strive to comply in all respects with the requirements but take comfort that the whole process will not be invalidated by minor errors.

Period of ballot's effectiveness

10. In section 234 (period after which ballot ceases to be effective) for subsection (1) there shall be substituted-

   "(1) Subject to the following provisions, a ballot ceases to be effective for the purposes of section 233(3)(b) in relation to industrial action by members of a trade union at the end of the period, beginning with the date of the ballot-

   (a) of four weeks, or
   (b) of such longer duration not exceeding eight weeks as is agreed between the union and the members' employer."

Period of Ballot's Effectiveness:
Para 10 – S.234(1) of the 1992 Act provides that in most cases ballots will cease to be effective at the end of the period of four weeks beginning with the date of the ballot. This can create practical difficulties, e.g. if shortly before expiry of the four week period, the parties are close to agreement but the Union feels obliged to re-ballot to preserve their options and negotiating leverage. Such re-balloting is not only inconvenient and expensive but may be viewed as an act of bad faith by the employer and introduce an additional barrier to settlement. Para 10 provides for the four week period to be lengthened by up to a maximum of four more weeks by agreement between the Union and employer. The text substituted in s.234 of the 1992 Act by para 10 permits extensions to be agreed separately where the ballot included the workers of two or more employers e.g. if one employer agrees an extension but another employer does not, the extension applies, but only in respect of the first employer's workforce.

Only sub section (1) of s.234 of the 1992 Act is amended; sub sections (2)-(6) are unaffected. They deal with the situation where a Court has lifted an injunction prohibiting a Union from calling industrial action.

Notice of industrial action

11.– (1) Section 234A (notice to employers of industrial action) shall be amended as follows.

(2) In subsection (3)(a) (notice relating to industrial action must describe employees intended to take part in industrial action) for "describes (so that he can readily ascertain them) the employees of the employer who" substitute "contains such information in the union's possession as would help the employer to make plans and bring information to the attention of those of his employees whom".

(3) After subsection (5) insert-

"(5A) These rules apply for the purposes of paragraph (a) of subsection (3)-

    (a) if the union possesses information as to the number, category or work-place of the employees concerned, a notice must contain that information (at least);

    (b) if a notice does not name any employees, that fact shall not be a ground for holding that it does not comply with paragraph (a) of subsection (3)."

(4) In subsection (7)-

    (a) insert at the beginning the words "Subject to subsections (7A) and (7B),", and

    (b) in paragraph (a) the words "otherwise than to enable the union to comply with a court order or an undertaking given to a court" shall cease to have effect.

(5) After subsection (7) insert-

"(7A) Subsection (7) shall not apply where industrial action ceases to be authorised or endorsed in order to enable the union to comply with a court order or an undertaking given to a court.

(7B) Subsection (7) shall not apply where-

    (a) a union agrees with an employer, before industrial action ceases to be authorised or endorsed, that it will cease to be authorised or endorsed with effect from a date specified in the agreement ("the suspension date") and that it may again be authorised or endorsed with effect from a date not earlier than a date specified in the agreement ("the resumption date"),

    (b) the action ceases to be authorised or endorsed with effect from the suspension date, and

   (c) the action is again authorised or endorsed with effect from a date which is not earlier than the resumption date or such later date as may be agreed between the union and the employer."

(6) In subsection (9) for "subsection (7)" substitute "subsections (7) to (7B)".

Notice of Industrial Action:

Para 11 – this section is a further initiative to promote negotiated settlements. S.234A of the 1992 Act requires a Trade Union to serve a written notification to an employer that the Union proposes to call on members of its workforce to take industrial action. The notice must specify whether the industrial action will be continuous or not and must be received at least seven days in advance of the start of the industrial action. Sub-section 234A(7) governs the situation where continuous industrial action is initially authorised or endorsed by the Union, then ceases to be authorised or endorsed and is then later authorised and endorsed again. The effect of sub section 234A(7) is that the initial authorisation/endorsement does not usually cover the later action under the later authorisation or endorsement and a fresh seven day notice has to be issued. This arrangement, in practice, discourages Unions from suspending industrial action during settlement negotiations because the industrial action cannot be immediately resumed if the negotiations fail i.e. a further seven day notice has to be issued.

By para 11(5) a new subsection (7A) is added to section 234A of the 1992 Act. S.234A(7A) provides for industrial action to be resumed in certain circumstances without the requirement of a fresh seven day notice where the specified period of suspension is extended by mutual agreement. It does not affect the existing exemption which permits a Union to reinstate industrial action which has been suspended in order to comply with an injunction or an undertaking given by the Union to a Court.

SCHEDULE 4

LEAVE FOR FAMILY REASONS ETC

PART I

MATERNITY LEAVE AND PARENTAL LEAVE

NEW PART VIII OF EMPLOYMENT RIGHTS ACT 1996

SCHEDULE 4

Part 1 deals with the amendment to the rules relating to maternity leave and the introduction of a right to parental leave. The parental leave rights are by way of compliance with Council Directive 97/75/EC amending and extending to the United Kingdom Directive 96/34/EC on the framework agreement on parental leave concluded by the Social Partners UNICE CEEP and the ETUC.

The combined effect of s.7, s.8, and s.9 of the 1999 Act is to replace the pre-existing text of Part VIII of the 1996 Act with a new Part VIII, set out in Part I of Schedule 4. Chapter I of the new Part VIII of the 1996 Act sets out the amended scheme for maternity leave and Chapter II introduces the parental leave scheme. Part II of Schedule 4 sets out the statutory scheme for time off for dependants in the form of a new s.57A inserted after s.57 of the 1996 Act.

The purpose of the new Chapter I Part VIII of the 1996 Act is to simplify the maternity leave scheme by providing a skeletal framework in primary legislation with the detail in a single set of Regulations made under the enabling provisions in the new Chapter I of Part VIII. The Secretary of State was empowered on 15 October 1999 under Commencement Order No. 2 to make the Regulations which, as The Maternity and Parental Leave etc. Regulations 1999 [SI 1999 No. 3312] (the MPL Regulations) which came into force on 15 December 1999. The principal provisions are summarised further on in this Schedule.

"PART VIII

CHAPTER I

MATERNITY LEAVE

71.– (1) An employee may, provided that she satisfies any conditions which may be prescribed, be absent from work at any time during an ordinary maternity leave period.

(2) An ordinary maternity leave period is a period calculated in accordance with regulations made by the Secretary of State.

(3) Regulations under subsection (2)-

(a) shall secure that no ordinary maternity leave period is less than 18 weeks;

(b) may allow an employee to choose, subject to any prescribed restrictions, the date on which an ordinary maternity leave period starts.

(4) Subject to section 74, an employee who exercises her right under subsection (1)-

(a) is entitled to the benefit of the terms and conditions of employment which would have applied if she had not been absent,

(b) is bound by any obligations arising under those terms and conditions (except in so far as they are inconsistent with subsection (1)), and

(c) is entitled to return from leave to the job in which she was employed before her absence.

(5) In subsection (4)(a) "terms and conditions of employment"-

(a) includes matters connected with an employee's employment whether or not they arise under her contract of employment, but

(b) does not include terms and conditions about remuneration.

(6) The Secretary of State may make regulations specifying matters which are, or are not, to be treated as remuneration for the purposes of this section.

(7) An employee's right to return under subsection (4)(c) is a right to return-

(a) with her seniority, pension rights and similar rights as they would have been if she had not been absent (subject to paragraph 5 of Schedule 5 to the Social Security Act 1989 (equal treatment under pension schemes: maternity)), and

(b) on terms and conditions not less favourable than those which would have applied if she had not been absent.

Section 71

New s.71 re-enacts the general right (set out in the original s.71 of the 1996 Act), of all pregnant employees to a period of maternity leave called, to distinguish it from other categories of maternity leave ordinary maternity leave. *The original s.72-s.76 of the 1996 Act are replaced by enabling provisions for Regulations to be made by the Secretary of State to establish comparable provisions which, like their predecessor provisions, will implement the requirements of the Pregnant Workers' Directive (Council Directive 92/85/EEC).*

72.– (1) An employer shall not permit an employee who satisfies prescribed conditions to work during a compulsory maternity leave period.

(2) A compulsory maternity leave period is a period calculated in accordance with regulations made by the Secretary of State.

(3) Regulations under subsection (2) shall secure-

(a) that no compulsory leave period is less than two weeks, and

(b) that every compulsory maternity leave period falls within an ordinary maternity leave period.

(4) Subject to subsection (5), any provision of or made under the Health and Safety at Work etc. Act 1974 shall apply in relation to the prohibition under subsection (1) as if it were imposed by regulations under section 15 of that Act.

(5) Section 33(1)(c) of the 1974 Act shall not apply in relation to the prohibition under subsection (1); and an employer who contravenes that subsection shall be-

(a) guilty of an offence, and
(b) liable on summary conviction to a fine not exceeding level 2 on the standard scale.

Section 72
This section and relevant provisions in the MPL Regulations replace the Maternity (Compulsory Leave) Regulations 1994 (SI 1994/2479) which implemented the health and safety requirement in the Pregnant Workers' Directive for there to be a minimum period of two weeks at the time of childbirth during which a woman must not work.

It is a criminal offence for an employer to allow an employee to work during her compulsory leave period. The maximum penalty is a fine not exceeding level 2 of the Standard Scale (currently £500).

73.- (1) An employee who satisfies prescribed conditions may be absent from work at any time during an additional maternity leave period.

(2) An additional maternity leave period is a period calculated in accordance with regulations made by the Secretary of State.

(3) Regulations under subsection (2) may allow an employee to choose, subject to prescribed restrictions, the date on which an additional maternity leave period ends.

(4) Subject to section 74, an employee who exercises her right under subsection (1)-

(a) is entitled, for such purposes and to such extent as may be prescribed, to the benefit of the terms and conditions of employment which would have applied if she had not been absent,
(b) is bound, for such purposes and to such extent as may be prescribed, by obligations arising under those terms and conditions (except in so far as they are inconsistent with subsection (1)), and
(c) is entitled to return from leave to a job of a prescribed kind.

(5) In subsection (4)(a) "terms and conditions of employment"-

(a) includes matters connected with an employee's employment whether or not they arise under her contract of employment, but
(b) does not include terms and conditions about remuneration.

(6) The Secretary of State may make regulations specifying matters which are, or are not, to be treated as remuneration for the purposes of this section.

(7) The Secretary of State may make regulations making provision, in relation to the right to return under subsection (4)(c), about-

(a) seniority, pension rights and similar rights;
(b) terms and conditions of employment on return.

Section 73
This section and the MPL Regulations 1999 made under it replace the provision for extended maternity absence for those with two years service contained in s.79-s.84 of the 1996 Act. This section renames this right of absence as additional maternity leave. The detailed provisions are contained in the MPL Regulations 1999. The principal change from the previous law made by the MPL Regulations is the reduction in the qualifying period of employment to one year. There are also substantial changes of detail in the operation of rights to additional maternity leave in the MPL Regulations. (The effect of the MPL Regulations is summarised in more detail in the note following s.75 below).

74.– (1) Regulations under section 71 or 73 may make provision about redundancy during an ordinary or additional maternity leave period.

(2) Regulations under section 71 or 73 may make provision about dismissal (other than by reason of redundancy) during an ordinary or additional maternity leave period.

(3) Regulations made by virtue of subsection (1) or (2) may include-

(a) provision requiring an employer to offer alternative employment;
(b) provision for the consequences of failure to comply with the regulations (which may include provision for a dismissal to be treated as unfair for the purposes of Part X).

(4) Regulations under section 73 may make provision-

(a) for section 73(4)(c) not to apply in specified cases, and
(b) about dismissal at the conclusion of an additional maternity leave period.

Section 74

This section empowers the Secretary of State to make Regulations covering the treatment of an employee absent from work at any stage during her maternity leave where a redundancy situation arises. The relevant provisions in the MPL Regulations are broadly the same as the original s.77 and s.81 of the 1996 Act, but with important changes in specific provisions.

75.– (1) Regulations under section 71, 72 or 73 may-

(a) make provision about notices to be given, evidence to be produced and other procedures to be followed by employees and employers;

(b) make provision for the consequences of failure to give notices, to produce evidence or to comply with other procedural requirements;

(c) make provision for the consequences of failure to act in accordance with a notice given by virtue of paragraph (a);

(d) make special provision for cases where an employee has a right which corresponds to a right under this Chapter and which arises under her contract of employment or otherwise;

(e) make provision modifying the effect of Chapter II of Part XIV (calculation of a week's pay) in relation to an employee who is or has been absent from work on ordinary or additional maternity leave;

(f) make provision applying, modifying or excluding an enactment, in such circumstances as may be specified and subject to any conditions specified, in relation to a person entitled to ordinary, compulsory or additional maternity leave;

(g) make different provision for different cases or circumstances.

(2) In sections 71 to 73 "prescribed" means prescribed by regulations made by the Secretary of State.

Section 75

This section further prescribes the regulation-making powers of the Secretary of State in respect of the three types of maternity leave:

- *Ordinary - (OML)*

- *Compulsory - (CML)*

- *Additional - (AML)*

Summary of the Maternity and Parental Leave etc Regulations 1999 by reference to the new Chapter I Part VIII Employment Rights Act 1996
The Regulations came into effect on 15 December 1999 and, like the 1999 Act, apply only to Great Britain. Equivalent primary and secondary legislation has been enacted in respect of Northern Ireland. Protection against being subjected to a detriment or being dismissed for any prohibited reason came into force on 15 December 1999. Otherwise the new law applies only to those employees with an expected week of childbirth commencing on or after 30 April 2000. However, it appears from the terms of Commencement (No. 2) Order that Regulations 17 and 18 are effective from 15 December 1999 (and not delayed until 30 April 2000), the significant effect of which is that the new provisions regarding the contractual status of an employee during AML apply between 15 December 1999 and 30 April 2000 as well as beyond.

- *Definitions of the different stages of maternity leave and other relevant terms e.g. "childbirth" are contained in Regulation 2. In this summary the abbreviation of EWC (Expected Week of Childbirth) is used, and OML, AML and CML for ordinary, additional and compulsory maternity leave.*

- *The principal maternity leave provisions are set out in Part II of the Regulations. The underlying design of the new legal scheme is to preserve the contract of employment throughout OML and AML subject to significant modifications during AML. Accordingly, the employment of an employee on maternity leave will only come to an end if she resigns or is dismissed, a fixed term contract expires or the contract terminates by mutual agreement. The complexities of concepts such as the "deemed dismissal" arising from a refusal to permit an employee to return to work after maternity leave will not longer be part of the legal scene of maternity leave issues*

- *All female employees are eligible for OML subject to giving statutory notice*

- *All such employees are eligible for AML provided they have one year's continuous employment as at 11 weeks before the beginning of the EWC provided the EWC is not earlier than 30 April 2000. Consistent with the theme of equal treatment for part-timers, continuous employment does not require any minimum number of weekly working hours or minimum level of earnings*

- *Notification need no longer be in writing unless requested by the employer. A MAT.B1 must be supplied to the employer if requested*

- *There are no separate notification requirements for AML. An employee entitled to take OML and AML need not say in advance whether she is intending to use part or all of her AML entitlement. She can return at the end of OML if she wishes but need not make a decision until after her baby is born. It would be prudent for employers to plan any necessary cover on the assumption that AML is being taken until the employee makes a firm decision and communicates it*

- *OML is 18 weeks, no longer 14 weeks*

- *AML is whatever period remains from the end of the OML period through to the end of the 29th week of a period of which the first week is the week (Sunday to Saturday) in which childbirth occurs*

- *The former procedure entitling the employer to require the employee to confirm in writing whether or not she intends to return after AML continues but the former sanction for failure to reply, i.e. loss of statutory right to return, is replaced by loss of the automatic protection against detriment and dismissal (contained in s.47C and s.99 of the 1996 Act and Regulations 19 and 20)*

- *At any time on or after 21 days before the end of OML the employer can write to the employee seeking confirmation of the date of childbirth and requesting her to state whether or not she intends to return to work after AML. The request must explain how to calculate the last date on which return from AML is permissible and must explain the consequences of a failure to respond in writing to the employer's request within 21 days of receipt of the request. The employer can only seek confirmation of whether the employee is to return to work and cannot be used as a device to extract the date of any planned early return to work prior to the expiry of AML*

- *The options available to an employer where an employee fails to comply are problematical. Disciplinary action would fall for consideration but the imposition of any sanction, (dismissal or a sanction short of dismissal), could constitute sex discrimination particularly in the context of EU case law on the protected period of pregnancy and maternity leave. Ultimately the practicalities of managing such issues within the law will be determined by future case law rulings*

- *If an employee intends to return before the end of OML or AML she is required to give 21 days notice which need not be in writing. If she fails to give any notice and simply returns or gives less than 21 days notice, the employer has the right to postpone her return to a date 21 days from when she first notified her intention or returned to work without notice. Alternatively the employer has the right to withhold pay for the period up to the end of the 21 days. Importantly, the right to return is not lost through the technical failure to give proper notice and the employee retains her protection from detriment or dismissal (unlike a breach of Regulation 12 i.e. the obligation to respond within 21 days to an employer's request for information about the date of childbirth and whether the employee intends to return to work at the end of AML)*

- *If an employee fails to return on her notified date of return or at the end of OML (if she is not entitled to AML) or at the end of her entitlement to AML, her employment does not automatically terminate. Such absence can be addressed through disciplinary process, including consideration of dismissal. To avoid such disciplinary action amounting to sex discrimination, the way in which she is treated should be the same way as a male with a comparable absence record would be treated, disregarding any absence during the pregnancy and disregarding the fact of the period of maternity leave. This further emphasises the need to maintain comprehensive and reliable workforce absence records across a range of fields including dates and reasons for absence*

- *The contract of employment, and terms and conditions of employment (including non-contractual terms) continue to apply throughout OML, except for those contractual terms relating to remuneration. The effect is that non-contractual terms relating to remuneration also continue in effect during OML e.g. discretionary benefits such as concessionary mortgage arrangements. For practical purposes the right to remuneration during OML is replaced by the right to receive SMP*

- *Regulation 9 defines remuneration as "sums payable to an employee by way of wages or salary" but no further assistance is available in the Regulations as to what this means. It is clear that normal salary is not payable, and that the provision of non-cash benefits (such as membership of schemes for permanent health insurance or private medical cover, use of the company's facilities and retention of a company car) remain intact. Various categories of other benefits must await case law rulings as in the case of Christmas bonus in the ECJ decision Lewen v. Denda 1999*

- *Contractual holiday entitlement accrues during OML. The contractual provisions regarding the organisation's holiday scheme will be applicable. Undoubtedly practical issues will arise such as whether an employer can apply a rule that does not permit untaken holiday to be carried beyond the end of the holiday year or whether the application of that rule would violate sex/ pregnancy protection rights. The assessment of the overall holiday position must involve a consideration of both the contractual position and the statutory holiday entitlement under the Working Time Regulations 1998*

- *In nearly all cases, OML will count as pensionable service*

- *The contract of employment continues during AML on a restricted basis*

- *During AML the employee continues to have the benefit of the employer's duty not to destroy mutual trust and confidence; terms as to notice of termination; disciplinary and grievance procedures; and any contractual redundancy benefits*

- *During AML the employer continues to have the benefit of the employee's obligation of good faith; and any terms as to the employee's notice of termination or any terms restricting participation in another business, disclosure of confidential information and the acceptance of gifts. This and the two preceding bullet points apply to any employee on AML on or after 15 December 1999*

- *The right to return to work on terms and conditions no less favourable than if she had been absent during OML or AML under Regulation 18 provides further benefits, e.g. the right to general pay increases and proper consideration under any PRP assessments*

- *It appears that the contractual entitlement to accrual of holiday is suspended during AML but the statutory right to four weeks paid leave under the Working Time Regulations 1998 remains intact. The practicalities of denying accrual of contractual holiday during AML and the impact on employee-relations may create a balance of advantage in favour of operating accrual*

- *The entitlement to return from OML is to return to the same job. In relation to OML "job" is not defined and must therefore bear its ordinary meaning "job" is defined in a particular sense for the purpose of AML. Accordingly, changing the job of an employee on OML may be more problematical for the employer e.g. the exercising of a contractual power to change the exact job undertaken by the employee on OML*

- *Regulation 10 regulates the situation where a redundancy situation arises during OML or AML and must be carefully observed by an employer*

- *An employee is protected from being subjected to any detriment (act or omission) for reasons relating to pregnancy, giving birth or having done so, or taking OML or AML or availing herself of any benefit under her contract during OML*

- *The protection against detriment for having given birth only applies to a detriment suffered during the period of the OML or AML. The other provisions e.g. detriment for having taken OML/AML are of unlimited duration. Accordingly a woman who, after return from maternity leave, is at some future date denied promotion or training opportunities because she took maternity leave would be entitled to make a claim of unlawful detriment under the victimisation provisions in s.47C of the 1996 Act and Regulation 19. In all probability such treatment would in any event amount to unlawful sex discrimination whatever the timing, during or beyond maternity leave, and an employer in such circumstances should anticipate a composite set of complaints being presented to the Employment Tribunal*

CHAPTER II

PARENTAL LEAVE

Parental Leave:
The new rights to parental leave implement the Parental Leave Directive (Council Directive 96/34/EC) which was applied to the UK by Council Directive 97/75/EC.

76.– (1) The Secretary of State shall make regulations entitling an employee who satisfies specified conditions-

(a) as to duration of employment, and
(b) as to having, or expecting to have, responsibility for a child,

to be absent from work on parental leave for the purpose of caring for a child.

(2) The regulations shall include provision for determining-

(a) the extent of an employee's entitlement to parental leave in respect of a child;
(b) when parental leave may be taken.

(3) Provision under subsection (2)(a) shall secure that where an employee is entitled to parental leave in respect of a child he is entitled to a period or total period of leave of at least three months; but this subsection is without prejudice to any provision which may be made by the regulations for cases in which-

(a) a person ceases to satisfy conditions under subsection (1);
(b) an entitlement to parental leave is transferred.

(4) Provision under subsection (2)(b) may, in particular, refer to-

(a) a child's age, or
(b) a specified period of time starting from a specified event.

(5) Regulations under subsection (1) may-

(a) specify things which are, or are not, to be taken as done for the purpose of caring for a child;
(b) require parental leave to be taken as a single period of absence in all cases or in specified cases;
(c) require parental leave to be taken as a series of periods of absence in all cases or in specified cases;
(d) require all or specified parts of a period of parental leave to be taken at or by specified times;
(e) make provision about the postponement by an employer of a period of parental leave which an employee wishes to take;
(f) specify a minimum or maximum period of absence which may be taken as part of a period of parental leave.

(g) specify a maximum aggregate of periods of parental leave which may be taken during a specified period of time.

S.76 *imposes a mandatory obligation on the Secretary of State to make the Regulations which are now incorporated in Part III of the Maternity and Parental Leave etc. Regulations 1999.*

77.– (1) Regulations under section 76 shall provide-

(a) that an employee who is absent on parental leave is entitled, for such purposes and to such extent as may be prescribed, to the benefit of the terms and conditions of employment which would have applied if he had not been absent,

(b) that an employee who is absent on parental leave is bound, for such purposes and to such extent as may be prescribed, by any obligations arising under those terms and conditions (except in so far as they are inconsistent with section 76(1)), and

(c) that an employee who is absent on parental leave is entitled, subject to section 78(1), to return from leave to a job of such kind as the regulations may specify.

(2) In subsection (1)(a) "terms and conditions of employment"-

(a) includes matters connected with an employee's employment whether or not they arise under a contract of employment, but

(b) does not include terms and conditions about remuneration.

(3) Regulations under section 76 may specify matters which are, or are not, to be treated as remuneration for the purposes of subsection (2)(b) above.

(4) The regulations may make provision, in relation to the right to return mentioned in subsection (1)(c), about-

(a) seniority, pension rights and similar rights;

(b) terms and conditions of employment on return.

S.77 *provides for the employment contract to continue throughout parental leave and the terms and conditions of employment, except those relating to remuneration, continue to apply in accordance with the MPL Regulations.*

78.– (1) Regulations under section 76 may make provision-

(a) about redundancy during a period of parental leave;

(b) about dismissal (other than by reason of redundancy) during a period of parental leave.

(2) Provision by virtue of subsection (1) may include-

    (a) provision requiring an employer to offer alternative employment;

    (b) provision for the consequences of failure to comply with the regulations (which may include provision for a dismissal to be treated as unfair for the purposes of Part X).

(3) Regulations under section 76 may provide for an employee to be entitled to choose to exercise all or part of his entitlement to parental leave-

    (a) by varying the terms of his contract of employment as to hours of work, or

    (b) by varying his normal working practice as to hours of work,

in a way specified in or permitted by the regulations for a period specified in the regulations.

(4) Provision by virtue of subsection (3)-

    (a) may restrict an entitlement to specified circumstances;

    (b) may make an entitlement subject to specified conditions (which may include conditions relating to obtaining the employer's consent);

    (c) may include consequential and incidental provision.

(5) Regulations under section 76 may make provision permitting all or part of an employee's entitlement to parental leave in respect of a child to be transferred to another employee in specified circumstances.

(6) The reference in section 77(1)(c) to absence on parental leave includes, where appropriate, a reference to a continuous period of absence attributable partly to maternity leave and partly to parental leave.

(7) Regulations under section 76 may provide for specified provisions of the regulations not to apply in relation to an employee if any provision of his contract of employment-

    (a) confers an entitlement to absence from work for the purpose of caring for a child, and

    (b) incorporates or operates by reference to all or part of a collective agreement, or workforce agreement, of a kind specified in the regulations.

> **S.78** *enables the Secretary of State to make special provision for particular cases such as redundancy, part-time working, the transfer of leave between one parent to another in exceptional circumstances.*

79.– (1) Regulations under section 76 may, in particular-

    (a) make provision about notices to be given and evidence to be produced by employees to employers, by employers to employees, and by employers to other employers;

(b) make provision requiring employers or employees to keep records;

(c) make provision about other procedures to be followed by employees and employers;

(d) make provision (including provision creating criminal offences) specifying the consequences of failure to give notices, to produce evidence, to keep records or to comply with other procedural requirements;

(e) make provision specifying the consequences of failure to act in accordance with a notice given by virtue of paragraph (a);

(f) make special provision for cases where an employee has a right which corresponds to a right conferred by the regulations and which arises under his contract of employment or otherwise;

(g) make provision applying, modifying or excluding an enactment, in such circumstances as may be specified and subject to any conditions specified, in relation to a person entitled to parental leave;

(h) make different provision for different cases or circumstances.

(2) The regulations may make provision modifying the effect of Chapter II of Part XIV (calculation of a week's pay) in relation to an employee who is or has been absent from work on parental leave.

(3) Without prejudice to the generality of section 76, the regulations may make any provision which appears to the Secretary of State to be necessary or expedient-

(a) for the purpose of implementing Council Directive 96/34/EC on the framework agreement on parental leave, or

(b) for the purpose of dealing with any matter arising out of or related to the United Kingdom's obligations under that Directive.

S.79 *makes supplementary provision as to the scope of the Regulation-making powers aimed at the practical operational aspects of the scheme together with a number of technical issues.*

80.– (1) An employee may present a complaint to an employment tribunal that his employer-

(a) has unreasonably postponed a period of parental leave requested by the employee, or

(b) has prevented or attempted to prevent the employee from taking parental leave.

(2) An employment tribunal shall not consider a complaint under this section unless it is presented-

(a) before the end of the period of three months beginning with the date (or last date) of the matters complained of, or

(b) within such further period as the tribunal considers reasonable in a case where it is satisfied that it was not reasonably practicable for the complaint to be presented before the end of that period of three months.

(3) Where an employment tribunal finds a complaint under this section well-founded it-

(a) shall make a declaration to that effect, and
(b) may make an award of compensation to be paid by the employer to the employee.

(4) The amount of compensation shall be such as the tribunal considers just and equitable in all the circumstances having regard to-

(a) the employer's behaviour, and
(b) any loss sustained by the employee which is attributable to the matters complained of."

The new s.80 provides for employees to present a complaint to an Employment Tribunal e.g. that the employer has obstructed the taking of parental leave or unreasonably postponed leave. The Employment Tribunal may award compensation and make a declaration, similar to the remedies available to Applicants in proceedings before an Employment Tribunal under s.57B (the enforcement provision in respect of the right to time off for dependants).

*   *The right to parental leave applies only in respect of a child born on or after 15 December 1999 or in the case of adoption, where the adoption takes place on or after 15 December 1999 regardless of when the child was born. There is a strong body of informed opinion that the Regulations, in denying parental leave to parents of children born before 15 December 1999, is in breach of the Parental Leave Directive. The European Commission has expressed that opinion in relation to the way in which Eire has implemented the Directive. Private sector employers will be entitled to rely on the terms of the UK Regulations until they are amended by Parliament but employers which are "State Authorities" in EU law may be faced with claims to directly enforce a Directive right which arguably has not been properly transposed into UK law. This presents a dilemma for public sector employers faced with applications for parental leave by employees in respect of children under the age of five born before 15 December 1999*

- *The right to parental leave is given to each person who has responsibility for the child as defined by Regulation 13(2) i.e. under the Children Act 1989 or the comparable Scottish legislation. The eligible persons therefore will be the mother, the father if he is married to the mother at the time of the birth, or if not, obtains a Court Order giving him parental responsibility, or makes a formal agreement with the mother giving him parental responsibility. Regulation 13(2) also defines responsibility for the child by reference to the father, if he is named on the birth certificate as such, and includes legal guardians of children whose parents have died*

- *The basic entitlement of each parent is as follows. "Parent" is used for ease of reference even though not every eligible person will be a parent (e.g. the sister and brother-in-law of a deceased mother who appointed them as the testamentary legal guardians of her children under the terms of her Will). There is a right to a maximum of 13 weeks leave for each child to be taken in units of not less than one week, during the period up to the child's fifth birthday, or the fifth anniversary of an adoption. These limits may only be overrun in consequence of an employer's postponement of a parent's request for leave. The Secretary of State has not used his discretion to introduce transferability of parental leave entitlement between those who have responsibility for the child*

- *Leave may only be taken at a maximum rate of four weeks per child per year*

- *The status of the contract during parental leave is the same as during AML (see above) i.e. for strictly limited purposes only. In particular parental leave confers no right to be paid (although the employer may agree to make it paid)*

- *The employer will be entitled to receive written evidence of the employee's responsibility for the child e.g. the father or the mother where the child was born before the date of joining the employer. In most cases the birth certificate will be sufficient but the employer is entitled to proper documentation evidencing parental responsibility*

- *Additional rights to leave (but still within the overall maximum of 13 weeks per child) are given if the child is disabled. In those circumstances leave can be taken at any time up to the child's eighteenth birthday and parental leave as short as a one day at a time can be taken. The child must be in receipt of Disability Living Allowance and the employer is entitled to evidence of receipt of this allowance*

- *The employer has a right to postpone the taking of parental leave in the circumstances set out below but has no right to postponement at the time of the child's birth nor can the employer postpone adoption leave at the time of completion of the adoption formalities. Further, the normal requirement of giving 21 days advanced notice is relaxed. 21 days notice has to be given of the EWC or the week in which adoption is expected to take place. Leave can start from the actual date of birth or adoption even if later or earlier than predicted*

- *The right to parental leave is dependant upon having at least one year's continuous service*

- *The year will run from the date the parent acquires a year's continuous employment. Subsequent years run from the anniversary of the start of the first year*

- *Where a parent takes some but not all of their parental leave entitlement and then changes employer the right to any untaken parental leave is preserved subject to the employee re-qualifying by a year's continuous employment and subject to the rights terminating on the child's fifth birthday*

- *Employers are under no legal obligation to keep any records of parental leave. The system will therefore depend on honesty and self-reporting. There is no obligation for employers to cooperate with the exchange of information about former employees. Employers are entitled to ask new employees what parental leave has been taken, (sensibly after recruitment to avoid any inference of sex discrimination) and to verify the information by appropriate enquiries. It may be advisable to require a new employee to sign a short form to certify the information, with an accompanying note that false information with would amount to gross misconduct. On the next revision of the organisation's rule book consideration could be given to extending the definition of gross misconduct to include false representations relating to entitlement to employee rights*

- *Seniority rights are frozen during parental leave; statutory continuity of employment is unbroken; periods on parental leave are not required to count as pensionable service unless they are paid (although administratively and in terms of employee relations, it may be sensible to treat the leave as counting for pensionable service) contractual holiday rights do not accrue, but bear in mind the underlying statutory holiday entitlement, (see commentary above regarding AML); benefits such as a company car or health care benefits are also suspended but it may not be practicable to apply suspension of benefits. If the organisation introduces or has a parental leave policy with more generous provision than the statutory minimum, a strategic view should be taken on what suspension, or otherwise, of contractual benefits is appropriate for the organisation*

- *The Regulations only affect contractual benefits and do not therefore affect purely discretionary benefits. As those benefits are discretionary it would however be lawful to provide in the organisation's policy that such benefits are also suspended during unpaid parental leave*

- *The right to return to work following parental leave differs according to the circumstances. If an employee does not return after AML because she takes a period of parental leave, the right to return is on the same terms as for a returner from AML i.e. to the same job, a defined by the Regulations subject to the right of redeployment if return to that job is not reasonably practicable. The same applies if an employee is allowed to take parental leave for a period of more than four weeks. However, for basic periods of parental leave not exceeding four weeks, the right to return is the same as the rather inflexible right to return from OML i.e. to the same job*

- *An aim of the MPL Regulations is to encourage employers to introduce in-house contractual schemes. The Regulations anticipate this will either be by way of a collective agreement or a workforce agreement (defined in the same was as in the Working Time Regulations 1998). If this is not done, the statutory scheme in Schedule 2 to the MPL Regulations applies automatically by default. Provided the collective or workplace agreement contains provisions at least as favourable as Schedule 2, parental leave will be governed by that agreement*

- *Under Schedule 2 the notice of intention to take leave does not have to be in writing but must specify the date the leave is to start and end (subject to the above exception regarding leave taken at the time of childbirth/adoption)*

- *The employer has the right to postpone the time at which leave is taken (other than at the time of childbirth/adoption) to a specified date up to six months later than the intended start date notified by the employee. The employer must give notice in writing within seven days of the employee's intention to take the leave. Postponement can only be imposed if the employer considers that its business would be unduly disrupted by the timing of the employee's parental leave*

- *The employer's counter-notice has to specify the dates of the postponed leave, fixed after consultation with the employee. In practice this could prove to be a very tight timescale. There is no definition of undue disruption. Complaints can be presented to the Employment Tribunal under s.80 of the 1996 Act in respect of an alleged unreasonable postponement of leave, as well as a refusal of leave. Although it is technically sufficient for the employer to show that it was genuinely considered that the timing of the parental leave would cause undue disruption (i.e. a subjective rather than objective test) in reality the Tribunal is likely to have doubts that the employer's belief is genuine unless the explanation is reasonably convincing*

- *Complaints to the Employment Tribunal must be made within a three month time limit. If the Tribunal decides that the complaint is well-founded it can award compensation, including compensation for injury to feelings as well as losses actually incurred by the employee. It is also unlawful to dismiss an employee for reasons related to taking parental leave, as it is to take action short of dismissal which subjects an employee to a detriment for having taken parental leave. Dismissal is automatically unfair under s.99 of the 1996 Act and detriment is prohibited under s.47C (see Regulations 19 and 20)*

- *There is considerable merit in introducing a collective or workplace agreement to avoid practical problems created by the default provisions in Schedule 2. For example if an organisation already provides contractual rights to childcare and/ or paternity leave, trying to operate two separate schemes (the organisation's contractual scheme and the statutory default scheme) is likely to be cumbersome, unhelpful to line managers and invite criticism of the HR Department. Further, the notice and postponement provisions in the default scheme in Schedule 2 are inflexible and could be readily designed to be more advantageous to the organisation and its workforce. Another consideration is that most current maternity policies will now require revision to ensure compliance with the statutory changes. There may be considerable merit in establishing one composite policy, not confined to pregnancy and maternity, but covering all aspects of family-related absence e.g. maternity leave, parental leave, and time off for family emergencies. An ambitious project would be to create one policy and procedure document (together with an operating manual for line managers including model documents and data reporting instructions) covering absence from work across the full spectrum of reasons including holidays, ill-health and issues such as bereavement and jury service. A collective or workplace agreement regarding parental leave could usefully examine the scope for reducing the impact upon the organisation by the parental leave obligations extending the period during which leave could be taken beyond five years, introducing a means of taking parental leave through part-time working and to use a negotiated scheme as a transitional option between expiry of statutory maternity leave and return to full-time working. Ultimately the attraction of a negotiated scheme will depend upon its ability to co-exist with and promote the overriding operational interests of the organisation*

PART II

TIME OFF FOR DEPENDANTS

PROVISIONS TO BE INSERTED AFTER SECTION 57 OF THE EMPLOYMENT RIGHTS ACT 1996

S.8 and Part II of Schedule 4 of the 1994 Act insert a new section s.57A after s.57 of the 1996 Act giving employees the right to take a reasonable amount of unpaid time off work to deal with specified matters affecting a dependant, thereby implementing the part of the Parental Leave Directive not implemented by the parental leave provisions. S.57A is relatively short and self-explanatory. Under s.57A(2), the employee's entitlement to take a reasonable amount of time off during working hours is dependent upon the employee telling the employer the reason for the absence as soon as reasonable practicable and unless it is not practicable to do so until after the employee has returned to work, telling the employer how long the employee expects to be absent. S.57A(3) defines what a "dependant" means and that definition is further extended by the terms of sub-paras 4 and 5. For the avoidance of doubt, sub-para 6 makes it clear that reference to illness or injury in s.57A includes mental illness or injury.

s.57B provides for an employee to present a complaint to an Employment Tribunal within 3 months of the refusal, that the employer has unreasonably refused time off.

"Dependants

57A.– (1) An employee is entitled to be permitted by his employer to take a reasonable amount of time off during the employee's working hours in order to take action which is necessary-

    (a) to provide assistance on an occasion when a dependant falls ill, gives birth or is injured or assaulted,

    (b) to make arrangements for the provision of care for a dependant who is ill or injured,

    (c) in consequence of the death of a dependant,

    (d) because of the unexpected disruption or termination of arrangements for the care of a dependant, or

    (e) to deal with an incident which involves a child of the employee and which occurs unexpectedly in a period during which an educational establishment which the child attends is responsible for him.

(2) Subsection (1) does not apply unless the employee-

    (a) tells his employer the reason for his absence as soon as reasonably practicable, and

    (b) except where paragraph (a) cannot be complied with until after the employee has returned to work, tells his employer for how long he expects to be absent.

(3) Subject to subsections (4) and (5), for the purposes of this section "dependant" means, in relation to an employee-

(a) a spouse,
(b) a child,
(c) a parent,
(d) a person who lives in the same household as the employee, otherwise than by reason of being his employee, tenant, lodger or boarder.

(4) For the purposes of subsection (1)(a) or (b) "dependant" includes, in addition to the persons mentioned in subsection (3), any person who reasonably relies on the employee-

(a) for assistance on an occasion when the person falls ill or is injured or assaulted, or
(b) to make arrangements for the provision of care in the event of illness or injury.

(5) For the purposes of subsection (1)(d) "dependant" includes, in addition to the persons mentioned in subsection (3), any person who reasonably relies on the employee to make arrangements for the provision of care.

(6) A reference in this section to illness or injury includes a reference to mental illness or injury.

57B.– (1) An employee may present a complaint to an employment tribunal that his employer has unreasonably refused to permit him to take time off as required by section 57A.

(2) An employment tribunal shall not consider a complaint under this section unless it is presented-

(a) before the end of the period of three months beginning with the date when the refusal occurred, or
(b) within such further period as the tribunal considers reasonable in a case where it is satisfied that it was not reasonably practicable for the complaint to be presented before the end of that period of three months.

(3) Where an employment tribunal finds a complaint under subsection (1) well-founded, it-

(a) shall make a declaration to that effect, and
(b) may make an award of compensation to be paid by the employer to the employee.

(4) The amount of compensation shall be such as the tribunal considers just and equitable in all the circumstances having regard to-

(a) the employer's default in refusing to permit time off to be taken by the employee, and
(b) any loss sustained by the employee which is attributable to the matters complained of."

The following points are noteworthy:

- *The right to time off for dependants has been in force since 15 December 1999*

- *The new right is a right to be permitted time off, not to be paid for it. Payment is a matter of negotiation or concession to be covered in the express terms and conditions or custom and practice of the organisation. A written policy is desirable to avoid doubt and to achieve consistency*

- *The amount of time off is a function of the particular circumstances i.e. an employee is entitled to be permitted whatever time off* is reasonable in the circumstances. *As the time off is permitted under s.57A(1) solely to* "take action which is necessary" *in relation to one of the five statutory sets of circumstances in s.57A(1) it should be relatively straightforward to control abuse*

- *Only s.57A(1)(e) is limited to dealing with a child-related situation. The remaining four purposes relate to a* "dependant"

- *S.57A(1)() which deals with the death of a dependent does not give a right to statutory leave to cope with the grief of bereavement. The statutory right to time off arises where the employee needs a reasonable amount of time off* in order to take action which is necessary *in consequence of the death of a dependant e.g. to make funeral arrangements*

- *The entitlement to a reasonable amount of time off in order to take action which is necessary to provide assistance on an occasion when a dependant gives birth raises interesting potential to avoid using any parental leave and to keep the 13 weeks entitlement intact for future use*

- *The definition of a dependant covers not only the predictable categories of child and spouse, but also a parent, and a person who lives in the same household as the employee otherwise than by reason of being an employee, tenant, lodger or border. This reflects the growth of atypical relationships and covers unmarried couples in both heterosexual and same-sex relationships. It would include certain flat-sharing arrangements. There are no age restrictions so that a dependant could be an adult child living, or staying with the parent-employee*

- *In the statutory set of circumstances set out in s.57A(1)(a) and (b) (i.e. providing assistance on an occasion when a dependant falls ill, gives birth or is injured or assaulted or to make arrangements for the provision of care for a dependant who is ill or injured), the definition of "dependant" is further extended to include any person who reasonably relies on the employee for assistance on an occasion when the person falls ill or is injured or assaulted or to make arrangements for the provision of care in the event of illness or injury. This could therefore include an elderly or infirm neighbour*

- For the statutory circumstances set out in s.57A(1)(d) (i.e because of the unexpected disruption or termination of arrangements for the care of a dependant), the definition of dependant is extended to include any person who reasonably relies on the employee to make arrangements for the provision of care

- A clear social purpose therefore is to promote care in the community where employees have assumed a responsibility for supporting others e.g. elderly relatives living elsewhere but alone, neighbours and friends where there is genuine commitment to assist in emergencies. However, time off is not for the provision of care but to assist in emergencies

- The circumstances envisaged by s.57A(1)(e) (loosely, incidents during school time) are not limited to accidents during school hours (or at nursery/play-school) but would also cover situations where the school and/or the Police summonsed the parent to deal with an offence at school .e.g fighting /drugs and also truanting

- There is much practical advantage to be gained by an organisation introducing a written policy and procedure (stand alone or within a wider family-friendly/ absence policy and procedure) so that employees and Line managers know exactly where they stand, the right of time off for dependants can be integrated into the organisation's systems and culture and the right to time off can be granted and policed consistently

PART III

CONSEQUENTIAL AMENDMENTS

Trade Union and Labour Relations (Consolidation) Act 1992 (c. 52)

1. The Trade Union and Labour Relations (Consolidation) Act 1992 shall be amended as follows.

2. In section 237(1A) (dismissal of those taking part in unofficial industrial action)-

   (a) for the words from "section 99(1) to (3)" to the end substitute "or under-

      (a) section 99, 100, 101A(d), 103 or 103A of the Employment Rights Act 1996 (dismissal in family, health and safety, working time, employee representative and protected disclosure cases),

      (b) section 104 of that Act in its application in relation to time off under section 57A of that Act (dependants);" and

   (b) at the end insert "; and a reference to a specified reason for dismissal includes a reference to specified circumstances of dismissal".

3. In section 238(2A) (dismissal in connection with other industrial action)-

(a) for the words from "section 99(1) to (3)" to the end substitute "or under-

    (a) section 99, 100, 101A(d) or 103 of the Employment Rights Act 1996 (dismissal in family, health and safety, working time and employee representative cases),

    (b) section 104 of that Act in its application in relation to time off under section 57A of that Act (dependants);" and

(b) at the end insert "; and a reference to a specified reason for dismissal includes a reference to specified circumstances of dismissal".

Employment Tribunals Act 1996 (c. 17)

4. In section 13(2) of the Employment Tribunals Act 1996 (costs and expenses) the following shall cease to have effect-

(a) the word "or" after paragraph (a),

(b) paragraph (b), and

(c) the words ", or which she held before her absence,".

Employment Rights Act 1996 (c. 18)

5. The Employment Rights Act 1996 shall be amended as follows.

6. In section 37 (contractual requirements for Sunday work: protected workers) omit the following-

(a) subsection (4),

(b) the word "and" after subsection (5)(a), and

(c) subsection (5)(b).

7. In section 43 (contractual requirements relating to Sunday work: opting out) omit the following-

(a) subsection (4),

(b) the word "and" after subsection (5)(a), and

(c) subsection (5)(b).

8. After section 47B (protection from detriment: disclosures) insert-

"**47C.–** (1) An employee has the right not to be subjected to any detriment by any act, or any deliberate failure to act, by his employer done for a prescribed reason.

(2) A prescribed reason is one which is prescribed by regulations made by the Secretary of State and which relates to-

    (a) pregnancy, childbirth or maternity,

    (b) ordinary, compulsory or additional maternity leave,

    (c) parental leave, or

    (d) time off under section 57A.

(3) A reason prescribed under this section in relation to parental leave may relate to action which an employee takes, agrees to take or refuses to take under or in respect of a collective or workforce agreement.

(4) Regulations under this section may make different provision for different cases or circumstances."

9. In section 48(1) (detriment: complaints to employment tribunals) for "or 47A" substitute ", 47A or 47C".

10. In section 88(1)(c) (notice period: employment with normal working hours) after "childbirth" insert "or on parental leave".

11. In section 89(3)(b) (notice period: employment without normal working hours) after "childbirth" insert "or on parental leave".

12. In section 92(4)(b) (right to written statement of reasons for dismissal) for "maternity leave period" substitute "ordinary or additional maternity leave period".

13. Omit section 96 (failure to permit return after childbirth treated as dismissal).

14. Omit section 97(6) (effective date of termination: section 96).

15. In section 98 (fairness of dismissal)-

(a) omit subsection (5), and
(b) in subsection (6) for "subsections (4) and (5)" substitute "subsection (4)".

16. For section 99 (unfair dismissal: pregnancy and childbirth) substitute-

"99.– (1) An employee who is dismissed shall be regarded for the purposes of this Part as unfairly dismissed if-

(a) the reason or principal reason for the dismissal is of a prescribed kind, or
(b) the dismissal takes place in prescribed circumstances.

(2) In this section "prescribed" means prescribed by regulations made by the Secretary of State.

(3) A reason or set of circumstances prescribed under this section must relate to-

(a) pregnancy, childbirth or maternity,
(b) ordinary, compulsory or additional maternity leave,
(c) parental leave, or
(d) time off under section 57A;

and it may also relate to redundancy or other factors.

(4) A reason or set of circumstances prescribed under subsection (1) satisfies subsection (3)(c) or (d) if it relates to action which an employee-

(a) takes,
(b) agrees to take, or

(c) refuses to take,

under or in respect of a collective or workforce agreement which deals with parental leave.

(5) Regulations under this section may-

(a) make different provision for different cases or circumstances;
(b) apply any enactment, in such circumstances as may be specified and subject to any conditions specified, in relation to persons regarded as unfairly dismissed by reason of this section."

17. In section 105 (unfair dismissal: redundancy) omit subsection (2).

18. In section 108 (qualifying period of employment) omit subsection (3)(a).

19. In section 109 (upper age limit) omit subsection (2)(a).

20. In section 114 (order for reinstatement) omit subsection (5).

21. In section 115 (order for re-engagement) omit subsection (4).

22. In section 118(1)(b) (compensation: general) omit ", 127".

23. In section 119 (compensation: basic award) omit subsection (6).

24. Omit section 127 (dismissal at or after end of maternity leave period).

25. Omit section 137 (failure to permit return after childbirth treated as dismissal).

26. In section 145 (redundancy payments: relevant date) omit subsection (7).

27. In section 146 (supplemental provisions) omit subsection (3).

28. In section 156 (upper age limit) omit subsection (2).

29. In section 157 (exemption orders) omit subsection (6).

30. In section 162 (amount of redundancy payment) omit subsection (7).

31. In section 192(2) (armed forces)-

(a) after paragraph (aa) insert-
  "(ab) section 47C,", and
(b) in paragraph (b) for "55 to 57" substitute "55 to 57B".

32. In section 194(2)(c) (House of Lords staff) for "and 47" substitute ", 47 and 47C".

33. In section 195(2)(c) (House of Commons staff) for "and 47" substitute ", 47 and 47C".

34. In section 199 (mariners)-

(a) in subsection (2) for "50 to 57" substitute "47C, 50 to 57B".
(b) in subsection (2) omit the words "(subject to subsection (3))", and
(c) omit subsection (3).

35. In section 200(1) (police officers)-

(a) after "47B," insert "47C,",
(b) for "to 57" substitute "to 57B",
(c) after "93" insert "and", and
(d) omit "and section 137".

36. In section 202(2) (national security)-

(a) in paragraph (b) for "and 47" substitute ", 47 and 47C",
(b) in paragraph (c) for "55 to 57" substitute "55 to 57B", and
(c) in paragraph (g) for sub-paragraph (i) substitute-

"(i) by section 99, 100, 101A(d) or 103, or by section 104 in its application in relation to time off under section 57A,".

37. In section 209 (power to amend Act) omit subsection (6).

38.– (1) Section 212 (weeks counted in computing period of employment) is amended as follows.

(2) Omit subsection (2).

(3) In subsection (3)-

(a) insert "or" after paragraph (b),
(b) omit "or" after paragraph (c), and
(c) omit paragraph (d).

(4) In subsection (4) omit "or (subject to subsection (2)) subsection (3)(d)".

39. In section 225(5)(b) (calculation date: rights during employment) for sub-paragraph (i) substitute-

"(i) where the day before that on which the suspension begins falls during a period of ordinary or additional maternity leave, the day before the beginning of that period,".

40. In section 226 (rights on termination) omit subsections (3)(a) and (5)(a).

41. In section 235(1) (interpretation: other definitions) omit the definitions of "maternity leave period" and "notified day of return".

42.– (1) Section 236 (orders and regulations) shall be amended as follows.

(2) In subsection (2)(a) after "order" insert "or regulations".

(3) In subsection (3)-

(a) after "and no order" insert "or regulations",
(b) for "72(3), 73(5), 79(3)," substitute "47C, 71, 72, 73, 76, 99,", and
(c) for "or order" substitute ", order or regulations".

Section 16.

SCHEDULE 5

Unfair Dismissal of Striking Workers

Trade Union and Labour Relations (Consolidation) Act 1992 (c. 52)

1. The Trade Union and Labour Relations (Consolidation) Act 1992 shall be amended as follows.

2. In section 238 (dismissals in connection with industrial action) after subsection (2A) there shall be inserted-

   "(2B) Subsection (2) does not apply in relation to an employee who is regarded as unfairly dismissed by virtue of section 238A below."

3. The following shall be inserted after section 238-

   "**238A.–** (1) For the purposes of this section an employee takes protected industrial action if he commits an act which, or a series of acts each of which, he is induced to commit by an act which by virtue of section 219 is not actionable in tort.

   (2) An employee who is dismissed shall be regarded for the purposes of Part X of the Employment Rights Act 1996 (unfair dismissal) as unfairly dismissed if-

   (a) the reason (or, if more than one, the principal reason) for the dismissal is that the employee took protected industrial action, and
   (b) subsection (3), (4) or (5) applies to the dismissal.

   (3) This subsection applies to a dismissal if it takes place within the period of eight weeks beginning with the day on which the employee started to take protected industrial action.

   (4) This subsection applies to a dismissal if-

   (a) it takes place after the end of that period, and
   (b) the employee had stopped taking protected industrial action before the end of that period.

   (5) This subsection applies to a dismissal if-

   (a) it takes place after the end of that period,
   (b) the employee had not stopped taking protected industrial action before the end of that period, and
   (c) the employer had not taken such procedural steps as would have been reasonable for the purposes of resolving the dispute to which the protected industrial action relates.

   (6) In determining whether an employer has taken those steps regard shall be had, in particular, to-

(a) whether the employer or a union had complied with procedures established by any applicable collective or other agreement;

(b) whether the employer or a union offered or agreed to commence or resume negotiations after the start of the protected industrial action;

(c) whether the employer or a union unreasonably refused, after the start of the protected industrial action, a request that conciliation services be used;

(d) whether the employer or a union unreasonably refused, after the start of the protected industrial action, a request that mediation services be used in relation to procedures to be adopted for the purposes of resolving the dispute.

(7) In determining whether an employer has taken those steps no regard shall be had to the merits of the dispute.

(8) For the purposes of this section no account shall be taken of the repudiation of any act by a trade union as mentioned in section 21 in relation to anything which occurs before the end of the next working day (within the meaning of section 237) after the day on which the repudiation takes place."

4.– (1) Section 239 (supplementary provisions relating to unfair dismissal) shall be amended as follows.

(2) In subsection (1) for "Sections 237 and 238" there shall be substituted "Sections 237 to 238A".

(3) At the end of subsection (1) there shall be added "; but sections 108 and 109 of that Act (qualifying period and age limit) shall not apply in relation to section 238A of this Act."

(4) In subsection (2) after "section 238" there shall be inserted "or 238A".

(5) At the end there shall be added-

"(4) In relation to a complaint under section 111 of the 1996 Act (unfair dismissal: complaint to employment tribunal) that a dismissal was unfair by virtue of section 238A of this Act-

(a) no order shall be made under section 113 of the 1996 Act (reinstatement or re-engagement) until after the conclusion of protected industrial action by any employee in relation to the relevant dispute,

(b) regulations under section 7 of the Employment Tribunals Act 1996 may make provision about the adjournment and renewal of applications (including provision requiring adjournment in specified circumstances), and

(c) regulations under section 9 of that Act may require a pre-hearing review to be carried out in specified circumstances."

Employment Rights Act 1996 (c. 18)

5.– (1) Section 105 of the Employment Rights Act 1996 (redundancy) shall be amended as follows.

(2) In subsection (1)(c) for "subsections (2) to (7)" there shall be substituted "subsections (2) to (7C).".

(3) After subsection (7B) (inserted by Schedule 3 to the Tax Credits Act 1999) there shall be inserted-

"(7C) This subsection applies if-

    (a) the reason (or, if more than one, the principal reason) for which the employee was selected for dismissal was the reason mentioned in section 238A(2) of the Trade Union and Labour Relations (Consolidation) Act 1992 (participation in official industrial action), and

    (b) subsection (3), (4) or (5) of that section applies to the dismissal."

SCHEDULE 5
Unfair Dismissal of Striking Workers:

Paras 1-5 - Most forms of industrial action involve a fundamental breach of obligations under an employee's contract of employment. This entitles the employer as a matter of contract law to lawfully dismiss. Further, an employee in such circumstances, is prevented from making an unfair dismissal claim other than in exceptional circumstances e.g. if at the time of the dismissal the employee is taking part in unofficial industrial action but the reason or the principal reason for the dismissal or selection for dismissal was one of the specified reasons in the 1996 Act (cases involving dismissal, maternity, health and safety, the employee's position as an employee-representative and "whistle-blowers"). Further, an employee can make an unfair dismissal claim if the employer dismisses selectively, or selectively re-engages, employees involved in official industrial action.

S.16 of the 1999 Act gives effect to Schedule 5 which widens the former legal provisions by providing a measure of, but not unlimited, protection against unfair dismissal for workers involved in industrial action. The widened protection does not apply to unofficial industrial action i.e. the scope of s.237 of the 1992 Act is unaffected. A new s.238A is added after s.238 of the 1992 Act which provides that in the following circumstances employees dismissed for taking part in "protected" industrial action will be regarded as having been unfairly dismissed:

- *Dismissal within eight weeks of the beginning of the industrial action*

- *Dismissal after eight weeks where the employee ceased industrial action before the eight week period ended; or*

- *The employee participates in industrial action beyond eight weeks but the employer has not followed all reasonable procedural steps to resolve the dispute. The industrial action is only "protected" where the employee is induced to participate by his Union and the Union's action itself is protected under s.219 of the 1992 Act (i.e. from liability to an action in tort for inducement to break, or interfere with, contractual obligations)*

The Employment Tribunal is required to have particular regard to the following matters when determining whether the employer has taken reasonable procedural steps to resolve the dispute, i.e. whether the employer and/or the Union:

- *Have followed agreed dispute resolution procedures*

- *Offered or agreed to commence or re-open negotiations after the industrial action has begun; and*

- *Unreasonably refused to involve a third party (probably ACAS) for dispute-resolution through conciliation or mediation*

Under s.238 mediators must confine their recommendations to procedural issues only.

S.238A(7) expressly provides that in Employment Tribunal proceedings, to determine whether an employer has taken those steps, no regard shall be had to the merits of the dispute. This provision is designed to distance the Employment Tribunal from the necessarily controversial function of making judgments about the merits of the dispute.

Where official industrial action becomes unofficial because the Union repudiates the action during the course of the dispute, employees lose the right to present a complaint of unfair dismissal in respect of any dismissal where they continue to take part in the industrial action after the day following the Union's repudiation. Where for example the Union repudiates the industrial action on a Wednesday, the protection against unfair dismissal would be lost to employees who took industrial action on or beyond the Friday of that week.

The effect of para 4 is to extend to scope of s.239 of the 1992 Act (supplementary provisions relating to unfair dismissal) to ensure that the unfair dismissal protection for striking workers fits into the scheme of unfair dismissal protection under Part X of the 1996 Act. However the unfair dismissal protection of striking workers is not service-related i.e. there is no requirement to have been employed for at least one year, nor does the upper age limit apply. The Employment Tribunal may undertake a full merits hearing under s.238A while industrial action is continuing but cannot consider re-employment remedies (reinstatement or re-engagement) until the dispute is over.

Para 4(5) also provides for Regulations to be made under s.7 of the Employment Tribunals Act 1996 to require Tribunals to carry out PHR's (pre-hearing reviews) and to enable Tribunals to adjourn cases in specified circumstances. It is expected that such Regulations will require PHR's in all s.238A claims of unfair dismissal and will also require Tribunals to adjourn proceedings where the lawfulness of the Union action is being challenged in the Courts.

S.105 of the 1996 Act, which provides the right not to be unfairly dismissed by means of selective redundancy, is amended by para 5 of this Schedule. Its effect is to provide a right not to be unfairly dismissed by selective redundancy where the reason for selection is a reason within s.238A(2).

SCHEDULE 6

THE CERTIFICATION OFFICER

Introduction

1. The Trade Union and Labour Relations (Consolidation) Act 1992 shall be amended as provided by this Schedule.

Register of members

2. In section 24 (duty to maintain register of members' names and addresses) the second sentence of subsection (6) (application to Certification Officer does not prevent application to court) shall be omitted.

3. In section 24A (securing confidentiality of register during ballots) the second sentence of subsection (6) (application to Certification Officer does not prevent application to court) shall be omitted.

4.– (1) Section 25 (application to Certification Officer for declaration of breach of duty regarding register of members' names and addresses) shall be amended as follows.

(2) In subsection (2)(b) (duty to give opportunity to be heard where Certification Officer considers it appropriate) omit "where he considers it appropriate,".

(3) After subsection (5) insert-

"(5A) Where the Certification Officer makes a declaration he shall also, unless he considers that to do so would be inappropriate, make an enforcement order, that is, an order imposing on the union one or both of the following requirements-

(a) to take such steps to remedy the declared failure, within such period, as may be specified in the order;

(b) to abstain from such acts as may be so specified with a view to securing that a failure of the same or a similar kind does not occur in future.

(5B) Where an enforcement order has been made, any person who is a member of the union and was a member at the time it was made is entitled to enforce obedience to the order as if he had made the application on which the order was made."

(4) After subsection (8) insert-

"(9) A declaration made by the Certification Officer under this section may be relied on as if it were a declaration made by the court.

(10) An enforcement order made by the Certification Officer under this section may be enforced in the same way as an order of the court.

(11) The following paragraphs have effect if a person applies under section 26 in relation to an alleged failure-

(a) that person may not apply under this section in relation to that failure;
(b) on an application by a different person under this section in relation to that failure, the Certification Officer shall have due regard to any declaration, order, observations or reasons made or given by the court regarding that failure and brought to the Certification Officer's notice."

5.– (1) Section 26 (application to court for declaration of breach of duty regarding register of members' names and addresses) shall be amended as follows.

(2) Omit subsection (2) (position where application in respect of the same matter has been made to Certification Officer).

(3) After subsection (7) insert-

"(8) The following paragraphs have effect if a person applies under section 25 in relation to an alleged failure-

(a) that person may not apply under this section in relation to that failure;
(b) on an application by a different person under this section in relation to that failure, the court shall have due regard to any declaration, order, observations or reasons made or given by the Certification Officer regarding that failure and brought to the court's notice."

Accounting records

6.– (1) Section 31 (remedy for failure to comply with request for access to accounting records) shall be amended as follows.

(2) In subsection (1) after "the court" insert "or to the Certification Officer".

(3) In subsection (2) (court to make order if claim well-founded) after "Where" insert "on an application to it" and for "that person" substitute "the applicant".

(4) After subsection (2) insert-

"(2A) On an application to him the Certification Officer shall-

(a) make such enquiries as he thinks fit, and
(b) give the applicant and the trade union an opportunity to be heard.

(2B) Where the Certification Officer is satisfied that the claim is well-founded he shall make such order as he considers appropriate for ensuring that the applicant-

(a) is allowed to inspect the records requested,
(b) is allowed to be accompanied by an accountant when making the inspection of those records, and
(c) is allowed to take, or is supplied with, such copies of, or of extracts from, the records as he may require.

(2C) In exercising his functions under this section the Certification Officer shall ensure that, so far as is reasonably practicable, an application made to him is determined within six months of being made."

(5) In subsection (3) (court's power to grant interlocutory relief) after "an application" insert "to it".

(6) After subsection (3) insert-

"(4) Where the Certification Officer requests a person to furnish information to him in connection with enquiries made by him under this section, he shall specify the date by which that information is to be furnished and, unless he considers that it would be inappropriate to do so, shall proceed with his determination of the application notwithstanding that the information has not been furnished to him by the specified date.

(5) An order made by the Certification Officer under this section may be enforced in the same way as an order of the court.

(6) If a person applies to the court under this section in relation to an alleged failure he may not apply to the Certification Officer under this section in relation to that failure.

(7) If a person applies to the Certification Officer under this section in relation to an alleged failure he may not apply to the court under this section in relation to that failure."

Offenders

7.– (1) Section 45C (application to Certification Officer or court for declaration of breach of duty to secure positions not held by certain offenders) shall be amended as follows.

(2) In subsection (2) (Certification Officer's powers and duties) insert before paragraph (a)-

"(aa) shall make such enquiries as he thinks fit,"

(3) In subsection (2)(a) (duty to give opportunity to be heard where Certification Officer considers it appropriate) omit ", where he considers it appropriate,".

(4) Omit subsections (3) and (4) (different applications in respect of the same matter).

(5) After subsection (5) insert-

"(5A) Where the Certification Officer makes a declaration he shall also, unless he considers that it would be inappropriate, make an order imposing on the trade union a requirement to take within such period as may be specified in the order such steps to remedy the declared failure as may be so specified.

(5B) The following paragraphs have effect if a person applies to the Certification Officer under this section in relation to an alleged failure-

(a) that person may not apply to the court under this section in relation to that failure;

(b) on an application by a different person to the court under this section in relation to that failure, the court shall have due regard to any declaration, order, observations or reasons made or given by the Certification Officer regarding that failure and brought to the court's notice.

(5C) The following paragraphs have effect if a person applies to the court under this section in relation to an alleged failure-

(a) that person may not apply to the Certification Officer under this section in relation to that failure;

(b) on an application by a different person to the Certification Officer under this section in relation to that failure, the Certification Officer shall have regard to any declaration, order, observations or reasons made or given by the court regarding that failure and brought to the Certification Officer's notice."

(6) In subsection (6) (entitlement to enforce order) after "been made" insert "under subsection (5) or (5A)".

(7) After subsection (6) insert-

"(7) Where the Certification Officer requests a person to furnish information to him in connection with enquiries made by him under this section, he shall specify the date by which that information is to be furnished and, unless he considers that it would be inappropriate to do so, shall proceed with his determination of the application notwithstanding that the information has not been furnished to him by the specified date.

(8) A declaration made by the Certification Officer under this section may be relied on as if it were a declaration made by the court.

(9) An order made by the Certification Officer under this section may be enforced in the same way as an order of the court."

Trade union administration: appeals

8. After section 45C there shall be inserted-

"45D. An appeal lies to the Employment Appeal Tribunal on any question of law arising in proceedings before or arising from any decision of the Certification Officer under section 25, 31 or 45C."

Elections

9. In section 54 (remedy for failure to comply with the duty regarding elections) the second sentence of subsection (1) (application to Certification Officer does not prevent application to court) shall be omitted.

10.– (1) Section 55 (application to Certification Officer for declaration of breach of duty regarding elections) shall be amended as follows.

(2) In subsection (2)(b) (duty to give opportunity to be heard where Certification Officer considers it appropriate) omit "where he considers it appropriate,".

(3) After subsection (5) insert-

"(5A) Where the Certification Officer makes a declaration he shall also, unless he considers that to do so would be inappropriate, make an enforcement order, that is, an order imposing on the union one or more of the following requirements-

(a) to secure the holding of an election in accordance with the order;
(b) to take such other steps to remedy the declared failure as may be specified in the order;
(c) to abstain from such acts as may be so specified with a view to securing that a failure of the same or a similar kind does not occur in future.

The Certification Officer shall in an order imposing any such requirement as is mentioned in paragraph (a) or (b) specify the period within which the union is to comply with the requirements of the order.

(5B) Where the Certification Officer makes an order requiring the union to hold a fresh election, he shall (unless he considers that it would be inappropriate to do so in the particular circumstances of the case) require the election to be conducted in accordance with the requirements of this Chapter and such other provisions as may be made by the order.

(5C) Where an enforcement order has been made-

(a) any person who is a member of the union and was a member at the time the order was made, or
(b) any person who is or was a candidate in the election in question,

is entitled to enforce obedience to the order as if he had made the application on which the order was made."

(4) After subsection (7) insert-

"(8) A declaration made by the Certification Officer under this section may be relied on as if it were a declaration made by the court.

(9) An enforcement order made by the Certification Officer under this section may be enforced in the same way as an order of the court.

(10) The following paragraphs have effect if a person applies under section 56 in relation to an alleged failure-

(a) that person may not apply under this section in relation to that failure;
(b) on an application by a different person under this section in relation to that failure, the Certification Officer shall have due regard to any declaration, order, observations or reasons made or given by the court regarding that failure and brought to the Certification Officer's notice."

11.– (1) Section 56 (application to court for declaration of failure to comply with requirements regarding elections) shall be amended as follows.

(2) Omit subsection (2) (position where application in respect of the same matter has been made to the Certification Officer).

(3) After subsection (7) insert-

"(8) The following paragraphs have effect if a person applies under section 55 in relation to an alleged failure-

(a) that person may not apply under this section in relation to that failure;
(b) on an application by a different person under this section in relation to that failure, the court shall have due regard to any declaration, order, observations or reasons made or given by the Certification Officer regarding that failure and brought to the court's notice."

12. After section 56 there shall be inserted-

"56A. An appeal lies to the Employment Appeal Tribunal on any question of law arising in proceedings before or arising from any decision of the Certification Officer under section 55."

Application of funds for political objects

13. After section 72 there shall be inserted-

"**72A.**– (1) A person who is a member of a trade union and who claims that it has applied its funds in breach of section 71 may apply to the Certification Officer for a declaration that it has done so.

(2) On an application under this section the Certification Officer-

(a) shall make such enquiries as he thinks fit,
(b) shall give the applicant and the union an opportunity to be heard,

(c) shall ensure that, so far as is reasonably practicable, the application is determined within six months of being made,

(d) may make or refuse the declaration asked for,

(e) shall, whether he makes or refuses the declaration, give reasons for his decision in writing, and

(f) may make written observations on any matter arising from, or connected with, the proceedings.

(3) If he makes a declaration he shall specify in it-

(a) the provisions of section 71 breached, and

(b) the amount of the funds applied in breach.

(4) If he makes a declaration and is satisfied that the union has taken or agreed to take steps with a view to-

(a) remedying the declared breach, or

(b) securing that a breach of the same or any similar kind does not occur in future,

he shall specify those steps in making the declaration.

(5) If he makes a declaration he may make such order for remedying the breach as he thinks just under the circumstances.

(6) Where the Certification Officer requests a person to furnish information to him in connection with enquiries made by him under this section, he shall specify the date by which that information is to be furnished and, unless he considers that it would be inappropriate to do so, shall proceed with his determination of the application notwithstanding that the information has not been furnished to him by the specified date.

(7) A declaration made by the Certification Officer under this section may be relied on as if it were a declaration made by the court.

(8) Where an order has been made under this section, any person who is a member of the union and was a member at the time it was made is entitled to enforce obedience to the order as if he had made the application on which the order was made.

(9) An order made by the Certification Officer under this section may be enforced in the same way as an order of the court.

(10) If a person applies to the Certification Officer under this section in relation to an alleged breach he may not apply to the court in relation to the breach; but nothing in this subsection shall prevent such a person from exercising any right to appeal against or challenge the Certification Officer's decision on the application to him.

(11) If-

(a) a person applies to the court in relation to an alleged breach, and

> (b) the breach is one in relation to which he could have made an application to the Certification Officer under this section,

he may not apply to the Certification Officer under this section in relation to the breach."

Political ballot rules

14. In section 79 (remedy for failure to comply with political ballot rules) the second sentence of subsection (1) (application to Certification Officer does not prevent application to court) shall be omitted.

15.– (1) Section 80 (application to Certification Officer for declaration of failure to comply with political ballot rules) shall be amended as follows.

(2) In subsection (2)(b) (duty to give opportunity to be heard where Certification Officer considers it appropriate) omit "where he considers it appropriate,".

(3) After subsection (5) insert-

> "(5A) Where the Certification Officer makes a declaration he shall also, unless he considers that to do so would be inappropriate, make an enforcement order, that is, an order imposing on the union one or more of the following requirements-
>
> > (a) to secure the holding of a ballot in accordance with the order;
> > (b) to take such other steps to remedy the declared failure as may be specified in the order;
> > (c) to abstain from such acts as may be so specified with a view to securing that a failure of the same or a similar kind does not occur in future.

The Certification Officer shall in an order imposing any such requirement as is mentioned in paragraph (a) or (b) specify the period within which the union must comply with the requirements of the order.

> (5B) Where the Certification Officer makes an order requiring the union to hold a fresh ballot, he shall (unless he considers that it would be inappropriate to do so in the particular circumstances of the case) require the ballot to be conducted in accordance with the union's political ballot rules and such other provisions as may be made by the order.
>
> (5C) Where an enforcement order has been made, any person who is a member of the union and was a member at the time the order was made is entitled to enforce obedience to the order as if he had made the application on which the order was made."

(4) After subsection (7) insert-

> "(8) A declaration made by the Certification Officer under this section may be relied on as if it were a declaration made by the court.

(9) An enforcement order made by the Certification Officer under this section may be enforced in the same way as an order of the court.

(10) The following paragraphs have effect if a person applies under section 81 in relation to a matter-

  (a) that person may not apply under this section in relation to that matter;

  (b) on an application by a different person under this section in relation to that matter, the Certification Officer shall have due regard to any declaration, order, observations, or reasons made or given by the court regarding that matter and brought to the Certification Officer's notice."

16.– (1) Section 81 (application to court for declaration of failure to comply with political ballot rules) shall be amended as follows.

(2) Omit subsection (2) (position where application in respect of the same matter has been made to Certification Officer).

(3) After subsection (7) insert-

"(8) The following paragraphs have effect if a person applies under section 80 in relation to a matter-

  (a) that person may not apply under this section in relation to that matter;

  (b) on an application by a different person under this section in relation to that matter, the court shall have due regard to any declaration, order, observations or reasons made or given by the Certification Officer regarding that matter and brought to the court's notice."

Political fund

17.– (1) Section 82 (rules as to political fund) shall be amended as follows.

(2) After subsection (2) insert-

"(2A) On a complaint being made to him the Certification Officer shall make such enquiries as he thinks fit."

(3) After subsection (3) insert-

"(3A) Where the Certification Officer requests a person to furnish information to him in connection with enquiries made by him under this section, he shall specify the date by which that information is to be furnished and, unless he considers that it would be inappropriate to do so, shall proceed with his determination of the application notwithstanding that the information has not been furnished to him by the specified date."

Amalgamation or transfer of engagements

18.– (1) Section 103 (complaints about procedure relating to amalgamation or transfer of engagements) shall be amended as follows.

(2) After subsection (2) insert-

"(2A) On a complaint being made to him the Certification Officer shall make such enquiries as he thinks fit."

(3) After subsection (5) insert-

"(6) Where the Certification Officer requests a person to furnish information to him in connection with enquiries made by him under this section, he shall specify the date by which that information is to be furnished and, unless he considers that it would be inappropriate to do so, shall proceed with his determination of the application notwithstanding that the information has not been furnished to him by the specified date.

(7) A declaration made by the Certification Officer under this section may be relied on as if it were a declaration made by the court.

(8) Where an order has been made under this section, any person who is a member of the union and was a member at the time it was made is entitled to enforce obedience to the order as if he had made the application on which the order was made.

(9) An order made by the Certification Officer under this section may be enforced in the same way as an order of the court."

Breach of union rules

19. In Part I, after Chapter VII there shall be inserted-

"CHAPTER VIIA

BREACH OF RULES

108A.– (1) A person who claims that there has been a breach or threatened breach of the rules of a trade union relating to any of the matters mentioned in subsection (2) may apply to the Certification Officer for a declaration to that effect, subject to subsections (3) to (7).

(2) The matters are-

(a) the appointment or election of a person to, or the removal of a person from, any office;
(b) disciplinary proceedings by the union (including expulsion);
(c) the balloting of members on any issue other than industrial action;
(d) the constitution or proceedings of any executive committee or of any decision-making meeting;
(e) such other matters as may be specified in an order made by the Secretary of State.

(3) The applicant must be a member of the union, or have been one at the time of the alleged breach or threatened breach.

(4) A person may not apply under subsection (1) in relation to a claim if he is entitled to apply under section 80 in relation to the claim.

(5) No application may be made regarding-

(a) the dismissal of an employee of the union;
(b) disciplinary proceedings against an employee of the union.

(6) An application must be made-

(a) within the period of six months starting with the day on which the breach or threatened breach is alleged to have taken place, or
(b) if within that period any internal complaints procedure of the union is invoked to resolve the claim, within the period of six months starting with the earlier of the days specified in subsection (7).

(7) Those days are-

(a) the day on which the procedure is concluded, and
(b) the last day of the period of one year beginning with the day on which the procedure is invoked.

(8) The reference in subsection (1) to the rules of a union includes references to the rules of any branch or section of the union.

(9) In subsection (2)(c) "industrial action" means a strike or other industrial action by persons employed under contracts of employment.

(10) For the purposes of subsection (2)(d) a committee is an executive committee if-

(a) it is a committee of the union concerned and has power to make executive decisions on behalf of the union or on behalf of a constituent body,
(b) it is a committee of a major constituent body and has power to make executive decisions on behalf of that body, or
(c) it is a sub-committee of a committee falling within paragraph (a) or (b).

(11) For the purposes of subsection (2)(d) a decision-making meeting is-

(a) a meeting of members of the union concerned (or the representatives of such members) which has power to make a decision on any matter which, under the rules of the union, is final as regards the union or which, under the rules of the union or a constituent body, is final as regards that body, or
(b) a meeting of members of a major constituent body (or the representatives of such members) which has power to make a decision on any matter which, under the rules of the union or the body, is final as regards that body.

(12) For the purposes of subsections (10) and (11), in relation to the trade union concerned-

(a) a constituent body is any body which forms part of the union, including a branch, group, section or region;
(b) a major constituent body is such a body which has more than 1,000 members.

(13) Any order under subsection (2)(e) shall be made by statutory instrument; and no such order shall be made unless a draft of it has been laid before and approved by resolution of each House of Parliament.

(14) If a person applies to the Certification Officer under this section in relation to an alleged breach or threatened breach he may not apply to the court in relation to the breach or threatened breach; but nothing in this subsection shall prevent such a person from exercising any right to appeal against or challenge the Certification Officer's decision on the application to him.

(15) If-

(a) a person applies to the court in relation to an alleged breach or threatened breach, and

(b) the breach or threatened breach is one in relation to which he could have made an application to the Certification Officer under this section,

he may not apply to the Certification Officer under this section in relation to the breach or threatened breach.

108B.– (1) The Certification Officer may refuse to accept an application under section 108A unless he is satisfied that the applicant has taken all reasonable steps to resolve the claim by the use of any internal complaints procedure of the union.

(2) If he accepts an application under section 108A the Certification Officer-

(a) shall make such enquiries as he thinks fit,

(b) shall give the applicant and the union an opportunity to be heard,

(c) shall ensure that, so far as is reasonably practicable, the application is determined within six months of being made,

(d) may make or refuse the declaration asked for, and

(e) shall, whether he makes or refuses the declaration, give reasons for his decision in writing.

(3) Where the Certification Officer makes a declaration he shall also, unless he considers that to do so would be inappropriate, make an enforcement order, that is, an order imposing on the union one or both of the following requirements-

(a) to take such steps to remedy the breach, or withdraw the threat of a breach, as may be specified in the order;

(b) to abstain from such acts as may be so specified with a view to securing that a breach or threat of the same or a similar kind does not occur in future.

(4) The Certification Officer shall in an order imposing any such requirement as is mentioned in subsection (3)(a) specify the period within which the union is to comply with the requirement.

(5) Where the Certification Officer requests a person to furnish information to him in connection with enquiries made by him under this section, he shall specify

the date by which that information is to be furnished and, unless he considers that it would be inappropriate to do so, shall proceed with his determination of the application notwithstanding that the information has not been furnished to him by the specified date.

(6) A declaration made by the Certification Officer under this section may be relied on as if it were a declaration made by the court.

(7) Where an enforcement order has been made, any person who is a member of the union and was a member at the time it was made is entitled to enforce obedience to the order as if he had made the application on which the order was made.

(8) An enforcement order made by the Certification Officer under this section may be enforced in the same way as an order of the court.

(9) An order under section 108A(2)(e) may provide that, in relation to an application under section 108A with regard to a prescribed matter, the preceding provisions of this section shall apply with such omissions or modifications as may be specified in the order; and a prescribed matter is such matter specified under section 108A(2)(e) as is prescribed under this subsection.

108C. An appeal lies to the Employment Appeal Tribunal on any question of law arising in proceedings before or arising from any decision of the Certification Officer under this Chapter."

Employers' associations

20.– (1) Section 132 (provisions about application of funds for political objects to apply to unincorporated employers' associations) shall be amended as follows.

(2) For "The" substitute "(1) Subject to subsections (2) to (5), the".

(3) After subsection (1) (as created by sub-paragraph (2)) insert-

"(2) Subsection (1) does not apply to these provisions-

    (a) section 72A;
    (b) in section 80, subsections (5A) to (5C) and (8) to (10);
    (c) in section 81, subsection (8).

(3) In its application to an unincorporated employers' association, section 79 shall have effect as if at the end of subsection (1) there were inserted-

"The making of an application to the Certification Officer does not prevent the applicant, or any other person, from making an application to the court in respect of the same matter."

(4) In its application to an unincorporated employers' association, section 80(2)(b) shall have effect as if the words "where he considers it appropriate," were inserted at the beginning.

(5) In its application to an unincorporated employers' association, section 81 shall have effect as if after subsection (1) there were inserted-

"(2) If an application in respect of the same matter has been made to the Certification Officer, the court shall have due regard to any declaration, reasons or observations of his which are brought to its notice."

21. In section 133 (provisions about amalgamations and similar matters to apply to unincorporated employers' associations) in subsection (2)(c) after "101(3)" there shall be inserted ", 103(2A) and (6) to (9)".

Procedure before Certification Officer

22. In section 256 (procedure before Certification Officer) for subsection (2) (provision for restricting disclosure of individual's identity) there shall be substituted-

"(2) He shall in particular make provision about the disclosure, and restriction of the disclosure, of the identity of an individual who has made or is proposing to make any such application or complaint.

(2A) Provision under subsection (2) shall be such that if the application or complaint relates to a trade union-

(a) the individual's identity is disclosed to the union unless the Certification Officer thinks the circumstances are such that it should not be so disclosed;
(b) the individual's identity is disclosed to such other persons (if any) as the Certification Officer thinks fit."

23. After section 256 there shall be inserted-

"Vexatious litigants.

256A.– (1) The Certification Officer may refuse to entertain any application or complaint made to him under a provision of Chapters III to VIIA of Part I by a vexatious litigant.

(2) The Certification Officer must give reasons for such a refusal.

(3) Subsection (1) does not apply to a complaint under section 37E(1)(b) or to an application under section 41.

(4) For the purposes of subsection (1) a vexatious litigant is a person who is the subject of-

(a) an order which is made under section 33(1) of the Employment Tribunals Act 1996 and which remains in force,
(b) a civil proceedings order or an all proceedings order which is made under section 42(1) of the Supreme Court Act 1981 and which remains in force,
(c) an order which is made under section 1 of the Vexatious Actions (Scotland) Act 1898, or

(d) an order which is made under section 32 of the Judicature (Northern Ireland) Act 1978.

256B.– (1) For the purposes of a relevant enactment an application to the Certification Officer shall be disregarded if-

(a) it was made under a provision mentioned in the relevant enactment, and
(b) it was refused by the Certification Officer under section 256A(1).

(2) The relevant enactments are sections 26(8), 31(7), 45C(5B), 56(8), 72A(10), 81(8) and 108A(13)."

Annual report by Certification Officer

24. In section 258(1) (Certification Officer: annual report) for "calendar year" there shall be substituted "financial year".

SCHEDULE 6
The Certification Officer:
Paras 1-19 – This is a technical Schedule which is unlikely to be of interest or concern to readers unless they have a requirement to be expert in the subject. For such readers, a useful starting point to achieving expertise is the summary in the statutory Explanatory Notes to the 1999 Act.

Section 31.   SCHEDULE 7

EMPLOYMENT AGENCIES

Introduction

1. The (1973 c. 35.)Employment Agencies Act 1973 shall be amended as provided in this Schedule.

SCHEDULE 7
Introduction:
Para 1 – S.37 gives effect to Schedule 7 which amends the Employment Agencies Act 1973 (the 1973 Act)

General regulations

2.– (1) Section 5 (power to make general regulations) shall be amended as follows.

(2) In subsection (1) there shall be substituted for paragraphs (f) and (g) and the proviso following paragraph (g)-

"(ea) restricting the services which may be provided by persons carrying on such agencies and businesses;

(eb) regulating the way in which and the terms on which services may be provided by persons carrying on such agencies and businesses;

(ec) restricting or regulating the charging of fees by persons carrying on such agencies and businesses."

(3) After subsection (1) there shall be inserted-

"(1A) A reference in subsection (1)(ea) to (ec) of this section to services includes a reference to services in respect of-

(a) persons seeking employment outside the United Kingdom;

(b) persons normally resident outside the United Kingdom seeking employment in the United Kingdom."

General Regulations:

Para 2 – S.5 of the 1973 Act (i.e. the power make to make Regulations under the 1973 Act) is amended to widen the regulation-making powers of the Secretary of State to regulate the provision of services covered by the 1973 Act to employers and those seeking work generally, rather than the restricted category expressly referred to in s.5 of the 1973 Act. The Secretary of State is also empowered to make Regulations restricting the services provided by agencies. There is much concern that the objectives of employment rights generally, and their application to atypical work relationships, is being thwarted through certain employment agency arrangements, and further concern about the fairness and integrity of certain working practices adopted by some employment agencies. No Regulations have been made at the time of publication.

An insight into the probable scope of such Regulations is to be found in the illustrations provided in the Explanatory Notes to the 1999 Act:

- *Restricting the ability of employment agencies/businesses to unilaterally vary the terms of their contracts of other arrangements with workers or hirers*

- *Restricting their ability to make payment to a worker for work done conditional upon undertaking other work*

- *Preventing agencies from purporting to enter into contracts on behalf of workers unless they are permitted to charge such workers for finding them work and have a binding contract with them giving them authority to enter into such contract; and*

- *Restricting the ability of employment agencies/businesses to impose terms on employers which seek to prevent or discourage them from dealing, whether directly or through other employment businesses or agencies, with workers supplied to them; or from referring such workers to other persons who might employ them*

Where businesses seek to impose charges in any of these circumstances, the Regulations may limit the size of those charges, time limit their application, or prohibit them altogether.

S.5(1A) is added to the 1973 Act, the effect of which is to establish that the Act also regulates services by UK based employment agencies providing services to clients seeking employment outside the UK and to clients normally resident outside the UK seeking employment in the UK.

Charges

3. For section 6(1) (restriction on demand or receipt of fee for finding or seeking to find employment) there shall be substituted-

   "(1) Except in such cases or classes of case as the Secretary of State may prescribe-

      (a) a person carrying on an employment agency shall not request or directly or indirectly receive any fee from any person for providing services (whether by the provision of information or otherwise) for the purpose of finding him employment or seeking to find him employment;

      (b) a person carrying on an employment business shall not request or directly or indirectly receive any fee from an employee for providing services (whether by the provision of information or otherwise) for the purpose of finding or seeking to find another person, with a view to the employee acting for and under the control of that other person;

      (c) a person carrying on an employment business shall not request or directly or indirectly receive any fee from a second person for providing services (whether by the provision of information or otherwise) for the purpose of finding or seeking to find a third person, with a view to the second person becoming employed by the first person and acting for and under the control of the third person."

Charges:

S.6(1) of the 1973 Act makes it unlawful for employment agencies/businesses to charge clients (i.e. clients looking for work) for the agency's service of finding *or* seeking *to find work for them. The Secretary of State is empowered to make exceptions. The text of s.6(1) of the 1973 Act is replaced by the substituted wording of s.6(1) set out in para 3. It makes it clear that the prohibition also extends to the* provision of information *by agencies and that the prohibitions apply not only to new job seekers but also those under contract with the employment agencies and those will be under contract once they have agreed to undertake an assignment with the hirer.*

An insight into the probable scope of such Regulations is again to be found in the illustrations provided in the Explanatory Notes to the 1999 Act:

- *The provision of employment agency services to entertainers, models, and certain other limited groups where it is the norm for an agent to be engaged to represent the worker, except where the agent charges the person who hires the worker;*

- *The inclusion of information about persons seeking work in publications made available to employers or potential employers; and*

- *The provision of information about work opportunities to persons seeking work where no other services are offered, and where the charge for such information is within prescribed limits*

Inspection

4.– (1) Section 9 (inspection) shall be amended as follows.

(2) In subsection (1) (power to inspect)-

  (a) for paragraph (a) there shall be substituted-

   "(a) enter any relevant business premises;", and

  (b) after paragraph (c) there shall be inserted-

     "; and
   (d) take copies of records and other documents inspected under paragraph (b).".

(3) After subsection (1) there shall be inserted-

  "(1A) If an officer seeks to inspect or acquire, in accordance with subsection (1)(b) or (c), a record or other document or information which is not kept at the premises being inspected, he may require any person on the premises-

    (a) to inform him where and by whom the record, other document or information is kept, and

    (b) to make arrangements, if it is reasonably practicable for the person to do so, for the record, other document or information to be inspected by or furnished to the officer at the premises at a time specified by the officer.

(1B) In subsection (1) "relevant business premises" means premises-

    (a) which are used, have been used or are to be used for or in connection with the carrying on of an employment agency or employment business,

    (b) which the officer has reasonable cause to believe are used or have been used for or in connection with the carrying on of an employment agency or employment business, or

    (c) which the officer has reasonable cause to believe are used for the carrying on of a business by a person who also carries on or has carried on an employment agency or employment business, if the officer also has reasonable cause to believe that records or other documents which relate to the employment agency or employment business are kept there.

(1C) For the purposes of subsection (1)-

    (a) "document" includes information recorded in any form, and

    (b) information is kept at premises if it is accessible from them."

(4) For subsection (2) (self-incrimination) there shall be substituted-

"(2) Nothing in this section shall require a person to produce, provide access to or make arrangements for the production of anything which he could not be compelled to produce in civil proceedings before the High Court or (in Scotland) the Court of Session.

(2A) Subject to subsection (2B), a statement made by a person in compliance with a requirement under this section may be used in evidence against him in criminal proceedings.

(2B) Except in proceedings for an offence under section 5 of the Perjury Act 1911 (false statements made otherwise than on oath), no evidence relating to the statement may be adduced, and no question relating to it may be asked, by or on behalf of the prosecution unless-

    (a) evidence relating to it is adduced, or

    (b) a question relating to it is asked,

by or on behalf of the person who made the statement."

(5) In subsection (3) (offence)-

    (a) for "or (b)" there shall be substituted ", (b) or (d)", and

    (b) after the words "paragraph (c) of that subsection" there shall be inserted "or under subsection (1A)".

(6) In subsection (4)(a) (restriction on disclosure of information) in sub-paragraph (iv) (exception for criminal proceedings pursuant to or arising out of the Act) the words "pursuant to or arising out of this Act" shall be omitted.

> **Inspection:**
> *Para 4 – S.9 of the 1973 Act contains the inspection powers and defines the range of premises which may be entered by inspectors, restricting inspection to "all reasonable times" and does not authorise forcible entry. Para 4 extends the range of premises which may be entered and authorises the inspectors to take copies of the agencies records and documents maintained by the agency as required by the 1973 Act. New obligations are imposed on agencies to disclose the whereabouts of documentation which ought to be on the premises and extends the definition of "document" to paperless forms e.g. electronic data systems.*
>
> *The provisions in s.9(2) of the 1973 Act protecting agencies against self-incrimination are replaced by new s.9(2), s.9(2A) and s.9(2B) accommodating the judgment of the European Court of Human Rights in Saunders v. the United Kingdom. The related offences of obstruction and non-compliance are extended to include obstruction and non-compliance under the new sections. Information obtained under the s.9 compulsory powers may now be used for the purpose of any criminal proceedings rather than restricted to 1973 Act offences.*

Offences

5. After section 11 there shall be inserted-

"**11A.**– (1) For the purposes of subsection (2) of this section a relevant offence is an offence under section 3B, 5(2), 6(2), 9(4)(b) or 10(2) of this Act for which proceedings are instituted by the Secretary of State.

(2) Notwithstanding section 127(1) of the Magistrates' Courts Act 1980 (information to be laid within 6 months of offence) an information relating to a relevant offence which is triable by a magistrates' court in England and Wales may be so tried if it is laid at any time-

    (a) within 3 years after the date of the commission of the offence, and
    (b) within 6 months after the date on which evidence sufficient in the opinion of the Secretary of State to justify the proceedings came to his knowledge.

(3) Notwithstanding section 136 of the Criminal Procedure (Scotland) Act 1995 (time limit for prosecuting certain statutory offences) in Scotland proceedings in respect of an offence under section 3B, 5(2), 6(2), 9(4)(b) or 10(2) of this Act may be commenced at any time-

(a) within 3 years after the date of the commission of the offence, and

(b) within 6 months after the date on which evidence sufficient in the opinion of the Lord Advocate to justify the proceedings came to his knowledge.

(4) For the purposes of this section a certificate of the Secretary of State or Lord Advocate (as the case may be) as to the date on which evidence came to his knowledge is conclusive evidence.

11B. The court in which a person is convicted of an offence under this Act may order him to pay to the Secretary of State a sum which appears to the court not to exceed the costs of the investigation which resulted in the conviction."

Offences:
Para 5 – Two new sections 11A and 11B are inserted into the 1973 Act extending the time in which an information laid before a Magistrates' Court, or a Sheriff Court in Scotland, is triable for any offence under the 1973 Act (except the s.9(3) offence) from six months. The new time limit is either three years from the date the offence was committed or six months from the date of which the Secretary of State comes to know of evidence sufficient to justify the prosecution, whichever is the earlier. The Court may award costs against the agency not exceeding the investigation costs.

Regulations and orders

6. For section 12(5) (regulations and orders: procedure) there shall be substituted-

"(5) Regulations under section 5(1) or 6(1) of this Act shall not be made unless a draft has been laid before, and approved by resolution of, each House of Parliament.

(6) Regulations under section 13(7)(i) of this Act or an order under section 14(3) shall be subject to annulment in pursuance of a resolution of either House of Parliament."

Regulations and Orders:
S.6(5) of the 1973 Act is replaced by the text in para 6 providing that Regulations under s.5(1) or s.6(1) of the 1973 Act are subject to the affirmative procedure whilst Regulations under s.13(7)(i) or an order under s.14(3) of the 1973 Act are subject to annulment.

Interpretation

7. In section 13(2) (definition of employment agency) for "workers" (in each place) there shall be substituted "persons".

> **Interpretation:**
> *Para 7 – The Definition of "employment agency" in s.13(2) is amended by substituting "workers" for "persons". This widens the definition of employment agency activity to include the supply of services to organisations as well is individuals in line with the definition of "employment business" activity in s.13(3) of the 1973 Act.*

Exemptions

8. For section 13(7)(i) there shall be substituted-

"(i) any prescribed business or service, or prescribed class of business or service or business or service carried on or provided by prescribed persons or classes of person."

> **Exemptions:**
> *Para 8 – The text in para 8 replaces the existing s.13(7)(i) of the 1973 Act to provide for greater flexibility and certainty regarding the exemptions which can be made from the provisions of the Act. The illustration given in the explanatory notes is that particular membership societies could be exempted from the Act to the extent that they provide services to their members but would remain subject to the legislation in respect of services provided to non-members. There is a useful comparative table for those involved in running, guiding or advising employment agencies/businesses, of the former text under the 1973 Act and the amended text as a result of the 1999 Act at pages 84-90 of the Explanatory Notes to the 1999 Act.*

SCHEDULE 8

NATIONAL SECURITY

1. The following shall be substituted for section 193 of the Employment Rights Act 1996 (national security)-

"**193.** Part IVA and section 47B of this Act do not apply in relation to employment for the purposes of-

(a) the Security Service,

(b) the Secret Intelligence Service, or

(c) the Government Communications Headquarters."

2. Section 4(7) of the Employment Tribunals Act 1996 (composition of tribunal: national security) shall cease to have effect.

3. The following shall be substituted for section 10 of that Act (national security, &c.)-

"National security.

10.– (1) If on a complaint under-

(a) section 146 of the Trade Union and Labour Relations (Consolidation) Act 1992 (detriment: trade union membership), or

(b) section 111 of the Employment Rights Act 1996 (unfair dismissal),

it is shown that the action complained of was taken for the purpose of safeguarding national security, the employment tribunal shall dismiss the complaint.

(2) Employment tribunal procedure regulations may make provision about the composition of the tribunal (including provision disapplying or modifying section 4) for the purposes of proceedings in relation to which-

(a) a direction is given under subsection (3), or

(b) an order is made under subsection (4).

(3) A direction may be given under this subsection by a Minister of the Crown if-

(a) it relates to particular Crown employment proceedings, and

(b) the Minister considers it expedient in the interests of national security.

(4) An order may be made under this subsection by the President or a Regional Chairman in relation to particular proceedings if he considers it expedient in the interests of national security.

(5) Employment tribunal procedure regulations may make provision enabling a Minister of the Crown, if he considers it expedient in the interests of national security-

(a) to direct a tribunal to sit in private for all or part of particular Crown employment proceedings;

(b) to direct a tribunal to exclude the applicant from all or part of particular Crown employment proceedings;

(c) to direct a tribunal to exclude the applicant's representatives from all or part of particular Crown employment proceedings;

(d) to direct a tribunal to take steps to conceal the identity of a particular witness in particular Crown employment proceedings;

(e) to direct a tribunal to take steps to keep secret all or part of the reasons for its decision in particular Crown employment proceedings.

(6) Employment tribunal procedure regulations may enable a tribunal, if it considers it expedient in the interests of national security, to do anything of a kind which a tribunal can be required to do by direction under subsection (5)(a) to (e).

(7) In relation to cases where a person has been excluded by virtue of subsection (5)(b) or (c) or (6), employment tribunal procedure regulations may make provision-

(a) for the appointment by the Attorney General, or by the Advocate General for Scotland, of a person to represent the interests of the applicant;

(b) about the publication and registration of reasons for the tribunal's decision;

(c) permitting an excluded person to make a statement to the tribunal before the commencement of the proceedings, or the part of the proceedings, from which he is excluded.

(8) Proceedings are Crown employment proceedings for the purposes of this section if the employment to which the complaint relates-

(a) is Crown employment, or

(b) is connected with the performance of functions on behalf of the Crown.

(9) The reference in subsection (4) to the President or a Regional Chairman is to a person appointed in accordance with regulations under section 1(1) as-

(a) a Regional Chairman,

(b) President of the Employment Tribunals (England and Wales), or

(c) President of the Employment Tribunals (Scotland).

10A.– (1) Employment tribunal procedure regulations may enable an employment tribunal to sit in private for the purpose of hearing evidence from any person which in the opinion of the tribunal is likely to consist of-

(a) information which he could not disclose without contravening a prohibition imposed by or by virtue of any enactment,

(b) information which has been communicated to him in confidence or which he has otherwise obtained in consequence of the confidence reposed in him by another person, or

(c) information the disclosure of which would, for reasons other than its effect on negotiations with respect to any of the matters mentioned in section 178(2) of the Trade Union and Labour Relations (Consolidation) Act 1992, cause substantial injury to any undertaking of his or in which he works.

(2) The reference in subsection (1)(c) to any undertaking of a person or in which he works shall be construed-

(a) in relation to a person in Crown employment, as a reference to the national interest,

(b) in relation to a person who is a relevant member of the House of Lords staff, as a reference to the national interest or (if the case so requires) the interests of the House of Lords, and

(c) in relation to a person who is a relevant member of the House of Commons staff, as a reference to the national interest or (if the case so requires) the interests of the House of Commons.

10B.– (1) This section applies where a tribunal has been directed under section 10(5) or has determined under section 10(6)-

(a) to take steps to conceal the identity of a particular witness, or
(b) to take steps to keep secret all or part of the reasons for its decision.

(2) It is an offence to publish-

(a) anything likely to lead to the identification of the witness, or
(b) the reasons for the tribunal's decision or the part of its reasons which it is directed or has determined to keep secret.

(3) A person guilty of an offence under this section is liable on summary conviction to a fine not exceeding level 5 on the standard scale.

(4) Where a person is charged with an offence under this section it is a defence to prove that at the time of the alleged offence he was not aware, and neither suspected nor had reason to suspect, that the publication in question was of, or included, the matter in question.

(5) Where an offence under this section committed by a body corporate is proved to have been committed with the consent or connivance of, or to be attributable to any neglect on the part of-

(a) a director, manager, secretary or other similar officer of the body corporate, or
(b) a person purporting to act in any such capacity,

he as well as the body corporate is guilty of the offence and liable to be proceeded against and punished accordingly.

(6) A reference in this section to publication includes a reference to inclusion in a programme which is included in a programme service, within the meaning of the Broadcasting Act 1990."

4. Section 28(5) of the Employment Tribunals Act 1996 (composition of Appeal Tribunal: national security) shall cease to have effect.

5.– (1) Section 30 of that Act (Appeal Tribunal Procedure rules) shall be amended as follows.

(2) In subsection (2)(d) for "section 10" substitute "section 10A".

(3) After subsection (2) insert-

"(2A) Appeal Tribunal procedure rules may make provision of a kind which may be made by employment tribunal procedure regulations under section 10(2), (5), (6) or (7).

(2B) For the purposes of subsection (2A)-

(a) the reference in section 10(2) to section 4 shall be treated as a reference to section 28, and

(b) the reference in section 10(4) to the President or a Regional Chairman shall be treated as a reference to a judge of the Appeal Tribunal.

(2C) Section 10B shall have effect in relation to a direction to or determination of the Appeal Tribunal as it has effect in relation to a direction to or determination of an employment tribunal."

6. After section 69(2) of the Race Relations Act 1976 (evidence: Minister's certificate as to national security, &c.) there shall be inserted-

"(2A) Subsection (2)(b) shall not have effect for the purposes of proceedings on a complaint under section 54."

7. Paragraph 4(1)(b) of Schedule 3 to the Disability Discrimination Act 1995 (evidence: Minister's certificate as to national security, &c.) shall cease to have effect.

SCHEDULE 8
National Security:

Prior to s.41, which gives effect to Schedule 8, Crown Servants (including staff of the Security and Intelligence Agencies) may be excluded by Ministers of the Crown from certain statutory employment rights on grounds of national security. The combined effect of s.41 and Schedule 8 is to remove some of these powers. Consequentially staff of the Security and Intelligence Agencies may present complaints of breach of employment rights such as unfair dismissal or unlawful discrimination. The Ministerial power under s.193 of the 1996 Act to exclude certain persons in Crown employment from any of the employment rights (excepting the rights created by the whistle-blower legislation, the Public Interest Disclosure Act 1998) is removed. Para 2 repeals s.4(7) of the 1996 Act which authorised a Minister to direct that Employment Tribunal proceedings must be heard and decided by the President of the Employment Tribunals.

S.10 of the Employment Tribunals Act 1996 is replaced with substituted text under para 3. The National Security *Defence to unfair dismissal complaints and complaints under s.146 of the 1992 Act (action short of dismissal on grounds related to Union membership or activities) is retained. However the power of Ministers to certify conclusively that an Act was done on grounds of national security i.e. unchallengeable by the claimant and not subject to assessment by the Employment Tribunal is removed. New safeguards to protect national security interests are introduced e.g. the Tribunal Procedure Regulations may be amended to empower Ministers to direct the Tribunal, in the interests of national security, that Crown employment proceedings should be heard by specially constituted Tribunals or that the anonymity of witnesses (or that all or part of the Tribunals Reasons for its decision) should be subject to secrecy. Exceptionally, an Applicant and his representative may be excluded under the proposed Regulations and there will be provision to appoint a special representative to represent the Applicant's interest and provision for the Applicant or his representatives to make a statement of case to the Tribunal before exclusion is implemented.*

New s.10A re-enacts s.10(2) and s.10(3) of the Employment Tribunals Act 1996 permitting the Tribunal to sit in camera (private) in certain circumstances. It is a criminal offence under new s.10B to publish anything likely to lead to the identification of a witness or a secret part of the reasons for the Tribunal's decision where the Tribunal has directed anonymity or such secrecy. Comparable provisions to those made in respect of Employment Tribunals apply, under para 5 in respect of appeals in national security cases to a specially constituted Appeal Tribunal. The Ministers' power to issue conclusive certificates in race relations and disability discrimination claims is removed by para 6 and 7.

SCHEDULE 9 — Section 44.

R<small>EPEALS</small>

1. B<small>ALLOTS AND</small> N<small>OTICES</small>

Chapter	Short title	Extent of repeal
1992 c. 52.	Trade Union and Labour Relations (Consolidation) Act 1992.	In section 226(2) the word "and" at the end of paragraph (b). Section 227(2). In section 234A(7)(a) the words "otherwise than to enable the union to comply with a court order or an undertaking given to a court".'.

2. L<small>EAVE FOR FAMILY REASONS ETC</small>

Chapter	Short title	Extent of repeal
1996 c. 17.	Employment Tribunals Act 1996.	In section 13(2)- the word "or" after paragraph (a), paragraph (b), and the words ", or which she held before her absence,".
1996 c. 18.	Employment Rights Act 1996.	In section 37, subsection (4), the word "and" after subsection (5)(a), and subsection (5)(b). In section 43, subsection (4), the word "and" after subsection (5)(a), and subsection (5)(b). Section 96. Section 97(6). Section 98(5). Section 105(2). Section 108(3)(a). Section 109(2)(a). Section 114(5). Section 115(4).

Chapter	Short title	Extent of repeal
1996 c. 18. – *contd.*		In section 118(1)(b), the word ", 127".
		Section 119(6).
		Section 127.
		Section 137.
		Section 145(7).
		Section 146(3).
		Section 156(2).
		Section 157(6).
		Section 162(7).
		In section 199, the words "(subject to subsection (3)" in subsection (2), and subsection (3).
		In section 200(1), the words "and section 137".
		Section 209(6).
		In section 212- subsection (2), in subsection (3), the word "or" after paragraph (c), and paragraph (d), in subsection (4) the words "or (subject to subsection (2)) subsection (3)(d)".
		Section 226(3)(a) and (5)(a).
		In section 235(1), the definitions of "maternity leave period" and "notified day of return".
S.I. 1994/2479.	Maternity (Compulsory Leave) Regulations 1994.	The whole instrument.

3. AGREEMENT TO EXCLUDE DISMISSAL RIGHTS

Chapter	Short title	Extent of repeal
1992 c. 52.	Trade Union and Labour Relations (Consolidation) Act 1992.	In Schedule A1, paragraph 163.
1996 c. 18.	Employment Rights Act 1996.	In section 44(4) the words from the beginning to "the dismissal,".
		In section 45A(4) the words from ", unless" to the end.
		In section 46(2) the words from the beginning to "the dismissal,".
		In section 47(2) the words from the beginning to "the dismissal,".
		In section 47A(2) the words from the beginning to "the dismissal,".
		In section 47B(2) the words from the beginning to "the dismissal,".
		Section 197(1) and (2).
		In section 197(4) the words "(1) or".
		In section 203(2)(d) the words "(1) or".
		In section 209(2)(g) the words "and 197(1)".
1999 c. 26	Employment Relations Act 1999.	Section 18(6).

4. Power to confer rights on individuals

Chapter	Short title	Extent of repeal
1996 c. 18.	Employment Rights Act 1996.	Section 209(7).

5. ACAS: general duty

Chapter	Short title	Extent of repeal
1992 c. 52.	Trade Union and Labour Relations (Consolidation) Act 1992.	In section 209 the words from ", in particular" to the end.
1993 c. 19.	Trade Union Reform and Employment Rights Act 1993.	Section 43(1).

6. Commissioners

Chapter	Short title	Extent of repeal
1967 c. 13.	Parliamentary Commissioner Act 1967.	In Schedule 2, the entries relating to- the Office of the Commissioner for Protection Against Unlawful Industrial Action, and the Office of the Commissioner for the Rights of Trade Union Members.
1975 c. 24.	House of Commons Disqualification Act 1975.	In Part III of Schedule 1, the entries relating to- the Commissioner for Protection Against Unlawful Industrial Action, and the Commissioner for the Rights of Trade Union Members.
1975 c. 25.	Northern Ireland Assembly Disqualification Act 1975.	In Part III of Schedule 1, the entries relating to- the Commissioner for Protection Against Unlawful Industrial Action, and

Chapter	Short title	Extent of repeal
1975 c. 25. – *contd.*		the Commissioner for the Rights of Trade Union Members.
1992 c. 52.	Trade Union and Labour Relations (Consolidation) Act 1992.	In section 65(3) the words "the Commissioner for the Rights of Trade Union Members or".
		In Part I, Chapter VIII.
		Sections 235B and 235C.
		Section 266 (and the heading immediately preceding it) and sections 267 to 271.
		In Schedule 2, paragraphs 1 and 4(4).
1993 c. 19.	Trade Union Reform and Employment Rights Act 1993.	In Schedule 7, paragraph 20.
		In Schedule 8, paragraphs 2, 6, 7, 58 to 60 and 79 to 84.

7. THE CERTIFICATION OFFICER

Chapter	Short title	Extent of repeal
1992 c. 52.	Trade Union and Labour Relations (Consolidation) Act 1992.	In section 24(6), the second sentence.
		In section 24A(6), the second sentence.
		In section 25(2)(b) the words "where he considers it appropriate,".
		Section 26(2).
		In section 45C(2)(a) the words ", where he considers it appropriate," and section 45C(3) and (4).
		In section 54(1), the second sentence.

Chapter	Short title	Extent of repeal
1992 c. 52. – *contd.*		In section 55(2)(b) the words "where he considers it appropriate,".
		Section 56(2).
		In section 79(1), the second sentence.
		In section 80(2)(b) the words "where he considers it appropriate,".
		Section 81(2).

8. EMPLOYMENT AGENCIES

Chapter	Short title	Extent of repeal
1973 c. 35.	Employment Agencies Act 1973.	In section 9(4)(a)(iv) the words "pursuant to or arising out of this Act".

9. EMPLOYMENT RIGHTS: EMPLOYMENT OUTSIDE GREAT BRITAIN

Chapter	Short title	Extent of repeal
1996 c. 18.	Employment Rights Act 1996.	Section 196.
		In section 199(6), the words "Section 196(6) does not apply to an employee, and".
		In section 201(3)(g), the word "196,".
		Section 204(2).
		In section 209(2)(g), the words "196(1) and".
		In section 209(5), the words ", 196(2), (3) and (5)".

10. Sections 33 to 36

Chapter	Short title	Extent of repeal
1992 c. 52.	Trade Union and Labour Relations (Consolidation) Act 1992.	Section 157. Section 158. Section 159. Section 176(7) and (8).
1996 c. 18.	Employment Rights Act 1996.	In section 117, subsection (4)(b) and the word "or" before it, and subsections (5) and (6). Section 118(2) and (3). Section 120(2). Section 124(2). Section 125. Section 186(2). Section 208. Section 227(2) to (4). Section 236(2)(c). In section 236(3) the words "120(2), 124(2)". In Schedule 1, paragraph 56(10) and (11).
1998 c. 8.	Employment Rights (Dispute Resolution) Act 1998.	Section 14(1).

11. Compensatory award: removal of limit in certain cases

Chapter	Short title	Extent of repeal
1996 c. 18.	Employment Rights Act 1996.	In section 112(4), the words "or in accordance with regulations under section 127B". In section 117(2) and (3), the words "and to regulations under section 127B".

Chapter	Short title	Extent of repeal
1996 c. 18. – *contd.*		In section 118(1), the words "Subject to regulations under section 127B,".
		Section 127B.
1998 c. 23.	Public Interest Disclosure Act 1998.	Section 8.
		Section 18(4)(b).

12. NATIONAL SECURITY

Chapter	Short title	Extent of repeal
1995 c. 50.	Disability Discrimination Act 1995.	Paragraph 4(1)(b) of Schedule 3, and the word "or" immediately before it.
1996 c. 17.	Employment Tribunals Act 1996.	Section 4(7).
		Section 28(5).
1998 c. 23.	Public Interest Disclosure Act 1998.	Section 11.

SCHEDULE 9
A Schedule of consequential repeals.

STATUTORY INSTRUMENTS

1999 No. 3312

TERMS AND CONDITIONS OF EMPLOYMENT

The Maternity and Parental Leave etc. Regulations 1999

Made .... *10th December 1999*

Coming into force .... *15th December 1999*

Whereas a draft of the following Regulations was laid before Parliament in accordance with section 236(3) of the Employment Rights Act 1996(**f001**) and approved by a resolution of each House of Parliament:

Now, therefore, the Secretary of State, in exercise of the powers conferred on him by sections 47C(2) and (3), 71(1) to (3) and (6), 72(1) and (2), 73(1), (2), (4) and (7), 74(1), (3) and (4), 75(1), 76(1), (2) and (5), 77(1) and (4), 78(1), (2) and (7), 79(1) and (2) and 99(1)(**f002**) of that Act and of all other powers enabling him in that behalf, hereby makes the following Regulations:-

PART 1

GENERAL

Citation and commencement

1. These Regulations may be cited as the Maternity and Parental Leave etc. Regulations 1999 and shall come into force on 15th December 1999.

Interpretation

2.– (1) In these Regulations-

"the 1996 Act" means the Employment Rights Act 1996;

"additional maternity leave" means leave under section 73 of the 1996 Act;

(**f001**) 1996 c. 18; section 236(3) was amended by paragraph 42 of Part III of Schedule 4 to the Employment Relations Act 1999 (c. 26).

(**f002**) Section 47C of the Employment Rights Act 1996 was inserted by paragraph 8 of Part III of Schedule 4 to the Employment Relations Act 1999; sections 71 to 79 of the 1996 Act were substituted by section 7 and Part I of Schedule 4 to the 1999 Act, and section 99 of the 1996 Act was substituted by paragraph 16 of Part III of Schedule 4 to the 1999 Act. The word "prescribed" in section 47C of the 1996 Act is defined in subsection (2) of that section; the same word in sections 71 to 73 is defined in section 75(2), and in section 99 it is defined in subsection (2) of that section.

"business" includes a trade or profession and includes any activity carried on by a body of persons (whether corporate or unincorporated);

"child" means a person under the age of eighteen;

"childbirth" means the birth of a living child or the birth of a child whether living or dead after 24 weeks of pregnancy;

"collective agreement" means a collective agreement within the meaning of section 178 of the Trade Union and Labour Relations (Consolidation) Act 1992(f003), the trade union parties to which are independent trade unions within the meaning of section 5 of that Act;

"contract of employment" means a contract of service or apprenticeship, whether express or implied, and (if it is express) whether oral or in writing;

"disability living allowance" means the disability living allowance provided for in Part III of the Social Security Contributions and Benefits Act 1992(f004);

"employee" means an individual who has entered into or works under (or, where the employment has ceased, worked under) a contract of employment;

"employer" means the person by whom an employee is (or, where the employment has ceased, was) employed;

"expected week of childbirth" means the week, beginning with midnight between Saturday and Sunday, in which it is expected that childbirth will occur, and "week of childbirth" means the week, beginning with midnight between Saturday and Sunday, in which childbirth occurs;

"job", in relation to an employee returning after additional maternity leave or parental leave, means the nature of the work which she is employed to do in accordance with her contract and the capacity and place in which she is so employed;

"ordinary maternity leave" means leave under section 71 of the 1996 Act;

"parental leave" means leave under regulation 13(1);

"parental responsibility" has the meaning given by section 3 of the Children Act 1989(f005), and "parental responsibilities" has the meaning given by section 1(3) of the Children (Scotland) Act 1995(f006);

"workforce agreement" means an agreement between an employer and his employees or their representatives in respect of which the conditions set out in Schedule 1 to these Regulations are satisfied.

(f003) 1992 c. 52.

(f004) 1992 c. 4.

(f005) 1989 c. 41.

(f006) 1995 c. 36.

(2) A reference in any provision of these Regulations to a period of continuous employment is to a period computed in accordance with Chapter I of Part XIV of the 1996 Act, as if that provision were a provision of that Act.

(3) For the purposes of these Regulations any two employers shall be treated as associated if-

(a) one is a company of which the other (directly or indirectly) has control; or
(b) both are companies of which a third person (directly or indirectly) has control;

and "associated employer" shall be construed accordingly.

(4) In these Regulations, unless the context otherwise requires,-

(a) a reference to a numbered regulation or schedule is to the regulation or schedule in these Regulations bearing that number;
(b) a reference in a regulation or schedule to a numbered paragraph is to the paragraph in that regulation or schedule bearing that number, and
(c) a reference in a paragraph to a lettered sub-paragraph is to the sub-paragraph in that paragraph bearing that letter.

Application

3.– (1) The provisions of Part II of these Regulations have effect only in relation to employees whose expected week of childbirth begins on or after 30th April 2000.

(2) Regulation 19 (protection from detriment) has effect only in relation to an act or failure to act which takes place on or after 15th December 1999.

(3) For the purposes of paragraph (2)-

(a) where an act extends over a period, the reference to the date of the act is a reference to the last day of that period, and
(b) a failure to act is to be treated as done when it was decided on.

(4) For the purposes of paragraph (3), in the absence of evidence establishing the contrary an employer shall be taken to decide on a failure to act-

(a) when he does an act inconsistent with doing the failed act, or
(b) if he has done no such inconsistent act, when the period expires within which he might reasonably have been expected to do the failed act if it was to be done.

(5) Regulation 20 (unfair dismissal) has effect only in relation to dismissals where the effective date of termination (within the meaning of section 97 of the 1996 Act) falls on or after 15th December 1999.

Part II

Maternity Leave

Entitlement to ordinary maternity leave

4.– (1) An employee is entitled to ordinary maternity leave provided that she satisfies the following conditions-

(a) at least 21 days before the date on which she intends her ordinary maternity leave period to start, or, if that is not reasonably practicable, as soon as is reasonably practicable, she notifies her employer of-
(i) her pregnancy;
(ii) the expected week of childbirth, and
(iii) the date on which she intends her ordinary maternity leave period to start,
and

(b) if requested to do so by her employer, she produces for his inspection a certificate from-
(i) a registered medical practitioner, or
(ii) a registered midwife,
stating the expected week of childbirth.

(2) The notification provided for in paragraph (1)(a)(iii)-

(a) shall be given in writing, if the employer so requests, and
(b) shall not specify a date earlier than the beginning of the eleventh week before the expected week of childbirth.

(3) Where, by virtue of regulation 6(1)(b), an employee's ordinary maternity leave period commences with the first day after the beginning of the sixth week before the expected week of childbirth on which she is absent from work wholly or partly because of pregnancy-

(a) paragraph (1) does not require her to notify her employer of the date specified in that paragraph, but
(b) (whether or not she has notified him of that date) she is not entitled to ordinary maternity leave unless she notifies him as soon as is reasonably practicable that she is absent from work wholly or partly because of pregnancy.

(4) Where, by virtue of regulation 6(2), an employee's ordinary maternity leave period commences with the day on which childbirth occurs-

(a) paragraph (1) does not require her to notify her employer of the date specified in that paragraph, but
(b) (whether or not she has notified him of that date) she is not entitled to ordinary maternity leave unless she notifies him as soon as is reasonably practicable after the birth that she has given birth.

(5) The notification provided for in paragraphs (3)(b) and (4)(b) shall be given in writing, if the employer so requests.

Entitlement to additional maternity leave

5. An employee who satisfies the following conditions is entitled to additional maternity leave-

    (a) she is entitled to ordinary maternity leave, and

    (b) she has, at the beginning of the eleventh week before the expected week of childbirth, been continuously employed for a period of not less than a year.

Commencement of maternity leave periods

6.– (1) Subject to paragraph (2), an employee's ordinary maternity leave period commences with the earlier of-

    (a) the date which, in accordance with regulation 4(1)(a)(iii), she notifies to her employer as the date on which she intends her ordinary maternity leave period to start, and

    (b) the first day after the beginning of the sixth week before the expected week of childbirth on which she is absent from work wholly or partly because of pregnancy.

(2) Where the employee's ordinary maternity leave period has not commenced by virtue of paragraph (1) when childbirth occurs, her ordinary maternity leave period commences with the day on which childbirth occurs.

(3) An employee's additional maternity leave period commences on the day after the last day of her ordinary maternity leave period.

Duration of maternity leave periods

7.– (1) Subject to paragraphs (2) and (5), an employee's ordinary maternity leave period continues for the period of eighteen weeks from its commencement, or until the end of the compulsory maternity leave period provided for in regulation 8 if later.

(2) Subject to paragraph (5), where any requirement imposed by or under any relevant statutory provision prohibits the employee from working for any period after the end of the period determined under paragraph (1) by reason of her having recently given birth, her ordinary maternity leave period continues until the end of that later period.

(3) In paragraph (2), "relevant statutory provision" means a provision of-

    (a) an enactment, or

    (b) an instrument under an enactment,

other than a provision for the time being specified in an order under section 66(2) of the 1996 Act.

(4) Subject to paragraph (5), where an employee is entitled to additional maternity leave her additional maternity leave period continues until the end of the period of 29 weeks beginning with the week of childbirth.

(5) Where the employee is dismissed after the commencement of an ordinary or additional maternity leave period but before the time when (apart from this paragraph) that period would end, the period ends at the time of the dismissal.

Compulsory maternity leave

8. The prohibition in section 72 of the 1996 Act, against permitting an employee who satisfies prescribed conditions to work during a particular period (referred to as a "compulsory maternity leave period"), applies-

(a) in relation to an employee who is entitled to ordinary maternity leave, and
(b) in respect of the period of two weeks which commences with the day on which childbirth occurs.

Exclusion of entitlement to remuneration during ordinary maternity leave

9. For the purposes of section 71 of the 1996 Act, which includes provision excluding the entitlement of an employee who exercises her right to ordinary maternity leave to the benefit of terms and conditions of employment about remuneration, only sums payable to an employee by way of wages or salary are to be treated as remuneration.

Redundancy during maternity leave

10.– (1) This regulation applies where, during an employee's ordinary or additional maternity leave period, it is not practicable by reason of redundancy for her employer to continue to employ her under her existing contract of employment.

(2) Where there is a suitable available vacancy, the employee is entitled to be offered (before the end of her employment under her existing contract) alternative employment with her employer or his successor, or an associated employer, under a new contract of employment which complies with paragraph (3) (and takes effect immediately on the ending of her employment under the previous contract).

(3) The new contract of employment must be such that-

(a) the work to be done under it is of a kind which is both suitable in relation to the employee and appropriate for her to do in the circumstances, and
(b) its provisions as to the capacity and place in which she is to be employed, and as to the other terms and conditions of her employment, are not substantially less favourable to her than if she had continued to be employed under the previous contract.

Requirement to notify intention to return during a maternity leave period

11.– (1) An employee who intends to return to work earlier than the end of her ordinary maternity leave period or, where she is entitled to additional maternity leave, the end of her additional maternity leave period, shall give to her employer not less than 21 days' notice of the date on which she intends to return.

(2) If an employee attempts to return to work earlier than the end of a maternity leave period without complying with paragraph (1), her employer is entitled to postpone her return to a date such as will secure, subject to paragraph (3), that he has 21 days' notice of her return.

(3) An employer is not entitled under paragraph (2) to postpone an employee's return to work to a date after the end of the relevant maternity leave period.

(4) If an employee whose return to work has been postponed under paragraph (2) has been notified that she is not to return to work before the date to which her return was postponed, the employer is under no contractual obligation to pay her remuneration until the date to which her return was postponed if she returns to work before that date.

Requirement to notify intention to return after additional maternity leave

12.– (1)Where, not earlier than 21 days before the end of her ordinary maternity leave period, an employee who is entitled to additional maternity leave is requested in accordance with paragraph (3) by her employer to notify him in writing of-

(a) the date on which childbirth occurred, and
(b) whether she intends to return to work at the end of her additional maternity leave period,

the employee shall give the requested notification within 21 days of receiving the request.

(2) The provisions of regulations 19 and 20, in so far as they protect an employee against detriment or dismissal for the reason that she took additional maternity leave, do not apply in relation to an employee who has failed to notify her employer in accordance with paragraph (1).

(3) A request under paragraph (1) shall be-

(a) made in writing, and
(b) accompanied by a written statement-

(i) explaining how the employee may determine, in accordance with regulation 7(4), the date on which her additional maternity leave period will end, and
(ii) warning of the consequence, under paragraph (2), of failure to respond to the employer's request within 21 days of receiving it.

PART III

PARENTAL LEAVE

Entitlement to parental leave

13.– (1) An employee who-

    (a) has been continuously employed for a period of not less than a year; and

    (b) has, or expects to have, responsibility for a child,

is entitled, in accordance with these Regulations, to be absent from work on parental leave for the purpose of caring for that child.

(2) An employee has responsibility for a child, for the purposes of paragraph (1), if-

    (a) he has parental responsibility or, in Scotland, parental responsibilities for the child; or

    (b) he has been registered as the child's father under any provision of section 10(1) or 10A(1) of the Births and Deaths Registration Act 1953**(f007)** or of section 18(1) or (2) of the Registration of Births, Deaths and Marriages (Scotland) Act 1965**(f008)**.

(3) An employee is not entitled to parental leave in respect of a child born before 15th December 1999, except for a child who is adopted by the employee, or placed with the employee for adoption by him, on or after that date.

Extent of entitlement

14.– (1) An employee is entitled to thirteen weeks' leave in respect of any individual child.

(2) Where the period for which an employee is normally required, under his contract of employment, to work in the course of a week does not vary, a week's leave for the employee is a period of absence from work which is equal in duration to the period for which he is normally required to work.

(3) Where the period for which an employee is normally required, under his contract of employment, to work in the course of a week varies from week to week or over a longer period, or where he is normally required under his contract to work in some weeks but not in others, a week's leave for the employee is a period of absence from work which is equal in duration to the period calculated by dividing the total of the periods for which he is normally required to work in a year by 52.

(f007) 1953 c. 20; sections 10 and 10A were substituted by the Family Law Reform Act 1987 (c. 42), sections 24 and 25.

(f008) 1965 c. 49; section 18(1) was substituted, and section 18(2) amended, by the Law Reform (Parent and Child) (Scotland) Act 1986 (c. 9).

(4) Where an employee takes leave in periods shorter than the period which constitutes, for him, a week's leave under whichever of paragraphs (2) and (3) is applicable in his case, he completes a week's leave when the aggregate of the periods of leave he has taken equals the period constituting a week's leave for him under the applicable paragraph.

When parental leave may be taken

15. An employee may not exercise any entitlement to parental leave in respect of a child-

(a) except in the cases referred to in paragraphs (b) to (d), after the date of the child's fifth birthday;

(b) in a case where the child is entitled to a disability living allowance, after the date of the child's eighteenth birthday;

(c) in a case where the child was placed with the employee for adoption by him (other than a case where paragraph (b) applies), after-

    (i) the fifth anniversary of the date on which the placement began, or

    (ii) the date of the child's eighteenth birthday,

whichever is the earlier.

(d) in a case where-

    (i) the provisions set out in Schedule 2 apply, and

    (ii) the employee would have taken leave on or before a date or anniversary referred to in paragraphs (a) to (c) but for the fact that the employer postponed it under paragraph 6 of that Schedule,

after the end of the period to which the leave was postponed.

Default provisions in respect of parental leave

16. The provisions set out in Schedule 2 apply in relation to parental leave in the case of an employee whose contract of employment does not include a provision which-

(a) confers an entitlement to absence from work for the purpose of caring for a child, and

(b) incorporates or operates by reference to all or part of a collective agreement or workforce agreement.

Part IV

Provisions Applicable In Relation To More
Than One Kind Of Absence

Application of terms and conditions during periods of leave

17. An employee who takes additional maternity leave or parental leave-

(a) is entitled, during the period of leave, to the benefit of her employer's implied obligation to her of trust and confidence and any terms and conditions of her employment relating to-

(i) notice of the termination of the employment contract by her employer;

(ii) compensation in the event of redundancy, or

(iii) disciplinary or grievance procedures;

(b) is bound, during that period, by her implied obligation to her employer of good faith and any terms and conditions of her employment relating to-

(i) notice of the termination of the employment contract by her;

(ii) the disclosure of confidential information;

(iii) the acceptance of gifts or other benefits, or

(iv) the employee's participation in any other business.

Right to return after additional maternity leave or parental leave

18.– (1) An employee who takes parental leave for a period of four weeks or less, other than immediately after taking additional maternity leave, is entitled to return from leave to the job in which she was employed before her absence.

(2) An employee who takes additional maternity leave, or parental leave for a period of more than four weeks, is entitled to return from leave to the job in which she was employed before her absence, or, if it is not reasonably practicable for the employer to permit her to return to that job, to another job which is both suitable for her and appropriate for her to do in the circumstances.

(3) An employee who takes parental leave for a period of four weeks or less immediately after additional maternity leave is entitled to return from leave to the job in which she was employed before her absence unless-

(a) it would not have been reasonably practicable for her to return to that job if she had returned at the end of her additional maternity leave period, and

(b) it is not reasonably practicable for the employer to permit her to return to that job at the end of her period of parental leave;

otherwise, she is entitled to return to another job which is both suitable for her and appropriate for her to do in the circumstances.

(4) Paragraphs (2) and (3) do not apply where regulation 10 applies.

(5) An employee's right to return under paragraph (1), (2) or (3) is to return-

(a) on terms and conditions as to remuneration not less favourable than those which would have been applicable to her had she not been absent from work at any time since-

(i) in the case of an employee returning from additional maternity leave (or parental leave taken immediately after additional maternity leave), the commencement of the ordinary maternity leave period which preceded her additional maternity leave period, or

(ii) in the case of an employee returning from parental leave (other than parental leave taken immediately after additional maternity leave), the commencement of the period of parental leave;

(b) with her seniority, pension rights and similar rights as they would have been if the period or periods of her employment prior to her additional maternity leave period, or (as the case may be) her period of parental leave, were continuous with her employment following her return to work (but subject, in the case of an employee returning from additional maternity leave, to the requirements of paragraph 5 of Schedule 5 to the Social Security Act 1989**(f009)** (equal treatment under pension schemes: maternity)), and

(c) otherwise on terms and conditions not less favourable than those which would have been applicable to her had she not been absent from work after the end of her ordinary maternity leave period or (as the case may be) during her period of parental leave.

Protection from detriment

19.– (1) An employee is entitled under section 47C of the 1996 Act not to be subjected to any detriment by any act, or any deliberate failure to act, by her employer done for any of the reasons specified in paragraph (2).

(2) The reasons referred to in paragraph (1) are that the employee-

(a) is pregnant;

(b) has given birth to a child;

(c) is the subject of a relevant requirement, or a relevant recommendation, as defined by section 66(2) of the 1996 Act;

(d) took, sought to take or availed herself of the benefits of, ordinary maternity leave;

(e) took or sought to take-

(i) additional maternity leave;

(ii) parental leave, or

(iii) time off under section 57A of the 1996 Act;

(f) declined to sign a workforce agreement for the purpose of these Regulations, or

(g) being-

(i) a representative of members of the workforce for the purposes of Schedule 1, or

(ii) a candidate in an election in which any person elected will, on being elected, become such a representative,

performed (or proposed to perform) any functions or activities as such a representative or candidate.

(3) For the purposes of paragraph (2)(d), a woman avails herself of the benefits of ordinary maternity leave if, during her ordinary maternity leave period, she avails herself of the benefit of any of the terms and conditions of her employment preserved by section 71 of the 1996 Act during that period.

(4) Paragraph (1) does not apply in a case where the detriment in question amounts to dismissal within the meaning of Part X of the 1996 Act.

(f009) 1989 c. 24.

(5) Paragraph (2)(b) only applies where the act or failure to act takes place during the employee's ordinary or additional maternity leave period.

(6) For the purposes of paragraph (5)-

(a) where an act extends over a period, the reference to the date of the act is a reference to the last day of that period, and

(b) a failure to act is to be treated as done when it was decided on.

(7) For the purposes of paragraph (6), in the absence of evidence establishing the contrary an employer shall be taken to decide on a failure to act-

(a) when he does an act inconsistent with doing the failed act, or

(b) if he has done no such inconsistent act, when the period expires within which he might reasonably have been expected to do the failed act if it were to be done.

Unfair dismissal

20.– (1) An employee who is dismissed is entitled under section 99 of the 1996 Act to be regarded for the purposes of Part X of that Act as unfairly dismissed if-

(a) the reason or principal reason for the dismissal is of a kind specified in paragraph (3), or

(b) the reason or principal reason for the dismissal is that the employee is redundant, and regulation 10 has not been complied with.

(2) An employee who is dismissed shall also be regarded for the purposes of Part X of the 1996 Act as unfairly dismissed if-

(a) the reason (or, if more than one, the principal reason) for the dismissal is that the employee was redundant;

(b) it is shown that the circumstances constituting the redundancy applied equally to one or more employees in the same undertaking who held positions similar to that held by the employee and who have not been dismissed by the employer, and

(c) it is shown that the reason (or, if more than one, the principal reason) for which the employee was selected for dismissal was a reason of a kind specified in paragraph (3).

(3) The kinds of reason referred to in paragraphs (1) and (2) are reasons connected with-

(a) the pregnancy of the employee;

(b) the fact that the employee has given birth to a child;

(c) the application of a relevant requirement, or a relevant recommendation, as defined by section 66(2) of the 1996 Act;

(d) the fact that she took, sought to take or availed herself of the benefits of, ordinary maternity leave;

(e) the fact that she took or sought to take-

(i) additional maternity leave;

(ii) parental leave, or

(iii) time off under section 57A of the 1996 Act;

(f) the fact that she declined to sign a workforce agreement for the purposes of these Regulations, or

(g) the fact that the employee, being-

(i) a representative of members of the workforce for the purposes of Schedule 1, or

(ii) a candidate in an election in which any person elected will, on being elected, become such a representative,

performed (or proposed to perform) any functions or activities as such a representative or candidate.

(4) Paragraphs (1)(b) and (3)(b) only apply where the dismissal ends the employee's ordinary or additional maternity leave period.

(5) Paragraph (3) of regulation 19 applies for the purposes of paragraph (3)(d) as it applies for the purpose of paragraph (2)(d) of that regulation.

(6) Paragraph (1) does not apply in relation to an employee if-

(a) immediately before the end of her additional maternity leave period (or, if it ends by reason of dismissal, immediately before the dismissal) the number of employees employed by her employer, added to the number employed by any associated employer of his, did not exceed five, and

(b) it is not reasonably practicable for the employer (who may be the same employer or a successor of his) to permit her to return to a job which is both suitable for her and appropriate for her to do in the circumstances or for an associated employer to offer her a job of that kind.

(7) Paragraph (1) does not apply in relation to an employee if-

(a) it is not reasonably practicable for a reason other than redundancy for the employer (who may be the same employer or a successor of his) to permit her to return to a job which is both suitable for her and appropriate for her to do in the circumstances;

(b) an associated employer offers her a job of that kind, and

(c) she accepts or unreasonably refuses that offer.

(8) Where on a complaint of unfair dismissal any question arises as to whether the operation of paragraph (1) is excluded by the provisions of paragraph (6) or (7), it is for the employer to show that the provisions in question were satisfied in relation to the complainant.

Contractual rights to maternity or parental leave

21.– (1) This regulation applies where an employee is entitled to-

(a) ordinary maternity leave;

(b) additional maternity leave, or

(c) parental leave,

(referred to in paragraph (2) as a "statutory right") and also to a right which corresponds to that right and which arises under the employee's contract of employment or otherwise.

(2) In a case where this regulation applies-

(a) the employee may not exercise the statutory right and the corresponding right separately but may, in taking the leave for which the two rights provide, take advantage of whichever right is, in any particular respect, the more favourable, and

(b) the provisions of the 1996 Act and of these Regulations relating to the statutory right apply, subject to any modifications necessary to give effect to any more favourable contractual terms, to the exercise of the composite right described in sub-paragraph (a) as they apply to the exercise of the statutory right.

Calculation of a week's pay

22. Where-

(a) under Chapter II of part XIV of the 1996 Act, the amount of a week's pay of an employee falls to be calculated by reference to the average rate of remuneration, or the average amount of remuneration, payable to the employee in respect of a period of twelve weeks ending on a particular date (referred to as "the calculation date");

(b) during a week in that period, the employee was absent from work on ordinary or additional maternity leave or parental leave, and

(c) remuneration is payable to the employee in respect of that week under her contract of employment, but the amount payable is less than the amount that would be payable if she were working,

that week shall be disregarded for the purpose of the calculation and account shall be taken of remuneration in earlier weeks so as to bring up to twelve the number of weeks of which account is taken.

Stephen Byers

Secretary of State for Trade and Industry

10th December 1999

SCHEDULE 1

REGULATION 2(1)

WORKFORCE AGREEMENTS

1. An agreement is a workforce agreement for the purposes of these Regulations if the following conditions are satisfied-

   (a) the agreement is in writing;
   (b) it has effect for a specified period not exceeding five years;
   (c) it applies either-
      (i) to all of the relevant members of the workforce, or
      (ii) to all of the relevant members of the workforce who belong to a particular group;
   (d) the agreement is signed-
      (i) in the case of an agreement of the kind referred to in sub-paragraph (c)(i), by the representatives of the workforce, and in the case of an agreement of the kind referred to in sub-paragraph (c)(ii), by the representatives of the group to which the agreement applies (excluding, in either case, any representative not a relevant member of the workforce on the date on which the agreement was first made available for signature), or
      (ii) if the employer employed 20 or fewer employees on the date referred to in sub-paragraph (d)(i), either by the appropriate representatives in accordance with that sub-paragraph or by the majority of the employees employed by him;
      and
   (e) before the agreement was made available for signature, the employer provided all the employees to whom it was intended to apply on the date on which it came into effect with copies of the text of the agreement and such guidance as those employees might reasonably require in order to understand it in full.

2. For the purposes of this Schedule-

   "a particular group" is a group of the relevant members of a workforce who undertake a particular function, work at a particular workplace or belong to a particular department or unit within their employer's business;

   "relevant members of the workforce" are all of the employees employed by a particular employer, excluding any employee whose terms and conditions of employment are provided for, wholly or in part, in a collective agreement;

   "representatives of the workforce" are employees duly elected to represent the relevant members of the workforce, "representatives of the group" are employees duly elected to represent the members of a particular group, and representatives are "duly elected" if the election at which they were elected satisfied the requirements of paragraph 3 of this Schedule.

3. The requirements concerning elections referred to in paragraph 2 are that-

   (a) the number of representatives to be elected is determined by the employer;

(b) the candidates for election as representatives of the workforce are relevant members of the workforce, and the candidates for election as representatives of a group are members of the group;

(c) no employee who is eligible to be a candidate is unreasonably excluded from standing for election;

(d) all the relevant members of the workforce are entitled to vote for representatives of the workforce, and all the members of a particular group are entitled to vote for representatives of the group;

(e) the employees entitled to vote may vote for as many candidates as there are representatives to be elected, and

(f) the election is conducted so as to secure that-

    (i) so far as is reasonably practicable, those voting do so in secret, and

    (ii) the votes given at the election are fairly and accurately counted.

SCHEDULE 2

REGULATION 16

DEFAULT PROVISIONS IN RESPECT OF PARENTAL LEAVE

Conditions of entitlement

1. An employee may not exercise any entitlement to parental leave unless-

    (a) he has complied with any request made by his employer to produce for the employer's inspection evidence of his entitlement, of the kind described in paragraph 2;

    (b) he has given his employer notice, in accordance with whichever of paragraphs 3 to 5 is applicable, of the period of leave he proposes to take, and

    (c) in a case where paragraph 6 applies, his employer has not postponed the period of leave in accordance with that paragraph.

2. The evidence to be produced for the purpose of paragraph 1(a) is such evidence as may reasonably be required of-

    (a) the employee's responsibility or expected responsibility for the child in respect of whom the employee proposes to take parental leave;

    (b) the child's date of birth or, in the case of a child who was placed with the employee for adoption, the date on which the placement began, and

    (c) in a case where the employee's right to exercise an entitlement to parental leave under regulation 15, or to take a particular period of leave under paragraph 7, depends upon whether the child is entitled to a disability living allowance, the child's entitlement to that allowance.

Notice to be given to employer

3. Except in a case where paragraph 4 or 5 applies, the notice required for the purpose of paragraph 1(b) is notice which-

    (a) specifies the dates on which the period of leave is to begin and end, and

(b) is given to the employer at least 21 days before the date on which that period is to begin.

4. Where the employee is the father of the child in respect of whom the leave is to be taken, and the period of leave is to begin on the date on which the child is born, the notice required for the purpose of paragraph 1(b) is notice which-

    (a) specifies the expected week of childbirth and the duration of the period of leave, and

    (b) is given to the employer at least 21 days before the beginning of the expected week of childbirth.

5. Where the child in respect of whom the leave is to be taken is to be placed with the employee for adoption by him and the leave is to begin on the date of the placement, the notice required for the purpose of paragraph 1(b) is notice which-

    (a) specifies the week in which the placement is expected to occur and the duration of the period of leave, and

    (b) is given to the employer at least 21 days before the beginning of that week, or, if that is not reasonably practicable, as soon as is reasonably practicable.

Postponement of leave

6. An employer may postpone a period of parental leave where-

    (a) neither paragraph 4 nor paragraph 5 applies, and the employee has accordingly given the employer notice in accordance with paragraph 3;

    (b) the employer considers that the operation of his business would be unduly disrupted if the employee took leave during the period identified in his notice;

    (c) the employer agrees to permit the employee to take a period of leave-

        (i) of the same duration as the period identified in the employee's notice, and

        (ii) beginning on a date determined by the employer after consulting the employee, which is no later than six months after the commencement of that period;

    (d) the employer gives the employee notice in writing of the postponement which-
        (i) states the reason for it, and
        (ii) specifies the dates on which the period of leave the employer agrees to permit the employee to take will begin and end,

  and

    (e) that notice is given to the employee not more than seven days after the employee's notice was given to the employer.

Minimum periods of leave

7. An employee may not take parental leave in a period other than the period which constitutes a week's leave for him under regulation 14 or a multiple of that period, except in a case where the child in respect of whom leave is taken is entitled to a disability living allowance.

Maximum annual leave allowance

8. An employee may not take more than four weeks' leave in respect of any individual child during a particular year.

9. For the purposes of paragraph 8, a year is the period of twelve months beginning-

   (a) except where sub-paragraph (b) applies, on the date on which the employee first became entitled to take parental leave in respect of the child in question, or

   (b) in a case where the employee's entitlement has been interrupted at the end of a period of continuous employment, on the date on which the employee most recently became entitled to take parental leave in respect of that child,

and each successive period of twelve months beginning on the anniversary of that date.

EXPLANATORY NOTE

(THIS NOTE IS NOT PART OF THE REGULATIONS)

These Regulations, together with provisions inserted into the Employment Rights Act 1996 ("the 1996 Act") by the Employment Relations Act 1999, confer new rights to maternity and parental leave. The provisions relating to parental leave implement Council Directive 96/34/EC on the framework agreement on parental leave (OJ No.L145, 19.6.96, p.4).

The provisions relating to ordinary maternity leave are derived from the maternity leave provisions in sections 72-78 of the 1996 Act as originally enacted, although the period of leave provided for is 18 weeks (reg.7(1)) rather than 14 weeks as under the Act. The provisions relating to additional maternity leave replace sections 79-85 of the 1996 Act as originally enacted; the new provisions differ principally in that the new right is a right to leave for a period of 29 weeks from the beginning of the week of childbirth (reg.7(4)) rather than a right to return within such a period, and that the new right is available to women who have been continuously employed for a year (reg.5) rather than for two years. The provision made for compulsory maternity leave (in new section 72 of the 1996 Act and reg.8) implements article 8.2 of the Pregnant Workers Directive (92/85/EEC; OJ No. L348,28.11.92, p.1), replacing the Maternity (Compulsory Leave) Regulations 1994 (S.I. 1994/2479) which originally implemented that provision.

The right to parental leave is available to employees who have been continuously employed for a year and have, or expect to have, parental responsibility (in Scotland, parental responsibilities) for a child (reg.13). The period of leave is 13 weeks (reg.14), and leave must generally be taken before the child's fifth birthday (reg.15, which sets out exceptions including provision for leave to be taken before the eighteenth birthday of a child entitled to a disability living allowance). Schedule 2 to the Regulations sets out provisions requiring that the employer must be notified of any proposal to take parental leave and may postpone it for up to six months; it also provides that (except in the case of a child entitled to a disability living allowance) parental leave may not be taken in periods other than a week or a multiple of a week. These provisions apply only to employees who are not subject to a collective or workforce agreement relating to parental leave.

In relation to both additional maternity leave and parental leave, provision is made for certain contractual rights and obligations to continue during the period of absence (reg.17), and for the employee to return to the same or an appropriate alternative job after that period (reg.18). The Regulations also make provision under sections 47C and 99 of the 1996 Act (both inserted by the Employment Relations Act 1999), identifying the cases where the protection against detriment or dismissal for which those sections provide is applicable (regs.19 and 20). The cases are not only cases connected with maternity or parental leave but also cases connected with the right to time off for dependants under new section 57A of the 1996 Act.

A Regulatory Impact Assessment of the costs and benefits that these Regulations would have is available to the public from Employment Relations 5A, Department of Trade and Industry, 1 Victoria Street, London SW1H 0ET.

0 11 085654 6

Index

making regulations 3–6, 8–11, 24–
25, 28–30, 152, 155, 160–63
relating to recognition requests 51–2
specifying collective bargaining
method 136–7
to issue guidance 136
security, national *see* national security
see also compensation; compensatory
awards
specific performance 65, 66, 81, 82
striking workers, unfair dismissal 177–81
supplementary awards 20

three-year principle 118
time off for dependants 169–72
advantage of written policy 172
complaints to Employment Tribunals
169, 170
compensation 170
definition of dependant 169, 170, 171,
172
no right to payment for 171
to assist in emergencies 172
to take action 171
trade union recognition *see* recognition
of trade unions
trade unions 7–11
action on behalf of members 9
application to CAC 53–8
balloting procedures 148
dismissal resulting from blacklisting 9
and employment rights 4–5
industrial action notices 149–50
procedures for statutory recognition 4,
49–53
prohibition of blacklists 8
see also recognition of trade unions;
training
training 11–15, 130
Transfer of Undertakings (Protection of
Employment) Regulations 1981
(TUPE) 44

unfair dismissal
compensation 44

additional awards 40
special awards 40
complaints to Employment Tribunal
178, 180
connected with right to be
accompanied 21
for health and safety matters 44
in maternity/parental leave cases 227–8
pregnancy and childbirth 174–5
and recognition
of striking workers 177–81
for taking part in industrial action 24
workers on fixed-term contracts 25–6,
27

voluntary recognition
agreements for 75–6, 77
applications to CAC
determination of agreements 77
to specify method 78–80, 81, 82
response to applications to CAC 80–82
termination of agreement for 78

waivers 27, 134, 210
whistle-blowing 44
workers
on board ships 39, 51, 52, 79, 104,
146–7
discrimination in recruitment/
treatment of 8
on fixed-term contracts 25–6, 27, 134
full-time 28
inside/outside Great Britain 79
in intelligence services 23, 46
number for recognition requests 51
part-time 28, 29, 30
in schools 46
workforce agreements 230–31
working day, definition 138
workplace, definition 144
workplace agreements 168